D1610921

Edwin James Aiken is a member of the School of Geography, Archaeology and Palaeoecology at The Queen's University of Belfast

Published and forthcoming in the Series:

1. *Zambesi: David Livingstone and Expeditionary Science in Africa* by Lawrence Dritsas

2. *New Spaces of Exploration: Geographies of Discovery in the Twentieth Century* by Simon Naylor and James Ryan (eds)

3. *Scriptural Geography: Portraying the Holy Land* by Edwin James Aiken

4. *Bringing Geography to Book: Ellen Semple and the Reception of Geographical Knowledge* by Innes Keighren

Scriptural Geography

Portraying the Holy Land

EDWIN JAMES AIKEN

I.B. TAURIS

LONDON · NEW YORK

Published in 2010 by I.B.Tauris & Co Ltd
6 Salem Road, London W2 4BU
175 Fifth Avenue, New York NY 10010
www.ibtauris.com

Distributed in the United States and Canada Exclusively by Palgrave Macmillan
175 Fifth Avenue, New York NY 10010

Tauris Historical Geography: 3

ISBN: 978 1 84511 818 1

A full CIP record for this book is available from the British Library
A full CIP record is available from the Library of Congress

Library of Congress Catalog Card Number: available

Printed and bound in Great Britain by
CPI Antony Rowe, Chippenham, Wiltshire
from camera-ready copy edited and supplied by the author

FSC
Mixed Sources
Product group from well-managed
forests and other controlled sources
Cert no. SGS-COC-2953
www.fsc.org
© 1996 Forest Stewardship Council

For my Father and Mother

Contents

Illustrations

Acknowledgements

In writing a book it is usual to acquire some debts, and this work is no exception. During the research and writing I was ably supported in different ways by a number of people. My first and greatest intellectual debt is to Professor David Livingstone, under whose guidance this research was carried out. He has ever remained a patient, resourceful and inspiring guide on the pilgrimage. Other individuals were extremely helpful in a variety of ways and they included: Emeritus Professor Rev Bill Addley, Dr Desi Alexander, Mrs Gill Alexander, Miss Alex Bulens, Professor Robin Butlin, Dr Mark Gardiner, Dr Haim Goren, Ms Florence Gray, Mr Stephen Gregory, Dr Pat Jess, Dr Nuala Johnson, Rev Charles McCurdy, Mrs Deborah Manley, Mr Alan Mauro, Mrs Virginia Murray, Ms Maura Pringle, Ms Yael Pritz, Mr Alan Ross, Professor Steve Royle, Dr Alastair Ruffell, Professor James Ryan, Ms Becky Stewart, Dr Jeanne-Marie Warzeski, Rev Dr Donald Watts, and Professor Charlie Withers. My family remained patient and supportive over many years of research and I thank them for that and so much more.

I gratefully acknowledge the financial support of the School of Geography, Queen's University, Belfast, which enabled me to carry out this research. I also made many demands (often awkward ones) upon various libraries, and would like to thank the library staffs at: Edinburgh University Library; The Gamble Library, Belfast; Glasgow University Library; The Main and Science Libraries, Queen's University, Belfast; The National Library of Scotland; New College Library, Edinburgh; The Presbyterian Historical Society, Belfast; The School of Geography Library, Queen's University, Belfast; and the

Staff of the Financial Secretary's Office of the Presbyterian Church in Ireland, Church House, Belfast.

Illustrations 1 and 2 are reproduced by kind permission of the Library of The Queen's University of Belfast.

Illustration 5 is reproduced from W. Walker, *Three Churchmen* (Edinburgh, 1893).

Illustration 6 is reproduced by kind permission of the Collection of the Queen's University of Belfast.

Illustration 7 is reproduced by kind permission of Mr Alan Ross.

Illustration 11 is reproduced by kind permission of the Trustees of the National Library of Scotland and Emeritus Professor A.D. Roberts.

Illustrations 12 and 14 are reproduced from L.A. Smith, *George Adam Smith* (London, 1943).

Illustrations 13, 15 and 17 are produced by kind permission of New College Library, University of Edinburgh.

All other illustrations are taken from copies in the author's possession.

The quotation from the Minutes of the Presbytery of Belfast on page 106 is reproduced by kind permission of the Clerk of the General Assembly of the Presbyterian Church in Ireland and the Presbyteries of North, South and East Belfast.

1 Introduction: Inscribing Terra Sancta

It is easy to find Palestine ... But how to find the Holy Land – ah, that is another question.[1]

PREAMBLE

This book sets out to find the Holy Land: to find it as it was understood and written about; not just as a Cartesian space, but as an intellectual, moral and discordant space; a space charged with the heat of religious debates, a space mapped by the exclusivist ideologies of religious apologetics, filled with the clamour of the engagements of those trying to understand the worst crises of Victorian society; a target for generations of pilgrims and also a space of inspiration and reflection. I intend to explore a topology of meaning – the management of a celestial landscape and the production of its geography. By doing so I hope to aid our understanding of the importance of the Holy Land in the long nineteenth century's story of social and religious upheaval and transformation, to demonstrate the significance of the geography of that space in Western thought and argument. My aim is to trace the genealogy of a particular representational practice of spatial knowledge: Scriptural Geography. For this purpose we will consider Scriptural Geographies to be non-fictional literary works dealing with the places in which the story, or narrative, of the Bible takes place.

In the midst of writing the history of an idea like the geography of the Holy Land, perspective must be borne in mind: the story must be told with an eye to the context of events, and a sensitivity to their chronology and the geography of their nascence and diffusion, rather more than the more mundane 'facts' involved in their occurrence. To obtain moment on the raw data of the texts our investigations must situate each author. Holy Land geography is a genre of literature which lends itself particularly well to such contextual analysis, comprising a lively combination of travel, science, archaeology, religion and literary studies, and this chapter will show how the faces of science and writing juxtapose, interact and react.

SCRIPTURAL GEOGRAPHY

By the nineteenth century books dealing with the Holy Land were widely distributed, enormously popular works; our studies will reveal enormous circulation figures for geographies of the Holy Land, reviews in the popular press, and evidence of the use of these works in school curricula. These works were, and are, important in the popularization of geographical knowledge. Apparently scientific, archaeological, topological and geological works became the regular reading matter of the large section of the Victorian population interested in matters as seemingly remote from the fieldwork of geography as preaching, philology, prophecy and social morality. To tell the story of the writing of the geography of the Holy Land we will attempt to trace the genealogy of this enormously popular literary (sometimes travel) genre.

Throughout this work the story of the huge project that was the production of Holy Land geographies will be constantly negotiated within the context of intellectual, social and religious currents, paying particular attention to the spatial and historical influences of the dissonance among religion, theology and science, which was a key factor in how the genre developed, and to which some forms of Holy Land geography owe their existence. Our history will focus on the nineteenth century, but before our detailed studies we will initially look at some of the ancestors of the Victorian works.

Writing geographies of the Holy Land is an activity that has a history stretching to antiquity. Butlin states that 'the origins of sacred geography date back ... to the Biblical toponymy ... compiled by

Eusebius, bishop of Caesarea early in the fourth century AD'.[2] He suggests that 'the use of historical and geographical skills to locate and characterize important Biblical places and events, continued through the Middle Ages to the early modern period (indeed continues in some countries to the present day.)'[3] Butlin further argues that this geographical project has been a key determinant in the development of Western geography more generally: 'In Europe, the concept and practice of historical geography in the seventeenth and eighteenth centuries, was closely associated with the scriptural or biblical geographies of the Old and New Testaments. This theme ... continued to figure in historical geography throughout the nineteenth and early twentieth centuries'.[4] The first Holy Land geographies of the early modern period were often simply assimilations of the notes of travellers and scholars of the classical period, reworked and set against the background of new maps of Palestine, as an aid to Biblical understanding. Their authors had rarely themselves ventured anywhere so dangerous as Palestine (as late as 1808 parties of explorers turned back at Malta, fearing the worst),[5] and they seem to have had little care for the empiricism and quasi-scientific method that dominated the outlook of their successors. These works were not scientific in any conventional sense: their observations are not generally based on direct experience or as the result of any methodologically controlled investigations. They could also draw on a theology which supported their project and did not present serious threats to the truth of the narratives they were trying to illustrate. At this juncture the investigation of the geography of the Holy Land was not an urgent pursuit or one of great apologetic moment. Natural theology, an enterprise devoted to explaining God's creation by scientific means, and to discerning evidence of design in the world, could happily produce lists of Holy Land flora and fauna and other natural phenomena: scientists had yet to begin to ask the awkward questions as to how these species arrived at their present state and location, and what this might mean for humans. This particular field of research evolved, as noted by Butlin, and 'European sacred geographies from the seventeenth and eighteenth centuries, though similar in purpose, were produced from within different traditions'.[6]

Furthermore Butlin argues for what he calls an 'Added energy' after the Reformation placed new emphasis on Biblical authority,

with 'a consequent intensification of interest in the detailed topographical and geographical environments of scripture'.[7] Later, in the
nineteenth century, intellectual currents ushered in 'attempts to re-
concile revealed knowledge and the authority of the sacred text with
the empirical knowledge and authority of the new science'.[8] Shepherd speaks of the authors of these geographies as 'a host of ... scholars and clergymen bent on authenticating the text of the Bible' and
argues that their work 'was chiefly the result of the confrontation in
the West between established religious beliefs and the latest discoveries in geology and human evolution'.[9] Oddly she goes on to
argue that 'Palestine provided no reassuring answers to their dilemma', which, as will be demonstrated below, is a sentiment
manifestly unsupported by the spirit in which these authors wrote
and by the content of their works.[10] However, it is probably not an
overstatement when Shepherd asserts:

> The most serious challenge to Turkish rule in the Near East since
> Napoleon took place at the time when the Protestant faith in the
> literal truth of the Scriptures was being put to the severest tests...
> Palestine was to be ransacked for 'evidence' of the accuracy of the
> Bible, not simply revered as the site of the Holy Places.[11]

The enthusiasm of the biblical geographers' quest at this point
cannot be doubted. The controversy surrounding the progress of
scientific thought was deep seated, 'the conclusions of geologists, in
particular, indicating through the study of fossils that the earth was
millions, not thousands, of years old, and had not been created in its
final form in a week were dismaying even to many of the scientists
themselves'.[12] And, even today, as Butlin points out, some works still
appear periodically which continue to set a biblical record cor-
roborated by Holy Land geography against scientific truth claims.[13]

The changing intellectual tastes of the audiences of Holy Land
Geographies, varying as did the social climate, dictated a change in
research methodology for the authors of the works over time. The
writers of later Scriptural Geographies conducted fieldwork with enthusiasm, enduring hardship, privation, loss and immense expense in
their quest for scientific accuracy and data worthy of the authority
granted by the highest levels of the new found notion of scientific

reliability. Now that pilgrimages were being undertaken 'not to worship, but to test and confirm the topographical truths of Scripture'[14] a different methodology was needed, and a different style had to be employed. The material needed not only to be proof against the criticisms of skeptical scientists, but also against critical theologians who would seek to deny that the cause was worthwhile at all. Careful fieldwork and conservative theological scholarship were the hallmarks of this enterprise.

Meanwhile, still later, in the latter nineteenth century, Holy Land Geographies interacted with science in an entirely different way. In these works the results of scientific investigation were integrated with the fieldwork carried out at biblical sites, as were the insights of critical theologians. This resulted in works which had little polemical charge, other than to exegete the Scriptures and the culture of the ancient Near East, but by that time acknowledging the negotiated nature of Scriptural knowledge, and that the productions of modernity could often be beneficial, rather than detrimental, to religious faith. These works contain 'important digests of up-to-date scientific description and explanation...'[15] and, as Butlin has noted, these works continued the Scriptural Geography project 'against a changing intellectual and theological climate'.[16]

This project's history can be traced through many phases and contexts, the details of which are not our primary concern here. However, it is useful by way of background to look at some Holy Land geographies from the whole sweep of the enterprise's long story. Initially an enthusiasm for pilgrimage to the Holy Land swept Christendom in the fourth century and pilgrims seemed to visit every site that could be imagined to be connected to any biblical event. At an early stage St Augustine 'secured the place of geography in the Christian system of knowledge'[17] as he felt that geography worked 'By providing information for understanding Scripture' and that therefore 'geographical studies eventually served biblical exegesis'.[18] By late medieval times however the pilgrims' routine route had contracted to include almost entirely sites from the New Testament, rather than the Old Testament. Most of the sites visited became concentrated in and around Jerusalem in what quickly became a well-trodden path, because '[a]s travel became more attractive owing to better roads, more facilities for shelter, more settled political conditions, and greater available wealth' the number of pilgrims soared.[19] The landscape became an actively and carefully managed and presented resource: a repository of sets of specific historical meanings, after all, as argued by Campbell, 'Like an archaeologist the Christian pilgrim is looking for the past, but it is a past made up of singular events and personalities, individual epiphanies, incarnations, and martyrdoms. Places are referred to as "witnesses" of those events and people'.[20] As our studies will reveal, this aspect of the 'witnessing' carried out by geographical places in the holy landscape became employed in a specific apologetic project of the nineteenth, twentieth and indeed twenty-first centuries. The nature of this enterprise required vast amounts of field data and this meant that the routes of travellers once more had to be extended to cover even the most obscure site of the most obscure biblical occurrence.

Ancient

Geographies of the Christian Holy Land have existed almost as long as Christianity itself. The earliest texts were born in the era of the Roman Empire which provided the communications network necessary for long distance travel with reasonable ease. A number of texts has survived, despite this however, ancient works on the Holy Land, like that of Eusebius, have proven the most difficult for scholars to contextualize and understand. Eusebius's famed work the *Onomasticon*, can only be dated imprecisely, and most writers consider it to have been composed sometime between 313 and 325.[21] Eusebius was Bishop of Caesarea from 313 and is more famed for his church histories than his *Onomasticon*. His work lists, in alphabetical order within each biblical book, the places mentioned in the Scriptures and other, associated, geographical features, like mountains and streams. It seems to be a reference work designed to meet the needs of a biblical scholar who reads of a place name in the Bible and wants to know more about it. The text itself is rich with the fruits of research: both textual interrogation and first-hand data collection conducted in the field. It seems likely that Eusebius used a variety of texts written by travellers, including some received at third-hand from Origen,[22] although there is also definite evidence within the text that

Eusebius did some travelling himself as many of the locations listed are accompanied by detailed information about routes. Entries can be as interesting as that for Ainan:

> *Ainan* (Gen. 38.14), which is in the passage of Thamna. Ainan is now a desert place lying beside Thamna, a very large village inhabited up to the present, lying between Ailia and Dispolis. There is a spring in the place called Ainan where there is an idol venerated by the country-folk.[23]

Or as dry as the entry for Souba: '*Souba* (2 Sam. 8.3), David attacked its king'.[24] Eusebius' work does not recommend that any particular veneration be given to any particular place, but he is often credited with resourcing the pilgrimage 'boom' of the fourth century AD.[25]

The first extant manuscript of a detailed pilgrim account, which can be considered travel writing per se, was written by an anonymous pilgrim who started his journey at Bordeaux, and is usually dated to AD 333.[26] The text consists mainly of a list of staging posts along the journey, with occasional comments, often displaying the beliefs of the age: 'There is [at Caesarea] the Bath of Cornelius the Centurion, who gave much alms. At the third milestone from there is Mount Syna, where there is a spring, and women who wash in it become pregnant'.[27] Despite such expressions of lore and myth the text has a real sense of the immediacy of a traveller who has been to the places that he describes. At times the tone almost reaches the conversational – 'Eighteen miles from Jerusalem is Jericho. Coming down the mountain range you reach a tomb on the right, and behind it is the sycamore tree which Zacchaeus climbed in order that he could see Christ...'[28] However, nothing is really known of the author's life or circumstances, and little can therefore be said about the context of the pilgrimage.

A fourth century nun, probably called Egeria, began an extensive tour of the Holy Land around the year 384. Her visit, of more than three years, to the holy sites comprised a tour of not only the principle biblical localities around Jerusalem, but it also extended as far south as Egypt. Egeria's manuscript, of which only the middle portion survives, is written in the form of a letter to the sisters of her convent who remained at home. Egeria's text was apparently written in Constantinople after her sojourn in Bible lands and prior to going on a further journey. The style is remarkably personal and enthusiastic and everywhere Egeria was welcomed by monks, priests and bishops who delighted her by showing her their local holy places. Remarkably her keenness remained unblunted by years of difficult journeys: as Hunt has described her endeavours – 'The driving force behind the *desiderium* of which she so frequently speaks, impelling her in pursuit of sacred places ... is the Bible: the urge to see and be shown in fullest detail every inch of a Scriptural landscape'.[29] With specific reference to her visit to the supposed site of Mount Sinai, Egeria neatly outlined what she wanted to achieve in her whole pilgrimage at each site:

> So this was our plan. When we had seen everything we wanted and come down from the Mount of God, we would come to the place of the [Burning] Bush. Then from there we would return through the middle of the valley now ahead of us and so return to the wadi with the men of God who would show us each one of the places mentioned in the Bible. And this is what we did.[30]

This is indeed what she did and she supplemented simply seeing the places with devotions particular to each one: 'And it was always our practice when we managed to reach one of the places we wanted to see to first have a prayer, then a reading from the [biblical] book, then to say an appropriate psalm and another prayer'.[31] Egeria showed no consternation when her guides pointed out to her places improbable in their triviality – 'Near by you are also shown the place where holy Moses was standing when God said to him, "Undo the fastening of thy shoes", and so on'[32] and she retained a keen interest in seeing every place that anyone was willing to point out to her. Egeria's work, while intended only for a small audience of people with whom she was closely acquainted, has remained a valuable source of information on just how Holy Land pilgrimages were conducted during the fourth century.

Medieval

Given the difficulties of travel in the medieval period it is understandable that many pilgrims wished to create written accounts for wide circulation and works of synthesis of pilgrim accounts. These allowed the medieval emphasis on the spiritual experience of pilgrimage, fostered by the period's religious enthusiasm, to benefit as many people as possible. Authority in texts was not then subject to the ideas of the privilege of actual experience and first hand knowledge, allowing many texts to be copied, edited and reworked over long periods of time. In this phase of the Holy Land geography genre Peter the Deacon wrote his book about Holy Land geography in 1137. It is mostly derived from the Venerable Bede's work on the Holy Places, and also has selections from Egeria's text and other, lost, texts. It is an important indicator of how such texts were recycled and reproduced throughout the medieval period. Peter himself apparently never travelled and created his work for readers who would never travel to the Holy Land either. Its text is densely packed with the places of Scripture and is keen to relay as much information as possible. To that end Peter's style is direct and informative, with little care for the niceties of elegant language or complexity of structure. He follows a 'route' through the landscape and notes the Bible stories connected with each place he encounters, rather than allowing the Bible to determine the order in which he deals with places. For example, his treatment of Jericho is a chronological jumble, but has a clear spatial pattern: 'It is still possible to see part of the foundations of the walls of the city of Jericho, the ones which were overthrown by Joshua son of Nun. And next to the house of Rahab is the sycamore tree into which Zacchaeus climbed'.[33] Peter seamlessly blends the stories of the Old and New Testaments with Rahab and Zacchaeus as near spatial neighbours, though temporally very distant. From here Peter jumps back in time again to the Prophets and Patriarchs, all without leaving the locality of Jericho: 'Not far from Jericho is the place where Elijah was caught up into heaven; and across the Jordan are some very high mountains, among them a specially lofty one called Nebo. This is the one which Moses climbed when he surveyed the Promised Land, and then died'. However, despite his privileging of space over time, no particular features of any place are noted and no actual travelled routes are detailed, allowing us to determine the nature of Peter's research.

The *Travels of Sir John Mandeville* has long been famed as 'one of the most popular and influential books of the later European Middle Ages'.[34] It deals with the journey of a fourteenth century noble man across Europe to Asia and back again, over a period of 35 years. Almost all scholars now believe Sir John Mandeville to be a fictitious character, and his journey to be largely fictitious as well. However, the book contains significant Holy Land material and, as this is derived from other sources, many of them genuine travel accounts, it is an important repository of medieval geographical knowledge concerning the Middle East, the author noting as he does that the Holy Land 'is the heart and midst of all the world'.[35] Like many medieval accounts the *Travels* is more of a list of data than a travel narrative. The text is rich with information about locality and history, without obvious immediate experience of the places: 'about Jerusalem is the Kingdom of Syria. And there beside is the land of Palestine, and beside it is Ascalon, and beside that is the land of Maritaine... About Jerusalem be these cities: Hebron, at seven mile; Jericho, at six mile; Beersheba, at eight mile...'[36]

Sir Richard Guylforde went on pilgrimage to the Holy Land in 1506 and his chaplain wrote an account of the trip. The unfortunate knight died at a fairly early stage on the outward journey, getting no further than Sion, but the rest of the party continued with unabated courage and left us a full and lively account. While the text contains much which bears obvious evidence of the writing of an eyewitness, there is also a certain amount of mythical material, such as the exit of the River Jordan from the Dead Sea. The author was keen to express the pilgrims' devotional exercises: '...as soon as we hadde syght of the Holy Lande we sange Te Deum, and thanked joyously Almyghty God, y^t had yeuen us suche grace to have ones ye sight of y^t most holy lande'.[37] Such notes permeate the text and are balanced by more geographical and biblical allusions which started as soon as the party landed –

At this Jaffe begynneth the Holy Lande; and to euery pylgryme at the first fote he setteth in londe there is granted plenary remyssion, de pena, and a culpa; and at this hauen Jonas ye prophet toke the see whan he fledde from the syght of our Lorde in Tharsis. And in the same Jaffe seynt Peter reysed from dethe Thabytam...[38]

The text also contains references to many extra-biblical traditions, such as the life of Mary after the death of Jesus Christ, which indicate for us the nature of the pilgrimage: Sir Richard's party was interested not only in seeing the scenes of Scripture, but also in seeing the scenes of Christian tradition. The author of the book was evidently keen to see a more contemporary Holy Land as well as the biblical one.

Early Modern

The vast developments in the state of geographical knowledge, and the equally enormous consequences for the authority of classical writers, ushered in by the Age of Reconnaissance had their effects on the enterprise of writing Holy Land geographies too. As new methods of questioning and observing the world and new conceptions of authority began to alter the traditional trust placed in authors like Strabo, Pliny and Ptolemy, new approaches were taken to thinking about the geography of the Holy Land as well. While purely religious pilgrim accounts continued to appear it is noteworthy that by the late sixteenth century some travellers were beginning to employ some of the concerns of natural philosophy both to inspire their journeys and to help structure their travel accounts. Leonhart Rauwolff was a German botanist and physician who toured the Near East from 1575–8 with the motive of collecting botanical specimens which he outlined early in his work:

> I found also those fruitful Places of the Eastern Countries described, which several Authors, and above all the Holy Scriptures have mentioned; and from thence I was enflamed with a vehement desire to search out, and view such plants growing spontaneously in their Native Places, and propounded also to myself to observe the Life, Conversation, Customs, Manners, and Religion of the inhabitants of these Countries.[39]

Rauwolff kept a pocket journal on his travels, and much of the book was written by aid of those notes. However, the anonymous editor of the work did need to make apologies for the tales of Prester John and the unicorn, pointing out that they were merely reports of other travellers' tales. Rauwolff was primarily on a mission to collect what could be thought of as scientific field data, about plants and herbal remedies, but he was also keenly aware of the religious associations of the landscapes he traversed and he noted his attitude of expectation as he approached the Holy Land –

> I found in me a great Desire to see these and other the like Holy Places; Not that I thought... to find their [sic] Christ our Lord ... but to exercise my outward Senses in the Contemplation thereof, that I might the more fervently consider with my inward ones ... Christ our Lord himself.[40]

Rauwolff's travels were a source for many later writers, and as Staphorst noted, 'this may very truly be said of Rauwolff, that whatever he writes upon his own Observations of Knowledge, is most faithful and sincere'.[41] These concerns for accuracy and reliability being important for scholars of the early modern period, many of them consciously contributing to 'the Republick of Learning' and 'Empire of Knowledge' which were the expressed reasons for Rauwolff's work being presented to the public.[42]

George Sandys was a traveller of a different variety than Rauwolff. His writings were of a more scholarly and less practical nature. Sandys travelled in 1610 around the Holy Land and as well as noting the events of his journey included much material from earlier authors, filling many pages with rich historical detail. Sandys was a skilled and elegant writer, and, this combined with his scholarly research has given a very poetically written book. The initial description of the Holy Land glows with the fruits of scholarship, though perhaps shows slightly less travel experience: 'A land that floweth with milk and honey: in the midst as it were, of the habitable world, and under a temperate Clime: adorned with beautiful Mountains and luxurious Vallies, the Rocks producing excellent waters, and no part empty of delight or profit'.[43] Sandys however did not believe all that previous writers had said of the Holy Land, and noted his reservations about

Sandys Travels,

CONTAINING AN

HISTORY

OF THE

Original and present State of the *Turkish* EMPIRE:
Their Laws, Government, Policy, Military Force,
Courts of Justice, and Commerce.

The *MAHOMETAN* RELIGION and CEREMONIES:

A DESCRIPTION of *CONSTANTINOPLE*,
The Grand Signior's *seraglio*, and his manner of living:

ALSO,

Of *GREECE*, With the RELIGION and CUSTOMS
of the *GRECIANS*.

Of *ÆGYPT*; the Antiquity, Hieroglyphicks, Rites, Customs,
Discipline, and Religion of the *Ægyptians*.

A VOYAGE on the River *NYLUS*:

Of *Armenia, Grand Cairo, Rhodes,* the *Pyramides, Colossus*;

The former flourishing and present State of *ALEXANDRIA*.

A Description of the *HOLY-LAND*; of the *Jews*, and several
Sects of *Christians* living there; of *Jerusalem, Sepulchre* of *Christ,*
Temple of *Solomon*; and what else either of Antiquity,
or worth observation.

LASTLY,

ITALY described, and the Islands adjoining; as *Cyprus, Crete,
Malta, Sicilia,* the *Æolian* Islands; Of *Rome, Venice, Naples, Syracusa,
Mysena, Ætna, Scylla,* and *Charybdis*; and other places of Note.

Illustrated with Fifty Graven Maps and Figures.

The Seventh Edition.

LONDON,
Printed for *John Williams Junior,* at the Crown in *Little-Britain.* 1673.

1: The title page of George Sandys's *Travels* (1673)

some assertions: '*Josephus* (and he that Country-man) reports that about [the Dead Sea] are fruits; and flowers, most delectable to the eye, which touched, fall into ashes. A Historian perhaps not always to be credited'.[44] Sandys did plenty of his own travelling, and provided accounts with a lot of colour, even if they are sparse in detail. He noted that 'Upon Easter-Monday we hired certain Asses to ride to Emaus [*sic*], accompanied by a Guard, and certain of the Fryars'. But the only further details of this trip that are given are that the party stopped for devotions on the way and that 'Emaus stands seven miles off and West of Jerusalem. The way thither mountainous; and in many places as if paved with a continual Rock; yet where there is earth, sufficiently fruitful'.[45] Much of Sandys' field observation seems to have been to confirm what he has read in other authors before setting out for the Holy Land.

Works of compilation were also important in the seventeenth-century knowledge of the Holy Land's geography. Heinrich Bünting's 1682 book on the travels described in the Bible is an important example of a work of synthesis. Like many before him Bünting set out to aid biblical scholars:

> It hath always been held a matter worth note (gentle Reader) even to the best Divines, to have the Typographical description of the Towns and Places, as they are mentioned in the Scriptures; and so much the rather, because by comparing the Actions of Men with the beginnings and endings of cities, they might the better understand the Prophets, and perceive the wonderful Providence of God.[46]

Bünting provided such material for his readers in two ways: first, Bünting gave his readers tables listing the journeys, as recorded in the Bible, of an amazing array of characters, with each journey's length in miles and a helpful computation of the total number of miles travelled by each individual, some of which figures seem improbably large, though this is not our concern. Second, he listed places mentioned in the Bible and provides as much geographical information as he can glean from classical writers about each one. Many places have, of necessity, decidedly short entries. Bünting anticipated the difficulty that his readers may have attributing much authority to his work, and fended off critics at an early stage –

> But if you question with me, How is it possible that I should come to the knowledge of those things, considering that Bablyon, Niniveh [sic], Jerusalem, and most of the Cities of the *Holy-Land*, are long since wasted and decayed? To this I answer; therein consists the greatness of Travel, because I have been constrained to use the help of many Authors.[47]

Bünting listed among his sources '*Strabo, Jerom, de Locis Hebraicis, Plinie, Livie, Plutarch...*' and many others.[48] He refers directly to no authors contemporary with himself, but does have some up to date information about the state of a few of the places in the Holy Land.

Frederick Hasselquist's journeys through the Levant were published in translation in London in 1766.[49] Hasselquist travelled in the East from 1749 until his death at Smyrna in 1752. He was a practically-minded and observant traveller, whose writings are peppered with the minutiae of all that he was exposed to and could analyse. His journeys were primarily to collect this information, rather than any sort of pilgrimage. Indeed he referred to the practice of pilgrimage as a 'kind of superstition'.[50] Predominantly Hasselquist was interested in botany, with a secondary interest in geology. These interests left him little time to consider what other writers think of as the sacredness of the landscape he observed; while he did visit the holy sites, it was in a cynical manner, and he tended to treat the Holy Land simply as a field site. His scorn came to the fore as the appointed monks showed him the sites of biblical stories: 'It would make me smile to be shewn a place where an affair happened, which perhaps never did happen; for [the monks] say this was the place where the man fell in amongst robbers, and was passed by the Priest, but taken up by the Samaritan...'[51] He devoted much more time to his botanical studies, but was often disappointed with the results: 'I botanized on the dry and poor Sion, and found some common plants there...'[52] He was also constantly engaged in making geological notes and reconstructed the holy landscape to a laboratory specimen with precision – '[The hills] nearer the Dead Sea, consist of a more loose limestone, sometimes white and sometimes greyish; between which

V O Y A G E S

A N D

T R A V E L S

In the L E V A N T;

In the YEARS 1749, 50, 51, 52.

C O N T A I N I N G

Obfervations in Natural Hiftory, Phyfick, Agriculture, and Commerce :

P A R T I C U L A R L Y

On the Holy Land, and the Natural Hiftory of the SCRIPTURES.

Written originally in the Swedifh Language, By the late FREDERICK HASSELQUIST, M. D. Fellow of the Royal Societies of UPSAL and STOCKHOLM.

Publifhed, by Order of her prefent Majefty the Queen of Sweden, By C H A R L E S L I N N Æ U S, Phyfician to the King of Sweden, Profeffor of Botany at Upfal, and Member of all the Learned Societies in Europe.

L O N D O N,

Printed for L. DAVIS and C. REYMERS, oppofite Gray's-Inn-Gate, Holborn, Printers to the ROYAL SOCIETY.

M DCC LXVI.

2: The title page of Frederick Hasselquist's
Voyages and Travels in the Levant (1766)

are layers of a reddish micaceous stone, or *Saxum purum micaceum'*. The effect of the nature of the geology on the plant life is also carefully noted – 'Near Jerusalem grow different sorts of plants on these hills, especially *Ceratonia*, Carob-tree; *Myrtus*, Myrtle; and *Terebinthus*, Turpentine tree; but farther towards Jericho, they are bare and barren'.[53]

Changing Modes

The ongoing project of textually portraying the geography of the Holy Land has been through many phases, each one producing works which demonstrate something of the broader intellectual, social and religious contexts of the time and place of their writing. Writers in the ancient world produced Holy Land works as aids to biblical understanding, as reference works, as repositories of mythology and as pilgrimage accounts. These works tended to use all of the holy sites, both Old and New Testament. Medieval writings were much more devotionally based, located around a much more centralized set of holy sites, and around a very clearly established pilgrimage tradition, built solidly into the Christian church's framework of belief. With the dawn of the Age of Reconnaissance, developments in geographical knowledge, authority and rationality served to undermine the influence of the Greek schoolmen's geographies and methods and to usher in new concerns, including the importance of first-hand experience, the collection of data for projects in natural philosophy and physick and the systematic recording of travel. Still later Holy Land books became entangled in concerns over the relationship between the Scriptural and scientific uses of the Holy Landscape. Our studies however will focus on these more recent expressions of the project, largely during the nineteenth century, and a more detailed and contextualized history of that era's Holy Land geographies now demands our attention.

2 A History of Scriptural Geography

Few travellers could resist the temptation to use modern Palestine as a living biblical commentary.[1]

DIDACTIC SCRIPTURAL GEOGRAPHIES

Didactic Scriptural Geographies are the earliest that we will consider. Scriptural Geography involving travel was perhaps initiated by the Empress Helena, mother of the Roman Emperor Constantine, who, in AD 326,

> assembled a lavish retinue for an imperial progress eastward through the land of her newly recognized Savior's birth. Unlike earlier Christian pilgrims, who were satisfied with the sometimes contradictory local traditions, Helena sought not merely to tread humbly in the legendary footsteps of Jesus, but to determine their actual locations and to enshrine them forever ... Her mission was deemed a complete success...[2]

This, argues Silberman, began a pilgrimage tradition which saw the first Scriptural Geographies published in early medieval times, but, for reasons of technology and literacy, the number published remained insignificant until it mushroomed soon after the Western 'rediscovery' of Palestine in the early nineteenth century, and this is where our detailed study begins.

Often the authors of these early works have never set foot in the Holy Land, and consider a literature review of available works on Palestine, many of these secondary as well, to be all that is necessary to satisfy the new craving to 'excavate more deeply the mines of Inspired Truth, and to traverse with a critical and observant eye the vast fields of Biblical research'.[3] Working within the conceptions that their day had of rationality, the location of truth and the dispensability of firsthand experience, these geographers were attempting to prosecute a didactic enterprise. Their concern was to aid students of the Bible by 'the use of geographical and historical skills to locate and characterize the important biblical places and events'.[4] This they did using the insights of a host of scholarly undertakings, including the science of their day. Modern Western science in its early stages of development did not, by and large, threaten the beliefs of even the most conservative Christians: scientists were as much part of a culture dominated by religion as anyone else, though geologists had been talking of a long earth history since the early 1800s. Science was seen as an undertaking which explained God's created world, and privileged the place of God's revealed truth in it. The common conception was of two Books of Revelation. One, a Book of Letters, was the Bible; the second, a Book of Nature, was the world and its apparent manifold evidence of a divine Creator.[5] The intellectual interchange which was promoted in using the two Books together is apparent in the commentary of Glacken that: 'The book of nature becomes a commentary, further substantiation of the truth of the revealed word ... Nature conceived of as a book thus often supplemented revelation as a means of knowing God'.[6] Essentially, the Book of Nature could be used to help explain the Book of Scripture, and this is just what the didactic Scriptural Geography enterprise was after. The way in which science was employed in these works is the key to why they can be considered together, as the genre of didactic Scriptural Geography. Science was the particular mode of inquiry through which the interchange between the two Books of Revelation was negotiated.

Bannister's 1844 *Survey of the Holy Land*, is a work of didactic Scriptural Geography. Bannister had not been to the Holy Land, and openly stated his 'aim to accumulate and compress into a single volume the cream of many larger ones; to educe from the writings of ancient and modern authors a succinct yet comprehensive epitome of the Geography, History, and Antiquities of Palestine; and establish the truth of the Inspired Records'.[7] Bannister's establishment of truth was not about a competition with a science which was seeking to usurp the Church's answers to questions of meaning – he never mentioned such an idea: he wanted to establish the truth of Scripture on the basis of using science to explore the Book of Letters. Bannister stated this goal saying that: 'A knowledge of the geography and history of the East, and of the civil and ecclesiastical usages of antiquity, will invest the narrations of Scripture with additional charms, by displaying the incomparable beauty and sublimity of its style, the aptness of its imagery, and the correctness of its allusions'.[8] This need for this simple, almost simplistic, scheme is borne out with example:

> Without some acquaintance with Sacred Geography, many of the finest passages in the Bible must be unintelligible and meaningless. The reader may test the correctness of this remark by a simple experiment. Let him ask himself the meaning of the following passages: – 'His seed shall be in many waters'. (Numb. xxiv. 7) 'Cast thy bread upon the waters: for thou shalt find it in many days'. (Eccles. xi. 1) ... We hazard nothing by the assertion, that a person entirely ignorant of the agricultural usages and atmospheric phenomena of the East would find it extremely difficult to give a correct explanation of these allusions.[9]

A SURVEY

OF THE

HOLY LAND;

ITS

GEOGRAPHY, HISTORY, AND DESTINY.

DESIGNED TO ELUCIDATE THE IMAGERY OF SCRIPTURE, AND
DEMONSTRATE THE FULFILMENT OF PROPHECY.

BY J. T. BANNISTER,

(Author of "Chart of the Holy Land," "Incidents of Jewish History," &c. &c.)

WITH AN INTRODUCTION

BY THE REV. W. MARSH, D.D.

VICAR OF ST. MARY'S, LEAMINGTON.

"Immensos Orientis thesauros, amplissimumque Scientiæ campum, cursumque ad laudem
patefaciet."—Lowth.

SECOND THOUSAND.

Mount Zion.

𝔈𝔪𝔟𝔢𝔩𝔩𝔦𝔰𝔥𝔢𝔡 𝔴𝔦𝔱𝔥 𝔐𝔞𝔭𝔰 𝔞𝔫𝔡 𝔈𝔫𝔤𝔯𝔞𝔟𝔦𝔫𝔤𝔰.

BATH:
BINNS AND GOODWIN.
LONDON: SIMPKIN, MARSHALL, AND CO.
1844.

3: The title page of J.T. Bannister's
Survey of the Holy Land (1844)

21

Demonstrative of the high rate of publication of these works, Rev Charles Forster's *Historical Geography of Arabia* appeared in two volumes in the same year.[10] Another exemplar of didactic Scriptural Geography, this work began with the claim that 'no opportunity (and they have been good and many) has been consciously allowed to escape of throwing light upon the sacred Volume',[11] and continued to explain that

> This remark peculiarly applies to some of the most interesting episodes of the Old and New Testaments ... the stories of Job, of Jethro, of the Queen of Sheba ... the site of Ophir ... the country and Abrahamic origin of the Gospel Magi: points, most of which have long and largely engaged the attention, and divided the opinions, of the commentators...[12]

Forster had an apologetic project, but it was a particular one, and not related to the theories of science, for he conducted his research 'with the sole object of illustrating ... by proofs actually existing in Arabia, the truth of the Mosaic accounts of the first peopling of Arabia'.[13] Forster was interested in the origins of the Islamic people. He was clearly not involved in a scientific project as such; even though he uses evidence from the field he did not go there himself. He does not mention contemporary scientific writers, and his entire engagement with his materials was through textual means.

A variation on approaching the questions of didactic Scriptural Geography is provided by Rev James Aitken Wylie's *The Modern Judea, Compared with Ancient Prophecy.*[14] This is a work with a similar theme, but Wylie was concerned with demonstrating the fulfilment of biblical prophecy in the Holy Land, after situating each prophecy in its geographical setting. However, he did not conduct his own fieldwork: 'Not having myself seen these countries, I judged that accuracy required that I should give the purely physical part of the description in most cases, in the words of the travellers themselves. This has given the volume a greater air of compilation than really belongs to it'.[15] This statement demonstrates that Wylie's relationship with science was one of almost ambivalence: he certainly did not feel threatened enough by it to launch his book against its assertions, indeed he discussed the place of the Bible in relation to science –

'Without professing to explain the order of the universe [the Bible] yet contains nothing at variance with external nature, as modern science has unveiled it'.[16] Wylie's was another work exploring the interchange between the Books of Revelation through the medium of the geography of the Holy Land.

The didactic project also assumed yet simpler forms, again indicating just how wide the section of the population was that consumed the works. The anonymously written *Scripture Sites and Scenes* was completed:

> To give the Bible student ... distinct and truthful ideas of the most important of these hallowed scenes ... It does not profess to be a systematic and scientific account of *all* the localities of the Old Testament, but in a brief compass to give lively impressions of some of the principal ones, *and that almost entirely from personal observation*.[17]

The note to the title that this work is *Chiefly for the Use of Sunday Schools*, indicates its didactic nature. In the text we follow the writer around the landscape, noting, with them, the salient features of the geography:

> It was towards evening that I reached the opening of the valley of Nabulus, running to the westward. This is a location powerfully stamped with Biblical associations: the eye of the mind rested with entire confidence on all its prominent features – the little round corn-covered plain, 'the parcel of ground' bought by Jacob, whose ruinous tomb ... appeared at a short distance.[18]

Similar textbook works also contributed to the 'Capes and Bays' tradition of rote-learning geography. Various volumes were produced for this sort of geographical education, of which John Bowes' work of 1867 is representative.[19] The book is simply a list of the places of the lands of the Bible with occasional notes as to what happened in each place for rote learning. Bowes himself set out his reasons for undertaking his task: 'Experience teaches us that the Volume of the Sacred Law cannot be intelligently read without a knowledge of geography'.[20] Such was the emphasis that Victorian society placed on

Scriptural Geography that it was evidently a key part of the curriculum in many schools.

A larger, more advanced educational text was provided by John Kitto's 1851 work,[21] which set out

> with the view of supplying what has been felt as a desideratum in schools – a History of Palestine, with accounts of the geography of the country, and of the customs and institutions of its ancient inhabitants; but it has been suggested by the Publishers, that the volume might be considered a valuable acquisition by readers of a more advanced class.[22]

Kitto's style remained pedagogical in nature, with numbered paragraphs, which amount to little more than short notes on places, customs and people.[23]

However, the adventure-seeking adult reader had to be considered as well, and a more exciting tone was adopted by John Lewis Burckhardt who travelled in the East, often disguised as Sheikh Ibrahim, between 1810 and 1816, and his accounts were published posthumously by his sponsors the Association for Promoting the Discovery of the Interior Parts of Africa.[24] They qualify as Scriptural Geography material, as pointed out by the editor, Leake,[25] in his prefatory remarks: 'our traveller ... has greatly improved our knowledge of Sacred Geography, by ascertaining many of the Hebrew sites in the once populous but now deserted region...'[26] Burckhardt's contribution was notable in that he, for most of his travels, explored land off the beaten tracks. Burckhardt gave the reader a very straightforward, if evidently partial, account of his activities. He was not apparently motivated by a desire to illustrate the Bible as his primary project, but did so as he went along, assuming that it would be of interest to his readers: 'Here is shewn the well into which Joseph was let down by his brothers; it is ... about three feet in diameter and at least thirty deep...'[27] or 'This is the *Cana* celebrated in the New Testament for the miracle at the marriage feast; and the house is shewn in which our Saviour performed it',[28] along with such allusions as: '...their eggs, which they lay in the rocky ground, are collected by the Arabs. It is not improbable that this bird is the Seloua, or quail, of the children of Israel'.[29]

After these earlier works the spread of literacy and falling book prices allowed books for a huge, general audience to be produced. Among these W.M. Thomson produced one of the best known didactic Scriptural Geographies in 1876.[30] Thomson launched his Scriptural Geography with an appeal to the authority of his text based on his own residence in the Holy Land:

> In many departments of Biblical literature the student in Europe or America, surrounded by ample libraries, is in a better situation to carry on profitable inquiry than the pilgrim in the Holy Land, however long his loiterings or extended his rambles. But it is otherwise in respect to the scenes and scenery of the Bible, and to the living manners and customs of the East which illustrate that blessed book. Here the actual observer is needed, not the distant and secluded student... A large part of these pages was actually written in the open country.[31]

Thomson went on to illustrate, minutely, the Bible from his own experience:

> In some part of these fields, which slope down southward into the valley of Jezreel, her only son, given in reward for her hospitality to Elisha, received a stroke of the sun while looking at the reapers, and this may well have been the case, for the valley glows like a furnace in harvest-time ... The scene is very natural, very graphic...[32]

Again and again Thomson's masterly pen is able to say of some obscure biblical reference that 'The cause is sufficiently obvious to anyone acquainted with the country'.[33]

Comparable with Thomson's work is W.H. Dixon's 1867 book *The Holy Land* which was written very much in the didactic tradition of Scriptural Geography. Dixon claimed for himself the authority of existential experience – 'These studies of the Scenery and Politics of the Sacred Story were made in the Holy Land – in the tent, the saddle, and the wayside khan...'[34] – but did not feel the need to enter into the contemporary debates that were, by then, raging around him. He chose the didactic form of Scriptural Geography deliberately:

I renounce the dream of instructing scholars in their craft; avoid dogma as beyond the province of a lay writer; and leave controversy for the most part to the critics. My aim is to afford the untravelled reader a little help in figuring to himself the country and the events which occupy so many of his thoughts.[35]

Dixon further explained the didactic nature of his work: 'In reading my camp Bible (with the help of Philo and Josephus), on the spots which it describes so well, I was surprised to find how much history lies overlooked in that vast treasury of truth. My book is a picture of what I then saw and read'.[36] His book is essentially a recreation of his experiences, packaged for those who would not be able to tour the Holy Land themselves. Dixon's didactic project meant that the questions that Dixon tried to settle were therefore different ones from those asked of the land's geography by an apologist:

Every hint afforded by the Bible narrative, as to local fact and local colour, helps to prove that the birthplace of David was the birthplace of JESUS, and that the khan, or residence of Jesse, in which these two men were born, stood here in Bethlehem, on the very ridge now crowned by the Basilica of St Helena, the church of the Holy Nativity.[37]

The didactic Scriptural Geography project consisted not only of narrative prose: atlases were also a tool of the trade. Richard Palmer began his *Bible Atlas* of 1831 by asserting that: 'As the study of Sacred Geography is highly interesting, and an acquaintance with it is quite necessary, in order to understand many parts of the Holy Scriptures, it is presumed that no apology is required for the publication of another SCRIPTURE ATLAS'.[38] It is interesting to note that, as late as 1831, and still in accordance with the ideals of the didactic Scriptural Geography project, Palmer finds it necessary to point out that: 'we have not followed the popular opinions concerning the situations of Paradise, Mount Ararat, and the original country of Abraham, &c. considering those which place them much further east, as being by far the best founded, and the most agreeable to Scripture History'.[39]

The notion of making the geography agree with Scripture history is one which would be anathema to later, polemical, Scriptural Geographers, whose earnest desire was that the biblical record would be shown to agree with the geography.

In this category must also come one Scriptural Geography by a female author. A. Goodrich-Freer provided an account of her early twentieth century pilgrimage in the company of an anonymous eminent epigrapher.[40] As noted by McEwan, the content of a woman's travel account can very often have a decidedly different flavour to that of a man.[41] Accordingly Goodrich-Freer's narrative, while encompassing the usual range of holy sites, dwelt also on other concerns, such as that, when resident in the Holy Land, 'You can return home in the afternoon with no anxious forebodings as to how much waste of time is awaiting you in the shape of cards and notes on the hall table...'[42]

Didactic Scriptural Geography can therefore be seen as a project whose aim was to acquaint the reading population with the geographical context of the Bible's stories. This textual project, often carried out by non-travellers, was part of a project of using the world's geography to explain the Bible.

POLEMICAL SCRIPTURAL GEOGRAPHIES

The nature of the polemical Scriptural Geography project is such that it requires an introduction to the nature of the relationship between science and religion in nineteenth century Britain, because the engagement of Christian theology with the new scientific ideas of the Victorian era is a crucial circumstance surrounding the birth of polemical Scriptural Geographies. Statements within the geographies – like '...a country which tells at every step, that THE WORD OF GOD IS TRUE'[43] – show the fear with which science and the new theology were regarded by many conservative biblical literalists, and the need to reiterate the special status of Scripture. Why was such a vehement, polemical line of argument deemed necessary? The importance of the project cannot be overestimated: at this time Britain was enduring a multifaceted intellectual crisis of hitherto unknown proportions. The spread of education and mass literacy were creating problems for the great institutions, as the 'Doctrines championed by established religious dignitaries who upheld the status quo were subjected to the radical critiques of self-taught working class intellectuals' and 'Revolution was in the air'.[44] For the first time, great ideas could be read about and manipulated on a large scale by those at the bottom of the social ladder, those who may have wished to change things, and the spirit of the age was thus determined on the back of reform, radicalism and renewal. In this world everything was up for criticism, and religious beliefs, and the particular religious belief in the inspiration of Scripture – a Scripture which seemed to say that it should be taken as the only source of truth – was only one of the many casualties of this notably freethinking period. These were restless times, and, because of the important role of the Church in the life of the nation at that time, it was inevitably embroiled with the emerging new force – modern Western science. Here, in the middle of the nineteenth century, says Livingstone, was an 'ongoing cultural conflict' a conflict centred on 'the role science was to play in the future of human society'.[45] This was a 'battle', in the terms of Bowler, 'in the ongoing war between science and religion for the control of the human mind'.[46] An almost adolescent intellectual crisis was one of the key symptoms, and it has been captured by Greene in terms of a dilemma: '*Either* mankind could have no knowledge whatever concerning values and the meaning of human existence, *or* science itself would have to derive meaning and value from the processes of nature-history... In either case the dilemma was real, the crisis severe'.[47] Because it was the Church that had, unquestioned, supplied so much of this information before from Scripture, a crisis of faith soon followed, and the certainty of the conservative Christian cosmography was thrown into question. Greene sees three elements to this crisis of faith. First, a challenge to the Victorian form of belief in the inspiration of Scripture, as increasingly science revealed a world which seemed to run on mechanistic principles, elucidated by the new positivistic epistemology. Second, a challenge to the discipline of natural theology and the supposed status of humankind in the Universe. Third, a 'challenge to the philosophical and religious foundations of Western moral and spiritual values implicit in the positivistic reduction of reality to the realm of sense experience': effectively, a denial of the spiritual.[48]

Initially a response to science had been unnecessary, as early in the century science was a discipline devoted to trying to see God in the world of nature – natural theology – an idea stretching back to the times of biblical antiquity,[49] and enthusiastically embraced by the clerics of the day and promoted by the Reformation and Puritanism.[50] The spirit of equality present in Puritanism, it has been argued, was strongly implicit in the growth of science.[51] However, as science came increasingly to favour more positivistic methods, eventually 'the religious burden placed on the sciences [essentially of proving God's existence and settling humankind's place in the universe] did prove too much to bear',[52] and conservative Christians had to respond to the criticisms levelled by a changed science at biblical truth. Nevertheless, many evangelical Christians, as pointed out by Livingstone, remained active in science, and simply altered their interpretations of Scripture.[53]

The publication of Darwin's theory of evolution by means of natural selection can be regarded as having brought matters to a head. It evacuated the force from the design argument of the natural theologians by showing how other means could bring about such a carefully structured world.[54] The epoch-defining *Origin of the Species* was published in 1859,[55] and, contrary to popular belief, the book created little immediate stir.[56] However, it was born into an age of turmoil, as we saw above, a society in which new ideas were rife, and a society of 'Victorian *laissez-faire* capitalism ... that was only too willing to see its own values provided with a "natural" justification'.[57]

Darwin had left Britain on 27 December 1831 on a voyage that would last almost five years and would change his life, and the science of biology, forever. He voyaged around the world on HMS *Beagle*, as a naturalist, and, on his return, 'As Falmouth hove into sight on the stormy night of 2 October [1836] he had questions enough for a career'.[58] Just more than twenty years later a theory about the natural world, making possible 'such transmutations (or evolution as we call it today) threatened Christian Britain at its core'.[59]

The importance of Darwin's theory was that it made evolution possible, gave it venom and gave such an idea's attacks on the scriptural truth, that God had made the earth and all of its inhabitants in seven days and that humans had a special place in it, plausibility. It gave the attacks enough plausibility to make it necessary for the con-servative Christian church to respond, since, society was such then that 'If the authority of the Bible as the inspired word of God were called into question, one of the major bulwarks of Western civil-ization would be undermined and millions of people would be set adrift in a sea of uncertainty'.[60]

The response was 'remarkable for its diversity',[61] and historians have come to see an increasing complexity of the debacle, as a range of sciences and religions interact with each other,[62] and even within what would normally be considered homogenous designations some authors show how a wide variety of responses was offered.[63] Among these responses were polemical Scriptural Geographies: they sought to limit science's role in the explanation of the place and origin of humankind, by demonstrating that the knowledge produced by sci-ence had an inferior status to the knowledge contained in the biblical text. Scientific fieldwork only proved what the Bible already said.

However, the implications of these different world views were so far reaching that they demanded to be judged by different standards. By the final third of the nineteenth century William Barton Rogers, at a meeting of the Boston Natural History Society, had 'succeed[ed] in establishing the point that the value of Darwin's views should be settled by scrutiny rather than authority, by science rather than by dogma'[64] and the stage was set for a sea change in how the world of religion engaged with the world of science.

Not only were problems for the conservative faithful created by scientists, but apparent attacks from theologians, on the issue of the interpretation of Scripture, and its truth content, and hence its story of the origins of the earth and interpretation of its present condition, became more intensive in this period as well. The German school of higher biblical criticism began to flourish about the middle of the nineteenth century, and had profound impacts on Victorian Chris-tianity.[65] It caused difficulties with many of the opinions traditionally held regarding the accuracy, authorship and authority of the Bible, and the movement was for a long time resisted by British theo-logians. Many Scriptural Geographies mention its threat specifically as their *raison d'être*, and the evidence from archaeology was particu-larly used to combat it.

These forces – scientific, social and theological – combined to compromise Scripture's monopoly on truth, and the clergy, together with a devout and scholarly section of the pious laity, reacted with swiftness and a characteristic praetorian vigour. They felt that the best way to fight science – essentially *geo*science – was with science – geography. Explorers and archaeologists were sent out with unbridled enthusiasm to make known the geography of the cradle of faiths, and, crucially, to show to what extent it was exactly as described in the Sacred Book, and was even now fulfilling some of the prophecies there contained. This massive project was undertaken, funded and pursued with immense energy. At the time this was the all-powerful conservative Christian Church ensuring its survival, even though, as Naomi Shepherd points out, 'Palestine was so small a country and so near Europe that it now seems absurd that it should have been one of the targets of great explorers'.[66] Yet this modern-day crusade, I argue, can only be understood if we are to accept that it had a lot more to do with the Jerusalem above, than the one which was carefully engraved, painted and photographed so many times from the Mount of Olives for the benefit of the faithful readership.

What was at stake was not the political allegiance of the space of Palestine, but of what it represented: this was not a crusade concerning a power struggle in Palestine, rather Palestine was but the space in which Western Christians fought their own intellectual civil war, symptomatic of the increasingly privileged role of science in Victorian cosmography. It was in Palestine that the conservatives sought ammunition directly from the patriarchs and heroes of the Bible, in the form of whatever remains they might have left in the landscape, and whatever of their cultural practices might have been bequeathed to the current inhabitants of the land. Palestine became a space for intellectual and moral posturing, in the same way as the Comaroffs have argued that southern Africa has been.[67] Palestine became the space in which the conservative ideas of Victorian society engaged with a new science, and with the social unrest of a newly educated and disenchanted section of the social system. Palestine became a battleground.

Amongst the literature produced by this crusade were polemical Scriptural Geographies. Historically these Scriptural Geographies appear just after the middle of the nineteenth century and are a clear response to the conflicts between the Church and geology. These works are full of blunt statements on just how successfully their authors have proved the accuracy of Scripture through their field-work, and are littered with an immense density of biblical quotations. This bolsters and modernizes the polemical Scriptural Geography pro-ject by adding a scientific element of fieldwork to the scholarly exam-ination of the Biblical texts.

These Scriptural Geographies, largely post-Darwinian, generally had a firm empirical base. Most of the authors had visited the Holy Land and rarely described places which they had not personally en-countered. They have been deeply engaged in the conflict of scien-tific and Biblical truth claims, usually travelling to the very battle-ground, the contested space of the Holy Land, onto which the meeting of mindsets was projected, in order to glean what they could from the spaces of Scripture. The spaces where divine revelation had once been so common, it was evidently thought, were the very sites where it might happen once more. Even as late as 1923, it was possible to write that 'A journey through the Holy Land may reason-ably be expected to be in some sort a sacramental event in a man's life...'[68]

A.P. Stanley's famous *Sinai and Palestine* was a mammoth contrib-ution to this tradition of polemical Scriptural Geography.[69] To him,

> This [recent recurrence of] interest in Sacred Geography ... is invited by the Scriptures themselves. From Genesis to the Apocalypse there are – even when not intending, nay even when deprecating, any stress on the local associations of the events recorded – constant local allusions, such as are the result of a faithful, and, as is often the case in the Biblical narrative, of a contemporary history.[70]

Stanley's use of geography was wary, and he was aware that:

> Those who visit or describe the scenes of Sacred history expressly for the sake of finding confirmations of Scripture, are often tempted to mislead themselves and others by involuntary exagger-ation or invention. But this danger ought not to prevent us from thankfully welcoming any such evidences as can truly be found to the faithfulness of the Sacred records.[71]

And so he used the facts of geography with a caution in his apologetic, aware that –

> there is a more satisfactory 'evidence' to be derived from a view of the sacred localities, which has hardly been enough regarded by those who have written on the subject. Facts, it is said, are stubborn, and geographical facts the most stubborn of all. We cannot wrest them to meet our views; but neither can we refuse the conclusions they force upon us. It is by more than a figure of speech that natural scenes are said to have 'witnessed' the events which occurred in their presence. They are 'witnesses' which remain when the testimony of men and books has perished. They can be cross-examined with the alleged facts and narratives.[72]

As Stanley conducted this enterprise of cross-examination upon his own travels in the Holy Land he considered it 'impossible not to be struck by the constant agreement between the recorded history and the natural geography both of the Old and New Testament'.[73] This led him to declare: 'The detailed harmony between the life of Joshua and the various scenes of his battles, is a slight but true indication that we are dealing not with shadows, but with realities of flesh and blood. Such coincidences are not usually found in fables'.[74] Again, it is Stanley's belief that –

> this evidence is, so far as it goes, incontestable. Wherever a story, a character, an event, a book is involved in the conditions of a spot or scene still in existence, there is an element of fact which no theory or interpretation can dissolve. 'If these should hold their peace, the stones would immediately cry out'.[75]

Stanley applied this apologetic strategy to practically every site he visited, as we witness in his account of the road along which Christ travelled:

> There can be no doubt that this ... is the road of the Entry of Christ, not only because, as just stated, it is, and must always have been, the usual approach for horsemen and for large caravans ... but also because this is the only one of the three approaches which meets the requirements of the narrative it follows... After this

scene, which, with the one exception of the conversation at the Well of Jacob, stands alone in the Gospel history for the vividness and precision of its localisation, it is hardly worth while to dwell on the spots elsewhere pointed out by tradition or probability on the rest of the mountain.[76]

Tristram's *Bible Places* is a comparable apologetic project in polemical Scriptural Geography which consistently and confidently affirmed that 'All research, whether topographical, physical, or archaeological, has uniformly illustrated the intense accuracy of Old Testament history and description...'[77] Tristram's conception of research should not be confused with the science against which his volume is pitted: by research he referred largely to the practices of field workers in the Holy Land, not the theories then being developed by geologists and naturalists which might have impacted on the acceptance of the entirety of the biblical narrative. Tristram himself was an evolutionist, and his concerns therefore were more with the moral aspects of Scripture's teaching. Tristram applied his own researches in Palestine to uncover scenes which will demonstrate the passages of Scripture that are set in them:

> The whole scene of the defiance of David by Goliath lies before us... A little way below Suweikeh, or *Socoh*, two other wadys fall into it, the whole forming an open space covered with fields, opposite which, probably, the Philistines encamped on the south side, at *Ephes-dammim*, now Damûn. In the centre is a pebbly torrent bed, 'smooth stones of the brook', and stunted acacias growing here and there. The Israelites were encamped nearer Socoh, on the north side. On the intervening open space the unequal contest took place between the champion of the Philistines and the youthful hero, described in 1 Sam. xvii.[78]

Tristram drew comfort from finding the scenery exactly as the Bible had led him to expect.

Samuel Kinns provides a further example of a polemical Scriptural Geographer, this time of the armchair variety. Yet he was a researcher who can claim credibility, as his research was carried out on archaeological materials in a museum setting.[79] His self-appointed task was to verify the truth of Scripture from archaeological inscriptions collected in the field: 'In these pages I shall endeavour to give some incidental and direct proofs of [the Bible's] historical accuracy; but it must not be supposed that I can in one volume meet all the objections urged against the Divine origin of this book...'[80] Kinns believed that he had proven that 'the scientific accuracy of the first chapter of Genesis is so remarkable that a Divine origin could alone account for the harmony of its statements with geological facts'.[81] His stated motivation was that: 'If these facts should by God's blessing be the means of assuring others, as they have still more fully convinced myself, of the Divine origin of the Bible, then I shall indeed be truly grateful that I have been led to pursue this special course of study...'[82]

Kinns dealt at length with the implications for Christian believers of Darwin's theory of Natural Selection, and concluded that it was entirely at odds with the Bible record, in contrast to Tristram: 'It seems, therefore, evident that if we accept as true the theories of evolution set forth by Darwin, we must give up all idea of the Bible being a Revelation from God to us'.[83] Kinns was able to demonstrate the accuracy of the Biblical narrative by reference to the inscriptions as in the following example drawn from his work, dealing with a passage in Genesis:

> I must now notice the *'seven years of great plenty'*, and the *'seven years of famine'*. Many, many times have defenders of the Biblical narrative been asked to show on the monuments any reference to these most remarkable events, and never did we doubt that some day confirmation would come, and now we have every reason to feel sure that it has come; ... There is in Elkab, or Eleithyia, a tomb, upon the walls of which is found an inscription relating to Aahmes, who was an officer in the army of the Pharaoh ... who promoted Joseph... What makes this inscription so intensely interesting is that we find no account on the monuments of any other famine 'lasting many years'. This must therefore be Joseph's famine...[84]

In 1857 Rev Horatio B. Hackett published a selection of his travel experiences in the Holy Land, 'which seemed to be capable, of being used with some advantage for the purpose of promoting a more earnest and intelligent study of the sacred volume'.[85] Hackett's work is marked as a polemical Scriptural Geography as he hoped that it would be a means of 'tracing out the proofs of the accuracy of the Bible in its allusions, customs, narratives, geographical notices...'[86] Hackett made his scheme clear as he outlined why he thought his study was important:

> Before entering on my immediate object here, I would premise a remark or two respecting the value of this agreement between the Scriptures and the geography of the Holy Land, as a testimony to the truth of the Bible... It not only frees the Bible from a class of objections which might be and have been urged against its claims to veracity, but, in so far as the agreement can be shown to be obviously unstudied, incidental, it furnishes a direct proof of the truthful character of the sacred Word.[87]

Hackett gave an example of how he saw the polemical Scriptural Geography project working:

> We read in the book of Genesis that when Sodom and Gomorrah were destroyed by fire from heaven, Abraham was dwelling in his tent by the oaks of Mamre, near Hebron ... On the morning after that awful catastrophe, it is said that 'he looked toward' the site of the cities, 'and all the land of the plain, and beheld, and lo, the smoke of the country went up as the smoke of a furnace'. (Genesis xix. 28.) Suppose travellers had now returned from the East, saying that the region of the Dead Sea is not visible from the neighbourhood of Hebron, and that Abraham, therefore, could never have seen any rising smoke from that position, what a shock this would give to our confidence in the Bible! Every one feels that such a representation, if true, would encumber the Scriptures with a serious difficulty. If such errors are to be found in them, if the writers betray such ignorance of the relative situation of the places which they mention, they would incur the suspicion of not having recorded facts, but inventions of their own, or mythic traditions in which they could no longer distinguish the true and false from each other. If convicted of mistakes here, who could resist the impression that they may be fallible also as religious teachers, and thus forfeit the whole character from which they claim their authority over the faith and consciences of men?[88]

However, Hackett was able to reassure his readers:

> From the height which overlooks Hebron, where Abraham stood ...
> the observer at the present day has an extensive view spread out
> before him towards the Dead Sea... A cloud of smoke rising from
> the plain would be visible to a person at Hebron now, and could
> have been, therefore, to Abraham, as he looked toward Sodom on
> the morning after its destruction by Jehovah.[89]

Hackett continued with his campaign around Bible sites:

> I spent a night and a part of two days in the vicinity of the Lake of
> Tiberias... In looking across the water to the other side, I had before
> me the country of the Gadarenes, where the swine, impelled by an
> evil spirit, plunged in to the sea. I was struck with a mark of ac-
> curacy in the sacred writers, which had never occurred to me till
> then... They state that 'the swine ran violently down the steep place
> or precipice' (the article being required by the Greek), 'and were
> choked in the sea'. It is implied here, first, that the hills in that
> region approach near the water; and, secondly, that they fall off so
> abruptly along the shore, that it would be natural for a writer, famil-
> iar with that fact, to refer to it as well known. Both these impli-
> cations are correct. [This demonstrates how the] exact knowledge of
> the Evangelists influenced their language.[90]

It was as he beheld such sights as this that Hackett regretfully stated:

> It may be necessary that one should stand on the spot and survey
> the landscape with his own eyes, in order to perceive the full effect
> of such a confirmation of the truth of the Bible; but surely no one
> who has done so – who has traversed the country and observed
> how its minutest geographical features are reflected back to us in
> the Scriptures – can doubt that the writers lived amid the scenes
> which they describe, and have interwoven in their narratives so
> many accurate allusions to them, because truth, always consistent
> with itself, was their guide.[91]

While the Palestine Exploration Fund, as a corporate body, had no
fixed opinion on the uses of data from exploration in apologetic

causes, many of its explorers had their own ideas. Claude Conder, one of the commanders of its Survey Expedition of 1871–5, wrote in his personal memoir of the Survey that:

> The main object of the Survey of Palestine may be said to have been to collect materials in illustration of the Bible. Few stronger confirmations of the historic and authentic character of the Sacred Volume can be imagined than that furnished by a comparison of the Land and the Book, which shows clearly that they tally in every respect. Mistaken ideas and preconceived notions may be corrected; but the truth of the Bible is certainly established, on a firm basis, by the criticism of those who, familiar with the people and the country, are able to read it, not as a dead record of a former world or of an extinct race, but as a living picture of manners and of a land, which can still be studied by any who will devote themselves to the task.[92]

Conder's task of surveying the Land and authenticating the Book also included analysing the accuracy of those Scriptural Geographers who have gone before: 'In [the cases of] Nob and Ajalon, Jerome's identifications are not in any way capable of being reconciled with the Scripture narrative'.[93] Conder privileged the authority of the scriptural record over the *Onomasticon* as he felt that the scriptural authors have been in the field, and have a familiarity with the places that they describe, which is an authority that Eusebius and Jerome cannot apparently claim. He was also critical of the fieldwork of others when not supported by reference to the biblical text:

> Shiloh lies in so remote a situation … that neither the early pilgrims nor the Crusaders seem to have known of its position … The Crusaders considered Neby Samwîl … to be Shiloh, and also Ramathaim Zophim, or, Gibeah of Saul. Such wild ideas are sufficient to show their ignorance of the Bible…[94]

Conder placed absolute authority in the Bible, using it to interpret the landscape, and to fix the sites of ancient places:

> There is no site in the country fixed with greater certainty that that of Shiloh. The modern name Seilûm preserves the most archaic

form which is found in the Bible in the ethnic Shilonite (1 Kings xi. 29) The position of the ruin agrees exactly with the very definite description given in the Old Testament of the position of Shiloh as 'on the north side of Bethel (now Betîn), on the east side of the highway that goeth up from Bethel to Shechem, and on the south of Lebonah' (Lubben) (Judges xxi. 19).[95]

Not only were explorations conducted by professionals employed on apologetics, smaller scale, private enterprise was at work as well: acting on his own initiative, William Wright made notable contributions to polemical Scriptural Geography. His work in the apologetic cause was conducted in a quite unique spirit, particularly his work on *Palmyra and Zenobia*, in which the stories of his travels are 'depicted with a humour which makes much of the book very good reading'.[96] Wright practised polemical Scriptural Geography in a manner which, while still attempting to authenticate the Bible, did so in a droll fashion, as, with immense frankness, he admitted that much of his exploratory work was carried out under a certain degree of duress:

> Around the base of the mountains, on all sides, these huge towers of death lifted their heads aloft, grim and inaccessible. I was in a dreadful dilemma. If, on the one hand, I attempted to scale the towers, I was certain to break my neck; and if I failed, I was certain to become an object of ridicule to my party ... who already had some misgivings about my sanity... it was my last hope, that should the towers prove unscalable we might somehow take them by screaming, as the French took the Bastille.[97]

However, after overcoming these and other difficulties (and secretly hoping for violent attacks on his party, to allow them to return home) Wright did make valuable discoveries and was invited to lecture to the PEF in 1892.[98]

Wright's methods may have been somewhat eccentric and often open to question, for instance his assertion that the discovery of a second female statue at Palmyra was 'too much of a good thing. The second discovery rendered the identification of the first with Zenobia as doubtful...'[99] which may demonstrate a certain methodological laxity, nonetheless, his work sets out its project as thoroughly experiential – 'This book was written partly in the saddle and partly in the tent, and almost wholly amid the scenes and adventures which it describes'.[100] Along with his writing equipment Wright brought on expedition 'a supply of sticking-plaster', and this might well be the best indicator of his approach to fieldwork.[101]

Wright began the book with the simple statement that 'The Bible tells us that Solomon built Tadmor in the wilderness, and classic authors inform us that Zenobia had her home there',[102] and ended with the equally simple assertion that 'I have thus endeavoured to present a simple picture of Bashan, its people and ruins, as I saw them'.[103] While Wright claimed that 'I have had no theory to support, and therefore I have had no inducement to distort facts to give colour to my own preconceived opinions', he then wrote: 'I have sought truth for its own sake, without any attempt to champion Scripture history, or prophecy, believing, as I do, that simple facts in every department of human research best illustrate the Divine Word'.[104] Wright went on to counsel that

> No one need be discouraged because the picture is poor in mechanical evidence of the pre-Ishmaelitish inhabitants of Bashan... is not the light shed in the Sacred Record by simple facts of a nature to satisfy the most utilitarian investigator? That Bashan contained an enormous number of towns is a fact proved beyond all cavil.[105]

In these, almost the final words of the book, we can see that Wright, while ostensibly pursuing purist research, was in fact out to prove the truth of the Bible in the face of adversity. This is the *raison d'être* of the polemical Scriptural Geography project.[106]

The polemical Scriptural Geography project continued well into the twentieth century, and still has its advocates today. By 1901 the enterprise was sophisticated and based on an established archive of tradition: in Saidian terms it had developed its own self-referentiality. In that year Frank Goodspeed published a series of lectures under the title *Palestine: 'A fifth Gospel'*[107] and he argued consistently in them that the geographical evidence in the Palestine of 1901 bears out the truth of the Gospel:

> In my discussion of the testimony which the land of Palestine as it is seen today bears to the Book, I shall hope to make clear four

particulars in which this is true: 1. First, the land itself is its own witness. 2. Second, the unchanging manners and customs of the people illustrate and enforce the credibility of the Bible record. 3. Third, we possess unmistakable evidence in fulfilled prophecy. 4. Fourth, modern excavation confirms the truthfulness of the Scriptures.[108]

In essence, Goodspeed's argument was that 'The [Bible] is a photograph of the land ... From the geographical standpoint the land and the Book are one'[109] because 'The stories, the events, the characters of the Book are bound up with localities and scenes still to be witnessed'[110] and so the opinions, record and authority of the Book could be trusted. Goodspeed had done his own fieldwork, and had evidently been deeply affected by the experience: 'I hope I may never forget the picture presented to my eye and imagination from Mount Olivet. That hill overlooks more territory which has contained the vital things of the world's faith than any other spot on earth'.[111]

Women also made contributions to the polemical Scriptural Geography project. Madeleine Sweeny Miller and her clergyman husband made many trips to the Holy Land in the first half of the twentieth century. Miller was a keen proponent of the value of geographical knowledge to students of the Bible, and enthusiastically declared that

Like a many-faceted jewel, Palestine flashes out new significances and colourful beauties with every change of light and angle. Social theorist, archaeologist, economist, historian, entrepreneur, artist, pilgrim – whatever your errand – you will find much for contemplation. So essential to an understanding of the Bible are its topography and folk-ways that I wish every bachelor of religion might be required to sojourn here before beginning his ministry – and be endowed with means for that sojourn.[112]

Miller was a polemical Scriptural Geographer, and enthused about the merits of archaeology as a tool in the apologetic project:

From broken pottery appearing in successive strata, from scarabs and seals, they are supplying blank pages of history; fixing pivotal dates; tracing lost migrations as well as modes of everyday living. Verification is coming to Old Testament narratives, which stand

out more brilliantly than ever against the new skyline of the ancient East. If 'higher criticism' a generation ago seemed to lower
the par value of the Bible in some quarters, certainly archaeology
has sent it up again in our day. We have more intellectual respect
for it than ever before.[113]

Following the establishment of Eretz-Israel in 1948 polemical
Scriptural Geography was able to point to this resettlement of the
land by the Jewish people as a fulfilment of Old Testament prophecy
and a further proof of the accuracy of such a document. G.T.B. Davis
is one author whose pamphlet *Seeing Prophecy Fulfilled in Palestine*
dealt with this issue.[114] Davis described the changes that had taken
place in the land of Israel since the establishment of Jewish set-
tlements and ends with the declaration that –

It is truly inspiring to be living in this age when prophecy is
fulfilled so wondrously before our very eyes. The fulfilment of Old
Testament predictions, uttered 2,500 years ago, proves beyond and
peradventure of doubt the truthfulness of the Word of God. The
record of these facts is a tonic to faith in these days of doubt and
unbelief.[115]

The polemical Scriptural Geography enterprise was thus one of
apologetics. Authors attempted, in a variety of ways, to use data from
both the physicality of the landscape and its archaeological remains
and the habits of its population to support their belief in the truth
claims of the Book whose story was set in that Land.

CONTEXTUAL SCRIPTURAL GEOGRAPHIES

Eventually, geography's ever-changing face filtered through to Scriptural Geography too, and the spatial context of revelation became
important, in works which were not afraid to assimilate the scientific
knowledge that polemical Scriptural Geographers found threatening,
and to gain insight from the theological ideas that polemical Scriptural Geographers found heretical. However, this does not mean that

this new set of Scriptural Geographers relied *only* on data from science and higher criticism, they used the biblical text too. The difference is in the way in which they use these various sources. As geography and theology developed in intellectual complexity, Scriptural Geography was not slow to pick up on these trends and assimilate them into its garderobe of techniques for engaging with the sacred space, and so contextual Scriptural Geography appeared.

As early as 1877 Selah Merrill was writing articles for the American Geographical Society which had a decided flavour of contextual Scriptural Geography. Merrill's sentiments were that 'it has taken not merely generations, but centuries, to raise up a class of men who would study Palestine in a religious, and at the same time in a thoroughly scientific spirit. Indeed, it is only in recent times that such a spirit has become prominent'.[116] Merrill championed the idea that Palestine had too long suffered from an idealized, imaginative geography. This geography, as it existed in the minds of the pious, 'has little likeness or relation to the actual Palestine which lies on the east and on the west of Jordan'.[117] In this imagined geography, argued Merrill, the land assumed an almost mythical and immutable quality, 'And an obstacle which the explorer sometimes meets is the reluctance on the part of such people to have anything done which may interfere with their ideal Holy Land'.[118]

Merrill had little time for traditional religious theories about the Holy Land, and felt that they were often misleading:

> if a person follows tradition as a sure guide, he must locate the cities of the plain at the south end of the Dead Sea, and do so in defiance of all the evidence which geology, physical possibilities, and archaeology have to present, which is opposed to tradition to such a degree as to be overwhelming.[119]

Thus Merrill prescribed that those who are to write Scriptural Geography must have 'a thorough personal acquaintance'[120] with the Land, and after such an acquaintance, Merrill wrote his own book of Eastern exploration, *East of the Jordan*.[121] This work was a mixture of field archaeology and erudite biblical and classical textual analysis.

In conducting his field work, Merrill's equipment was that of the scientist:

My sun-umbrella, ... my gun, and two pockets full of cartridges; my compass and field glass. In my saddle bags I carry a geological hammer, extra ammunition, thermometer, guide-book, a large note-book with pens and ink, also string and cotton to plug the wounds in birds that are shot, and paper with which to wrap them up.[122]

No mention is made of a Bible which would usually be among the most important part of a polemical Scriptural Geographer's baggage. Among his party's duties Merrill stated that 'Archaeology and topography have the first claim upon our attention, and after them, natural history'.[123] Merrill did not mention apologetics or anything approaching it. He did not feel threatened by the new scientific ideas, indeed, when discussing the relative patience of his men and his camp donkeys he can joke about them: 'If it is true that men came up from the lowest order of creation, then it is certainly true that at that stage which the life of the donkey represents, the race of human beings left behind many noble qualities'.[124] And so, unthreatened by science he was able to use it to dispel the myths of his predecessors:

Until recently, the opinion held by a majority of the best Biblical scholars was a modification of that just stated. Namely, that the shallow water south of the promontory El Lisan covered the sites of the doomed cities. But the geological researches that have been carried on about the Dead Sea during the past few years have made both these theories no longer tenable... During past geological ages the surface of the sea has contracted to its present limits. The destruction of these cities took place within historical times; but within historical times there has been no convulsion in that region, or change in the sea or land about it, to justify either of the opinions to which reference has been made.[125]

Merrill's reliance on field data outweighed his respect for his predecessors in Scriptural Geography:

To the suggestion that Nawa might be the site of Golan, 'J.L.P.', in Smith's 'Bible Dictionary', says very decidedly: 'For this there is not a shadow of evidence, and Nawa, besides, is much too far to the eastward'. But since these words were written, the ground has been thoroughly examined, and the objection of its being too far east is not a good one.[126]

He even used his field data to correct the allusions of respected commentators:

> In Hosea vi. 8. we find Gilead mentioned as a city ... The majority of commentators say (among them, for example, Keil and Delitzsch) that 'Gilead is not a city, for no such city is mentioned in the Old Testament'. We consider it best, however, to take the statement of Hosea in a literal sense.[127]

This was not a decision made on the basis of a naive literalism, but on the basis of field evidence, and of having visited the site. Merrill elsewhere demonstrates his respect of the scholarship of Delitzsch, and makes use of his interpretation of the Talmud, and evidently entered into direct correspondence with this 'eminent commentator'.[128]

Merrill showed no concern to authenticate the Bible from his experience of the archaeology and geography. Rather he used the Bible's allusions, often after their modification by higher critics, along with his existential experiences in the Land, to help situate the places mentioned in the Biblical text. This is a contextual project: his aim was to illustrate rather than to authenticate.

A.H. Sayce, Professor of Assyriology at Oxford from 1891–1933,[129] was likewise an enthusiastic contextual Scriptural Geographer. His 1894 book, *Higher Criticism and the Monuments*, was a substantial contribution to the project. In the preface he stated quite simply that:

> I cannot refrain from drawing attention to the remarkable way in which archaeological discovery has confirmed the judgment of the Jewish Church... The distinction ... drawn by the Jewish Church between the Hagiographa and the earlier books of the Old Testament is strikingly reflected in the results of archaeological research... In one case we have history, in the other case history transformed in to a parable.[130]

Sayce aimed to write, 'as an archaeologist rather than a theologian, treating the books of the Hebrew Bible as I should any other oriental literature which laid claim to similar antiquity, and following the archaeological evidence whithersoever it may lead'.[131] However, even though Sayce did not buy wholesale into the arguments of higher criticism and modern scientific research, he nonetheless employed them in his work. 'It may often happen', he stated,

> that the ancient book we are examining may be, in its present form, of comparatively late date, and yet contain older documents, some of them indeed being earlier than itself by several centuries. Modern research has shown that a considerable part of the most ancient literature of all nations was of composite origin, more especially if it was of a historical or religious character.[132]

This was the influence of higher criticism at work. Sayce spoke in support of higher criticism, arguing that –

> The arrogancy of tone adopted at times by the 'higher criticism' has been productive of nothing but mischief; it has aroused distrust even of its most certain results, and has betrayed the critic into a dogmatism as unwarranted as it is unscientific... If the archaeologist ventured to suggest that the facts he had discovered did not support the views of the critic, he was told that he was no philologist. The opinion of a modern German theologian was worth more, at all events in the eyes of his 'school' than the most positive testimony of the monuments of antiquity.[133]

Sayce's project however was a more nuanced and sophisticated argument for the use of higher criticism and modern science, and he went on to argue that in the early days of higher criticism,

> ...the fault lay not with the 'higher criticism' but with the 'higher critic'. He had closed his eyes to a most important source of evidence, that of archaeology, and had preferred the conclusions he had arrived at from a narrower circle of facts to those which the wider circle opened out by oriental discovery would have forced him to adopt.[134]

He therefore argued for the use of a combination of modern methods to help contextualize the Bible stories. His argument was that: 'The period of scepticism is over, the period of reconstruction has begun. We shall find that the explorer and decipherer have given us back the old documents and the old history, in a new and changed form it may be, but nevertheless substantially the same'.[135] Sayce supported his argument that the Scriptures can be more fully understood by a combination of critical and scientific means with numerous examples:

> Two or three years ago it would have seemed a dream of the wildest enthusiasm to suggest that light would be thrown by modern discovery on the history of Melchizedek. Whatever lingering scruples the critic might have felt about rejecting the historical character of the first half of the fourteenth chapter of Genesis, he felt none at all as to the second half of it. Melchizedek, 'King of Salem' and 'priest of the most high God', appeared to be altogether a creature of mythology. And yet among the surprises which the tablets of Tel el-Amarna had in store for us was the discovery that after all Melchizedek might well have been a historical personage.[136]

Less overtly scholarly works are also part of the contextual Scriptural Geography project, as it authors were trying to benefit a broad range of Christian readers. Cunningham Geikie's Scriptural Geography was founded on the straightforward premise that:

> Nothing is more instructive or can be more charming, when reading Scripture, than the illumination of its texts from such sources [data from personal travel], throwing light upon its constantly recurring Oriental imagery and local allusions, and revealing the exact meaning of words and phrases which otherwise could not be adequately understood. Its simple narratives, its divine poetry, its prophetic visions, its varied teachings, alike catch additional vividness and force when read with the aid of such knowledge. The Land is, in fact, a natural commentary on the sacred writings which it has given to us, and we study them as it were amidst the life, scenery, and the local peculiarities which surrounded those to whom the Scriptures were first addressed.[137]

Geikie's was a contextualization project; he felt no need to authenticate the Scriptures by his travels, symptomatic of this was Geikie's assertion that – 'It would be interesting to go through the Gospels and note the strict correctness of their allusions to the scenery, topography, and customs of the people round the lake in old times'.[138] It 'would' said Geikie. He took on no such task, and evidently felt no compulsion to do so.

PROBABLE SITE OF GATH (p. 107).

4: Illustration from page 113 of Cunningham Geikie's
The Holy Land and the Bible

In 1899 an important collection of essays was published, concerned with the authority of the documents of antiquity in the light of recent archaeological discovery, and particularly the Bible, within the context of both modern archaeological work and critical biblical scholarship. Because they make use of the data from field expeditions and archaeological investigations, the essays are a form of Scriptural

Geography. S.R. Driver, a noted critical scholar, opened his section on the Old Testament with the bold assertion:

> There are many representations and statements in the Old Testament which only appear in their proper perspective when viewed in the light thrown upon them by archaeology. And in some cases, as will be seen, it is not possible to resist the conclusion that they must be interpreted in a different sense from that in which past generations have commonly understood them.[139]

Driver quickly followed this with an example of such a passage –

> The Book of Genesis opens with a Cosmogony (i.1–ii.4a), which for sublimity alike of conception and expression stands unique in the literature of the world. While for long this cosmogony was regarded as a literally true description of the manner in which the earth was gradually adapted to become the habitation of man, the progress of science during recent years has shewn this view of it to be no longer tenable; the order in which the several creative acts are represented as having taken place conflicting too seriously with the clearest teachings of astronomy and geology for it to be regarded as possessing and value as a scientific exposition of the past history of the earth. And hardly had science established this conclusion, when archaeology opportunely disclosed the source from which the Hebrew cosmogony was derived.[140]

Driver went on to show how archaeology has uncovered inscriptions in ancient Babylon which tell essentially the same creation narrative as Genesis, and predate it considerably, and so Driver was forced to conclude that the Genesis narrative is derived from a Babylonian creation story, and that its significance must be symbolic, rather than literal:

> The progress of Babylonian and Egyptological research has strikingly confirmed the results obtained by anthropologists upon other *data* respecting the immense antiquity of man upon this earth. The chronology of the Book of Genesis forms, however, it is evident, a carefully constructed scheme ... and if it deviated from the reality ... by whole centuries, it materially confirms the con-

clusion, reached in the first instance upon other considerations, respecting the symbolical character of the narrative...[141]

Driver's conception of the authority of the Bible has been forged by a combination of higher criticism, archaeological field work and religious tradition. Of these three he appears to grant the highest authority to archaeology:

> Now while, as need hardly be said, there are many points on which, as between what may be termed the traditional and the critical views of the Old Testament, the verdict of archaeology is neutral, on all other points the facts of archaeology, so far as they are at present known, harmonize entirely with the opinions generally adopted by the critics. The contrary is, indeed, often asserted: it is said, for example, that the discoveries of Oriental archaeology are daily refuting the chief conclusions reached by critics, and proving them one after another to be untenable: but if the grounds on which such statements rest are examined in detail, it will be found that they depend almost uniformly upon misapprehension...[142]

In 1901 A.W. Cooke published *Palestine in Geography and in History*, and Cooke stated his project in the preface:

> This Handbook has been written for the help of Bible readers and students who desire to form a clear picture of the country in which most of the events about which they read occurred. It is an attempt to enable them to follow the narratives on the Old and New Testaments, with their eyes upon the actual scenery.[143]

Cooke's work aims to 'bring the latest results of Palestinian research within the reach of readers who have neither time nor opportunity to consult larger works for themselves'.[144] This use of field research to contextualize, rather than authenticate the Scriptures, is what makes Cooke a contextual Scriptural Geographer. Furthermore, in Cooke's 'historical discussions, the works of Kittel, Graetz, Schürer, Wellhausen and Ewald have chiefly been consulted'.[145] These are all critical scholars, and Cooke's use of them is important, as he tries to contextualize the biblical narrative. And so Cooke treats the history and geography of Palestine, contextualizing the Bible's stories with a full historical and geographical analysis of how so many of the places had come to be as they were. No polemic was thought necessary.

Later works in this tradition decry the practices of the polemical Scriptural Geographers, among them John Kelman, who deplored the 'mistaken zeal of the huntsmen of the fields of prophecy, who cannot see a bat fluttering about a ruin or a mole turning up the earth without turning ecstatically to the Hebrew prophetic books, – as if these were not the habits of bats and moles all the world over'.[146]

By 1935 the Bishop of Bradford, in an Introduction to S.L. Caiger's work on biblical archaeology was able to say that –

> It is a serious mistake … to set archaeology and criticism against one another. Both are needed as helps to understand the Bible story. Without higher criticism, Old Testament history would still be largely a chaos: criticism has introduced order and development into the story. Archaeology does not disprove criticism: it only contributes additional data for the problems which criticism has to solve; and the finds of the excavator have to be set side by side with the literary evidence of the Bible itself, in order to obtain what every student, critic, or archaeologist desires, a trustworthy account…[147]

The contextual nature of the understanding of the influence of the Holy Land on the Holy Book is demonstrated by G.E. Wright's 1960 work dealing with biblical archaeology. Wright noted that 'The Bible, unlike other religious literature of the world, is not centered on a series of moral, spiritual, and liturgical teachings, but in the story of a people who lived at a certain time and place'.[148] In order to thoroughly contextualize this emplaced narrative, Wright argues that the methods of archaeology are necessary to run the, often unwritten, history to earth:

> The study of archaeology, however, involves the theologian in certain risks. The first is that he may find that the biblical events did not occur at all, that the Bible is little more than a congeries of myth and legend. For the most part archaeology has substantiated and illumined the biblical story at so many points that no one can seriously take this position. Nevertheless, the role of archaeology

has sometimes been negative. For example, it has lent its support to the evidence of geology and biology that man and the earth have a much longer past than the traditional biblical chronology allowed.[149]

Wright draws on the specific nature of religious experience to help found his discussion of the contextualizing merits of archaeological discourse:

> The resurrection of Christ was an inner certainty for early Christians, but it is something which archaeology can do nothing to illuminate. Hence the support archaeology can give to the biblical record is limited. It cannot 'prove the bible true', but it can illuminate the historical setting, the events themselves, and the cultural background.[150]

Wright's argument was that apologetics could not, in the intellectual climate of the second half of the twentieth century, proceed on the basis of archaeological investigation. By then field science had a different role: that of contextualizing the Bible.

In de Boer's preface to Franken and Franken-Battershill's study of the same topic in 1963, the conclusion was reached that – '[Now] the door opens for collaboration between archaeology and exegesis. Both branches of the same discipline belong together and their going hand in hand promises to be a success if each of them respects the law of scientific research: openness to verification'.[151] It is appropriate that our study of contextual Scriptural Geography should end with a passage from the same book, which neatly summarizes the development of much of the Scriptural Geography project, from within the perspective of contextual Scriptural Geography:

> Archaeologically speaking, Palestine has suffered from her unique position in the sphere of world religions. Instead of being treated as a practical aid to history, helping to push back the frontiers of prehistory, archaeology in Palestine has in the past – and in some instances even now – been used to shore up an interpretation of the authority of the Old Testament... Archaeology is a costly business, and its patrons often had some religious axe to grind, or some pet theory to prove... Executors of such pursuits pay little

attention to 'irrelevant' archaeological evidence and their publications have often little value.[152]

Contextual Scriptural Geography is a project about explanation
and situation of the biblical text, using the methods of modern science and theological scholarship. Its authors do not attempt apologetics or deny that the truth claims of the Bible have been compromised by both science and some theological scholarship. Their task is
rather to work within a radically altered intellectual framework, and
show how the insights of geosciences can help readers to understand
the Bible.

LINKING SCRIPTURAL GEOGRAPHIES

The genealogy of the Scriptural Geography project can thus be traced
through the ages, with an eye to the context of the project's existence. My argument hinges around the changing role of science in
Scriptural Geography. Initially science was, through natural theology,
the ally of the faithful, allowing Scriptural Geographers to explore
and document the Holy Land, even if through secondary texts. Subsequently science began to prove threatening to the religious faith of
many and Scriptural Geography was employed to combat the growing dissatisfaction with Victorian Christian society's values and
failings. Eventually, science, both in the field and employed in understanding the biblical text, came to be seen once more as the ally of
faith, and was used to help contextualize the Bible, and allow for a
fuller understanding of its stories, in conjunction with critical scholarship and a spirit of devout reverence.

I want to argue on the basis of this brief introductory survey that
Scriptural Geographies can be divided into three separate and distinct
categories: those *didactic* works, whose aim is simply to inform the
reader about the landscape of the Holy Land, or as much of it as is
imagined to remain in a similar condition to the ancient landscape,
using mainly textual sources; those specifically and openly *polemical*,
seeking to prove Scriptural truth in the face of a threatening science;
and those whose concern is to *contextualize* the site of divine reve-

lation, using the insights of science, in geographical and historical ways, for the benefit of Biblical scholars. To support this assertion of a threefold categorization of distinct orders of Scriptural Geography a more detailed analysis will now be undertaken and a representative variety of the multitude of Scriptural Geographies published will be surveyed and analyzed. While my taxonomy is conceptual and genetic rather than historical, the three orders of Scriptural Geography do roughly fall into three time periods: initially prior to 1850, before science was a serious threat to religion and was practised, at least in Britain, within a natural theology context; between 1850 and about 1880, when the friction of modern theology, science and religion was at its height; and after about 1880, when scientific ideas were assimilated into the religious narratives of many of the writers. However, this chronology is of secondary importance to the analysis, and some works were published in each period which lie outside the time frame that they might be expected to reflect: in our dealings with Scriptural Geographies we must treat them as contextually situated works, having, along with Livingstone, an awareness of the 'situated messiness' of the circumstances of their creation, as with all geographical knowledge.[153]

INSTANCES IN THE SCRIPTURAL GEOGRAPHY PROJECT

Now that this work's triumvirate classification of Scriptural Geographies has been advanced and supported, an emblematic contributor to each order of Scriptural Geography will be dealt with in detail, to aid our understanding of the process of the negotiation of this particular form of geographical knowledge at specific points in its genealogy. The story of Scriptural Geography will be told with reference to the wider contexts of social theory and travel writing theory, of time, space and the changing nature of knowledge and authority. All of these are apparent in the biographies of three individual Scriptural Geographers, whose lives compare and contrast. The three are Protestant clerics of the nineteenth century; they were all biblical scholars, all Old Testament specialists; they all made significant scholarly contributions to the world in their day; they were all

Western Europeans and they all viewed the Holy Land as a special space. Their motivations to write about the Holy Land were united by a single factor. They wanted to benefit Christian believers. They were all Scriptural Geographers. And yet they lived in profoundly different times, and had profoundly different ideas about their Christian faith, and about the world around them, which meant that they wrote profoundly different types of Scriptural Geography.

Michael Russell

Bishop Michael Russell wrote prolifically in a short, but very full, life. His writings covered an almost unbelievable range of topics in depth and clarity, and yet today, because of a changing intellectual climate, they are largely forgotten. His biography exists only in a short essay published more than a century ago, and this is perhaps a reflection of the relative obscurity of the Scottish Episcopal Church, in which he served as a bishop. Russell is a figure whose life and writings repay earnest study, as an insight into how didactic Scriptural Geography works. A fully contextually-aware study of his life is a fruitful undertaking, and will cast light on the nature of geography, theology and their relationship to the Holy Land in the early nineteenth century.

Josias Leslie Porter

As a Vice-Chancellor, Education Commissioner and Presbyterian Moderator, J.L. Porter is a figure not without significance in Irish history. While no biography exists, it is possible to reconstruct his fascinating life from archival and documentary sources and to see the contrasts of a life spent in Ireland, Scotland, England, and the Holy Land. He was a mammoth contributor to polemical Scriptural Geography, and his work is well overdue a new analysis. The peripherality of his publishing career (the majority of his works were published in Belfast) has meant that he has not yet received the attention which should be the due of such a significant scholar. An assessment of his work is provided here, and it is hoped that it will demonstrate the uses of geographical knowledge in Christian apologetics and the social and intellectual forces behind this particular employment of the tools of students of space and culture in the third quarter of the nineteenth century.

George Adam Smith

George Adam Smith was a well known and highly respected scholar of the late nineteenth century. His many works were immensely popular and poetically written and his notable scholarly career was marked by countless accolades and awards. His writings have received much scholarly attention, and it is hoped that this work breaks new ground by bringing a new set of theoretical apparatus to their study. In spatial terms George Adam Smith's life stretched from British India to Scotland to Germany to the Holy Land and it will be argued that the effects of this spatially-fluid existence are seen in his theology and in his Scriptural Geography, through a geographical study of the expression of the late Victorian intellectual sensibility.

A comparison of these three figures, their biographies and their Scriptural Geographies, will reveal the genealogy of the Scriptural Geography project in more detail, at crucial points in its existence. Our studies will therefore detain us at three key points in Scriptural Geography's story, and we will note the extent to which our three emblematic Scriptural Geographers follow the salient features of the different forms of the project noted in our analysis, along with more specific theoretical and biographical contexts for each of the three, which will allow us to begin to understand just why and how they wrote about the geography of the Bible in the particular ways that they did.

3 The Didactic Order: Michael Russell

The chapter on Natural History has no pretensions to scientific argument or technical precision ... Its main object is to illustrate the Scriptures...[1]

MICHAEL RUSSELL

An unbounded enthusiasm for geographical knowledge and the approach of an erudite scholar can be sensed in the opening of two works of the nineteenth century: 'In many respects Egypt has long appeared to the scholar, the antiquary, and the philosopher, the most interesting country on the face of the earth'[2] and 'There is no country in the world more interesting to the antiquary and scholar than that which was known to the ancients as "Ethiopia above Egypt", the Nubia and Abyssinia of the present day'.[3] The author of these words, Bishop Michael Russell, was a Scottish clergyman whose intense fascination with scholarship and whose unremitting literary labours were generally considered to be the cause of his early death.[4]

He was firstborn to John and Euphan (née Hamilton) Russell on 12 August 1781, in Edinburgh.[5] His was a Presbyterian family, and Russell was brought up a Presbyterian.[6] The next event in his life that has been recorded is that he matriculated at Glasgow University at the beginning of the academic year 1800–01. His studies at Glasgow were protracted, lasting a total of five years, instead of the usual four.[7] Most probably this was on account of his poor circumstances, which meant that while studying the young Russell had simultaneously to tutor pupils to provide income to continue his education. That Russell actually took his degree at all was unusual for a student at a southern Scottish university at that period, and serves to indicate his scholarly inclinations and personal determination. The curriculum demonstrates the scope of the content of the Scottish higher education system at the time: Russell's first year was spent in studying Latin, his second Greek, followed by a year of Logic, then a year's study of Ethics, and his course finished with a year's study of Physics.[8] He graduated with an MA with High Honours in 1806.[9]

In the same year Russell was appointed Second Master of Stirling Grammar School, a position he secured largely on the merit of his bookish reputation. He was generally considered to be overqualified for the job.[10] During his time at Stirling he came into contact with Episcopalians, and, in due course shifted his denominational allegiance. This meant that his teaching job became untenable, as to work in a state-run grammar school like Stirling, it was necessary to be a Presbyterian. Russell responded to this challenge with characteristic creativity and established a private school in his house at Stirling. The venture was very successful and most of his pupils were the sons of Presbyterian merchants from Glasgow.[11] His activities however were soon to be directed to another sphere.

In 1808 Russell was given charge of the small congregation of Alloa, a few miles from Stirling, after being admitted to deacon's orders in the Scottish Episcopal Church. Since the congregation was small and his stipend slender, he continued to maintain his private school and apparently only travelled to Alloa to take services.[12] The Alloa congregation was still in its earliest phase and 'Mr Russell's charge of Alloa seems to have been from the first only of a partial and quasi-missionary nature'.[13] Sadly, 'there is at Alloa no trace left of his brief ministry' and the congregation has no documentary sources at all going back any further than 1837.[14]

In November 1809 Russell was elected to be the incumbent of St James' Church in Leith, after preaching for the pulpit, and he continued to live there for the rest of his life. This was a larger congregation with a more generous income, and he was able to quit his school-teaching activities for the first time since he had gone to Glasgow University. It was a prestigious charge, and had previously been

5: Bishop Michael Russell

in the care of Bishop Robert Forbes.[15] Russell's ministry at St James' was evidently a success, and here

> he found ample scope for his best energies every day of the week; and his steady, faithful ministry of forty years was abundantly blessed to the Church. All ministerial duties, including the keeping and preservation of registers, were duly and regularly attended to.[16]

At Leith Russell engaged avidly in erudite pursuits and took on the editorship of *The Scottish Episcopal Review and Magazine*. This strange publication, which in one form or another has continued to the present day, was, at the time of Russell's editorship, remarkable in that it included 'little ... that is distinctively either Scottish or Episcopal ... there is less reference to the Scottish Episcopal Church than is to be found in any English ecclesiastical magazine of the present day [1893]'.[17] It is notable that the publication is at pains to distance itself from its church, and 'Even those contributors who ... had the closest connection with the "Episcopal Church in Scotland" seem to make themselves strangers to their own flesh, and write or designate themselves as if "spectators *ab extra*"'.[18] The journal was 'only in a negative sense ... an organ of the "Scottish Episcopal Church". It admitted nothing that was directly opposed to the principles or claims of that Church...'[19] However, the publication did have a solid intellectual content, and discussed the burning issues of the day.

Russell's scholarly efforts and speedy rise through the church were recognized, as in February 1820 his Alma Mater, Glasgow, recognized the quality of his work with the honorary degree of LLD, and indeed Russell published regularly, in an enormously productive life. His range of topics varied from his influential *History of the Church in Scotland*, which appeared in 1834,[20] through to a work on *The Barbary States*, which formed part of The Edinburgh Cabinet Library.[21]

PUBLICATIONS

In 1827 Russell produced the first of two volumes of one of his great works. *A Connection of Sacred and Profane History* was to become the work with which his reputation as a scholar was firmly established.[22] While this work is of little direct interest to our inquiries here, an understanding of its content will allow us to see how Russell's interest in the geography of the Holy Land was first stimulated. Russell set out to finish the works of Dr Shuckford, whose book linking the history contained in the Bible with secular historical accounts remained incomplete at the time of his death. Russell bemoaned that

> The numerous events, therefore, which took place under the government of the Judges; in the brilliant reigns of Saul, David, and Solomon; as well as during those of the successive princes of Israel and Judah, till the ascendancy of the Assyrian power threatened the liberty of both these nations, remained to be embodied in a continuous narrative...[23]

Russell set out to fill this gap and provide a work which continued Shuckford's project. Ten years later Russell added a second volume to this work, and so was able to connect sacred and profane history from the time of Joshua to the time of Christ, drawing on and complementing the work of Prideaux, whose writings filled in the historical detail of the period between the close of the Old and opening of the New Testament. Given the familiarity with some of the most obscure documentation of Eastern history that Russell demonstrated in this work, it is perhaps natural that publishers would subsequently turn to him when a work dealing with the East was required.

The year 1829 saw the publication of Russell's *Life of Oliver Cromwell*, in two volumes, in the Constable's Miscellany series.[24] The work is interesting to the present project in that it shows us what type of scholar Russell was: how he dealt with texts and what sort of authority he gave them, how he conceived of history, and how his perspective on the historiographical angles available to authors came through in his work.

The tomes in question are heavy with scholarship and erudition. Their tone is self-consciously historical and learned, with frequent, highly detailed footnotes and a painstaking level of detail. At the beginning of the first volume Russell immediately set out to demonstrate his methodological approach to the reader; he says that in this biography, Cromwell's story is fully illustrated by a perusal of the works of Clarendon, Heath, Bates, Dugdale, Hollis, Coke, and Slingsby Bethel, compared with those of Milton, Clement Walker, Winstanly, Sydenham, Dawbeny, the author of the Unparalleled Monarch, Gibson, May, and Ricraft. In later times ... the conclusions, as to the character and policy of Cromwell which have been drawn by Hume and Echard, on the one hand, and Macaulay, Laing, Brodie and Godwin on the other...[25]

These sources are not however taken at face value: their content is evidently carefully scrutinized and more trust is placed in some than others, apparently on the basis of the supposed rigour of their scholarship –

The industry of Mark Noble, too, has brought to light many interesting facts respecting the genealogy and descendants of Oliver; and he has never rested satisfied without an authentic reference, the various notices with which he has imbodied [sic] his book may be confidently received as the materials of history.[26]

It seems that, for Russell, a work qualifies as part of 'the materials of history' merely by having a thorough attitude to referencing and a rigorous research programme; no attention is paid to the provenance of the materials or the niceties of the historiographical narrative into which they are woven. In Russell's conception there is not so much a problem of there being 'no history on the mortuary table',[27] rather, the questions at stake are easily and quickly answered by a fleeting glimpse of the 'body', as they tend to be of a superficial nature. Therefore, as Russell comes to write his own account of Cromwell's life, he does it in the following manner:

It has been the study of the present author, while he availed himself of the labours of his predecessors, to avoid the two extremes ... and to give an unbiased view of Cromwell's conduct ... His character throughout is made to depend upon his actions; and the reader, accordingly, is everywhere supplied with evidence by means of which he may at once form his own judgment, and also ascertain the accuracy of the opinions which have been propagated by others.[28]

Russell's historiography leans towards a naive and uncomplicated conception of sources, contexts and ideas, with, at times, a poorly-justified reliance on textual authorities. However, where available, Russell is not slow to use the results of field-based inquiries: 'The reader will be pleased with the following notice, conveyed to me by a gentleman who has recently inspected the edifice and adjacent grounds, as well as all the records which respect the family of Crom-well in the neighbour hood of Huntingdon...'[29] Russell's reliance here on the field reports of others engaged in primary research will be seen to be symptomatic of his other works as well. Even when writing explicit geography, Russell never ventured into the field himself.

In short, Russell's method is one of compilation and synthesis. His works are not based on original research, and as we shall see below, this practice is what governs his particular form of didactic Scriptural Geography as well.

An important collection of sermons was published by Russell in 1830.[30] *Discourses on the Millennium* became one of his most notable works, not so much for the content of the sermons, but because of the introduction to the work. In this Russell published his 'Rules of Interpretation', which plainly disclosed his liberal approach to the interpretation of Scripture. He saw that the doctrine of the verbal in-spiration of the Scriptures 'could not be maintained in the face of advancing science, and, equally in the interests of the Scriptures and of truth, he urged the duty of recognising the necessary modif-ications of the theory of inspiration'.[31]

In 1831 Russell was appointed as Dean of Edinburgh, in succession to Dr Walker. This was Russell's stepping stone to a diocese of his own, and his rise through the ranks of the Scottish Episcopal Church was now well on its way. In that year he published his first volume in The Edinburgh Cabinet Library, with the Edinburgh publisher, Oliver & Boyd, on *Egypt*. The work was Volume 3 of the Library, and was also published as Volume 23 of Harper's Family Library in North America. This work is characterized by its reliance on other sources to tell its story; just like Russell's biography of Cromwell, its strategy is one of assimilation. Robert Mayhew has dealt with the concept of geographies which are based primarily on synthesis.[32] His analysis is based on tracing the footnotes of various authors of geographical texts, and demonstrating how the sources used indicated a 'geography of scholarly exchange among the authors of geography books'.[33] Mayhew is interested in 'the impressive degree to which eighteenth-century scientists ignored war and xenophobia to exchange ideas, thereby enacting the cosmopolitan ideal of a Republic of Letters', and the same can apply to the Scriptural Geographers of the early nineteenth century.[34] While Mayhew does also allow that the Republic of Letters was 'undermined by national antagonisms and religious schisms',[35] the idea still has a certain moment, as the entire history of science may be said to be similarly marked. Mayhew's work also emphasizes that 'a humanist Republic of Letters saw experimental work as merely mechanical, and thus outside the scholarly ambit...'[36] The nature of this Republic is explained further, as 'an imagined community, wherein all scientists and scholars were in theory connected despite the fact that they might never hear of each other, let alone meet or communicate. Scientists were a community held together by ink, both on the printed page and in the written letter'.[37] And so, Mayhew can argue that 'The scholarly authorities whom an author chose to cite must tell us something of their scientific self-fashioning, of their intellectual tastes and imagination, of the sense they had of whom they were in dialogue with as they composed their books'.[38]

These notions resonate strongly with the methods Russell deployed in the production of a range of Scriptural Geographies. His work on Egypt is heavily derivative and ripe for such analysis. In his preface to the book he sets out his more contemporary literature reviewing project, assuring that –

> The reader will find that we have not neglected any source of information in respect to the learning and science of the Egyptians ... In collecting material for the history of Modern Egypt, we placed the greatest reliance on the works of such writers as had lived for some time in the country ... In this point of view the successive communications of Mr Salt are extremely valuable; as are also the several notices which have been received in this country through the medium of France. Among these last a distinguished place is due to the 'Histoire de la Régénération de l'Égypte,' written in the form of letters by Jules Planat, a staff-officer in the service of the pasha.[39]

For the non-travelling Russell, Egypt exists primarily as a virtual space, a space of the imagination,[40] a textual space, inscribed on the pages of travellers' works,[41] and a performed space.[42] Russell here privileges the experience he can have of Egypt through textual sources above any notion of the direct existential experience of being in Egypt and observing for himself.

The sources that Russell chose are significant as well. A certain moral topography can be sensed in Russell's textual world. The British respectability of Henry Salt is obviously part of his ticket to credibility, along with his residence in Egypt. The reference to works from France, including Planat's work, shows Mayhew's Republic of Letters at work. French-British relations at this time remained strained after the Napoleonic wars and disturbances in France, as recently as 1830, would have caused Britain to look suspiciously upon her revolutionary neighbour. However, Russell, as a citizen of the Republic of Letters, evidently realized the quality of French scholarship respecting Egypt.

These are the sources mentioned and justified in the preface, however, other sources are felt to need no preliminary justification as to their reliability. Russell cites the classical sources like Herodotus and Clio,[43] Eratosthenes,[44] Philadelphus, Euthemenes, Pomponius Mela, and Pliny,[45] Lucan and Lucretius,[46] without feeling the need to justify their credibility or authority. Just as in the case of his biography of Cromwell, Russell relies on earlier texts, often without giving solid reasons for this practice. The same textualizing strategy surfaces in his discussion on the supposed source of the Nile (still undiscovered in 1831): he considered the ideas of Herodotus, Pomponius Mela, Euthemenes, Lucretius and 'many modern authors'[47] (who he neglects to name), and reaches a conclusion, with Herodotus, that the Nile probably rises in Libya.

As Russell's more contemporary footnotes are commonly simply a surname or a couple of keywords from a title, it is useful to expand on these in order to aid our understanding of his self-constructed intellectual world. Among his more modern sources are Mr Browne,[48] M Savary,[49] Dr Shaw,[50] Volney,[51] Belzoni,[52] Antis [sic],[53] Denon,[54] Felix Mengin,[55] and Malte Brun.[56] Among other classical sources introduced in the text are Josephus, Manetho, Syncellus, Africanus and Eusebius.[57] These lists show a cosmopolitan array of sources, including British, French and Italian authors. Russell is also perhaps in a minority in the early nineteenth century, in that he uses sources written by women.[58] Some sources are however, discredited:

> The reader may be surprised that, in describing the manners and customs of the Modern Egyptians, we have not taken any notice of a volume by the late Mr Burckhardt on this very subject. Suffice is to observe that the work in question is simply a collection of Arabic proverbs, which illustrate the sentiments of the people rather than their customs or manners, and was therefore altogether unsuitable or the purpose which we had in view.[59]

Whether this exclusion was, in reality, for other reasons is a question of interest. It may have been that Burckhardt's apparent conversion to Islam made his works distasteful to Russell, or perhaps Burckhardt's tactic of disguising himself as an Arab when travelling, in order to collect information more freely, caused Russell to reject Burckhardt's work as unscholarly.

However, many sources, those which perhaps form the higher points of the moral textual topography, are judged worthy of inclusion, and Russell does not consider the use of such a variety of textual sources a simple matter –

> The chronologer [of Egypt] pursues his way, trusting now to one guide, and at another time to a second who appears to have opened the path under a clearer light; but, unfortunately, he soon becomes convinced that the authorities who oppose him, in whatever direction he may choose to proceed, are more numerous than those who favour him with their aid, and on whose reputation he had thought it safe to rely. As he advances, he is further dismayed by the unwelcome discovery that all his guides become more and more ignorant, and also that their confidence increases in proportion to the obscurity in which they are enveloped. Their statements abound with fictions sufficient to stagger the strongest belief.[60]

These are the sources upon which Russell's work is based, after he has filtered them on the bases of 'reputation', favourable opinions and supposed fictionality. The manner in which he uses these sources, demonstrated in the actual structure of the book itself must now claim our attention.

Like all the works in The Edinburgh Cabinet Library, *Egypt* is a small book, comprising only 480 foolscap octavo pages,[61] and Russell must frequently apologize for leaving out many issues in a work of its size; however, he manages to pack a surprising amount of material into the book. After a general introduction on the importance of the subject and the scope of the work, the first substantive chapter is on the geographical and physical properties of Egypt, looking at the layout of the country, and a few of its most striking geographical features. This is followed by a chapter on the ancient history of Egypt, tracing it from the land's earliest mortal ruler up to the Saracen period. A chapter on the 'Mechanical labours of the ancient Egyptians' comes next, encompassing a survey of what might be referred to as the engineering projects of ancient Egypt, from the pyramids to the canals to the tombs and Sphinx. The next chapter deals with the literary and scientific endeavours of ancient Egypt, including hieroglyphs, the history of the Egyptian nation's historical studies and the early development of arithmetic in ancient Egypt. A sixth chapter deals with the remains of ancient Egyptian art and temples. A further chapter tells the history of modern Egypt, from the time of the Saracens to the time of Mohammed Ali, the Egyptian ruler in 1831. Logically this is followed by a chapter on 'The actual state of Egypt under the government of Mohammed Ali'. Somewhat anomalously the next chapter returns us to ancient history and geography, with information on oases, ancient buildings and desert places. The tenth chapter returns to the present and looks at 'Manners and customs of the Egyptians' in a contemporary setting. The final chapter looks at the natural history of Egypt, with sections on geology, zoology and botany. In common with other Edinburgh Cabinet Library works the volume lacks any conclusion, and ends abruptly.

Russell's Egypt is a land of inscription,[62] and scholastic endeavour. His own imagined geography of Egypt is what the book is based on. As we have seen he outlines the story of Egypt, and much of its geography, in terms of ancient scholarly texts. While writing about a land less mentioned in the Bible than some others, he is keen to illustrate biblical texts with his newly acquired knowledge of Egypt:

In the sacred writings of the Hebrews [Egypt] is called Mizraim, evidently the plural form of the oriental noun Mizr, the name which is applied to Egypt by the Arabs of the present day. The Copts retain the native Chemia, which, perhaps, has some relation to Cham, the son of Noah...[63]

And, further, 'The Nile, we may observe, was described, even among the descendants of Jacob, by the term Sichor...'[64] When discussing the Israelite exodus from Egypt, Russell clears up a common historical misunderstanding about this event, describing in detail another with which it is apparently often confused, and then states that 'the true exode of the Chosen People, with all the demonstrations of miraculous agency by which it was accomplished, is too well known to require from us even the most abbreviated narrative'.[65]

In addition to religion, the way in which Russell treats science in his work is of interest to us. Russell, it must be remembered, belonged to that period of the early nineteenth century when a still newly-developing science – largely comprising of natural theology – was not thought of as a threat to religious belief, and he is accordingly enthusiastic about the scientific enterprise. He remarks that his own science, contained in the 'Chapter on Natural History, is meant entirely for popular use, and has no claims to scientific precision, either in the description or arrangement',[66] but he praises the scientific achievements of others, including the ancient Egyptians,[67] and is critical of the lack of scientific practice among the contemporary travellers whose works he uses: 'It is to be regretted that our travellers, generally speaking, have not bestowed that degree of attention upon the geological structure of Eastern Africa which it unquestionably deserves'.[68] And, even beyond geology, in the sciences of botany and zoology, '...there is still a complete want of systematic views in all the descriptions and details with which we have been hitherto supplied; and thus we are compelled to rest satisfied with conjecture when we are most desirous to attain the means of establishing a philosophical principle'.[69] He is equally critical of the state of contemporary Egyptian science, informing that in the mosques 'lectures are read on all subjects which among Mohammedan churchmen continue to be regarded as scientific, although entirely unconnected with the improvements of modern times'.[70] And this example of Russell's Orientalist perspective is prevalent throughout his work. For Russell the Orient is an inferior, sadly decayed place, just as Edward Said might expect him to believe.[71] At the outset he laments that

> it requires great effort of imagination to combine the ideas of that magnificence and power which must have distinguished the epoch when Thebes was built, and the splendid monuments of her kings erected, with the facts which meet the view of the traveller in our own days, amid the desolations of Karnac and the ruins of Luxor.[72]

The wording demonstrates a scholar who laments that the current inhabitants of the land of Egypt have fallen from the glory of their ancestors, and that they have been careless with the landscape; they have allowed ruin to creep over it, thus leaving Western tourists less impressed than they really should be, and thus hampering Western scholarship. Explicitly put, 'The actual inhabitants of Egypt sink into insignificance when compared with the mouldering dust of their ancestors'.[73] In Russell's terms, the indigenous peoples have not properly preserved those parts of their past that we, in the West, value. In his view it has obviously been easy for this state of affairs to develop, as the government has been deficient by Western standards, and yet:

> In a country where the administration of law depends almost entirely upon the character of an individual, and where at the same time the nomination to the supreme authority is usually determined by intrigue or in the field of battle, the mere form of government cannot be of very much consequence.[74]

To Russell's Western mind, the political intrigues of Egypt seem impenetrable and must therefore be illogical, irrational and inferior.

By contrast, Russell's opinion of the pasha, Mohammed Ali, is high.[75] This is in stark opposition to Russell's opinion of the pasha's subjects:

> It is sometimes a misfortune for a man to live in advance of his age; and we accordingly find that the pasha is not only far from being popular, but that he is disliked by the more influential classes of his subjects on account of his most meritorious exertions. The indulgence, for example, which he grants to religious

sects of every denomination; the use of the vaccine discovery as well as of other surgical practices borrowed from Europe; and above all the school of anatomy recently founded, which creates a necessity for human subjects even in addition to the waxen models which he has procured from Italy, are innovations highly disagreeable to the bigoted Mussulmans. In fact they perceive that he [the pasha] is a Turk only to his own countrymen, with whom he is rigidly strict; whilst to all others he displays a degree of liberality to which they are disposed to give the name of dis-honesty or indifference.[76]

The pasha's Western values put him ahead of his time, as the rest of Egypt's population is, in Russell's conception, backward, timeless and unprogressive, a nation which does not praise progress in the Western manner. Many of these apparent defects may be partly blamed on the Egyptian climate according to Russell:

The effect, it is admitted, whether it be of climate, of education, or of government, is the same among all the settlers in Egypt except the Arabs, – a disposition to exist without exertion of any kind, – to pass whole days upon beds and cushions, – smoking and count-ing beads. This is what Maillet termed the Egyptian taste; and that it may be acquired by residing among the native inhabitants of Cairo is evident, from the appearance exhibited by Europeans who have passed some years in that city.[77]

Obviously this is why 'Cairo is the dirtiest city in the whole earth'.[78]

However, there is a lighter side to the Oriental life depicted by Russell: he talks of professional Nile swimmers, who 'sometimes float down the river on their backs, with a cup of coffee in one hand and a pipe in the other, while their feet are tied together with a rope'.[79] And yet the houses of Cairo hide activities which Russell refers to only in glancing terms:

We shall take no further notice of the disgraceful scenes which too often accompany the exhibitions of these dancing-women, nor shall we draw aside the veil which conceals from the common eye the sensualities of the Egyptian capital. It would be almost equally disagreeable to copy the descriptions given by several British

travellers of the sufferings inflicted upon the senses and imagination of a European by the reptiles, flies, fleas, and other more
nauseous vermin.[80]

The veiled mysticism of the East is here tantalizingly displayed and
what is, for the residents of Cairo, everyday life, is exoticized and
problematized by Russell. Derek Gregory's conception of Orientalism
and of the Western understanding of issues like climatic influences,
sensuality and timelessness is of a 'complex web of textualizations in
which dreams of the fantastic were captured in intricate display' – a
world of an imaginary, where everything is Other and exotic.[81] This is
a rich exhibition of Said's thesis: Russell's work is one of high
Orientalism.

To conclude our analysis of this work, Russell's preface, initially,
set out to show how his sources for the ancient history of Egypt,
including the Bible, may be illustrated by a knowledge of the present
geography of the country:

> we have spared no pains to illustrate the descriptions of Grecian,
> Roman, and Arabian historians, by reference to the actual
> condition of that singular country [Egypt] in our own times;
> attempting by these means to supply the reader of Herodotus,
> Diodorus, Siculus, Strabo, Pliny, Abdollatiph, a light reflected from
> the ruins of those splendid monuments which they were the first
> to make known to the great body of their less-informed
> contemporaries.[82]

Here is an example of Russell using the present geography of Egypt,
mediated through other writers, to explain ancient texts. This, as well
as setting out the knowledge created by contemporary travellers to
the same purpose, is his overarching aim.

Russell's project can be seen as a didactic enterprise. In his version
of the Scriptural Geography project, his work's relationship with
knowledge is simply one of transfer. He doesn't feel threatened by
scientific knowledge, or that his faith is in need of geographical
apologetic: his narrative is one of teaching and informing, nicely
uncomplicated by the more complex concerns that successive Scriptural Geographers would find so absorbing.

In the same year (1831) Russell published a work on *Palestine*, as Volume 4 in the Edinburgh Cabinet Library.[83] In Russell's style, this was also a work of synthesis and amalgamation, but differed from *Egypt* in that it also benefited from personal interaction with many of the authors whose works were used and some of them also acted in a consultative capacity in reviewing the content of the book. At the outset Russell opined that

> In giving an account of the Holy Land, an author, upon examining his materials, finds himself presented with the choice either of simple history on the one hand, or of merely local description on the other ... But it occurred to the writer of the following pages, that the expectations of the general reader would be more fully answered, were the two plans to be united; combining an account of the constitution, the antiquities, the religion, the literature, and even the statistics of the Hebrews, with a narrative of their rise and fall in the sacred land bestowed upon their fathers.[84]

This goal, of informing 'the general reader' about the Israelites and the Holy Land, Russell set out to achieve by

> leav[ing] no source of information unexplored, which might supply the means of illustrating the political condition of the Twelve Tribes immediately after they settled on the banks of the Jordan.[85]

Indeed, 'the reader will find in a narrow compass the substance of the extensive works of Fuller,[86] Wilken,[87] Michaud,[88] Mills,[89] and Hogg'.[90] The book is a true work of synthesis from a range of French and English sources. Also, Russell outlined how:

> The topographical description of the Holy Land is drawn from the works of numerous travellers and pilgrims, who, since the time of the faithful Doubdan,[91] have visited the interesting scenes where the Christian faith had its origin and completion. On this subject Maundrell[92] is still a principal authority; for, while we have the best reason to believe that he recorded nothing but what he saw, we can trust implicitly to the accuracy of his details in describing every thing which fell under is observation. The same high character is due to Pococke[93] and Sandys,[94] writers whose sim-

plicity of style and thought afford a voucher for the truth of their narratives. Nor are Thevenot,[95] Paul Lucas,[96] and Careri,[97] though less frequently consulted, at all unworthy of confidence as depositories of historical facts. In more modern times we meet with equal fidelity, recommended by an exalted tone of feeling, in the volumes of Chateaubriand[98] and Dr Richardson.[99]'[100]

These are the works upon which Russell's volume is based. However, he was at pains to note that his choice was selective, as he has 'carefully rejected all such speculations or conjectures as might gratify the curiosity of learning without tending to edify the youthful mind'.[101] Quite why Russell was considering a youthful audience is not clear, as the Edinburgh Cabinet Library was not intended for the young, however, at various points in the work this is the audience for which he chose to cater.

This work, unlike Russell's others, profited from consultation. In the first edition of 1831 Clarke, Burckhardt, Buckingham, Legh, Henniker, Jowett, Light, Macworth, Irby, Mangles, Carne and Wilson are named; by the fourth edition of 1837 Maden, Madox, Spence, Hardy, the anonymous author of *Three Weeks in Palestine*, Delamartine and Bové are mentioned as being among those who 'have not only contributed valuable materials, but also lent the aid of their names to correct or confirm the statements of some of the more apocryphal among their predecessors'.[102]

As may be supposed, in a work written by a cleric, 'The history of Palestine, prior to the fall of Jerusalem, rests upon the authority of the inspired writers, or of the those annalists, such as Josephus and Tacitus, who flourished at the period of the events which they describe'.[103]

The sources of this work can be viewed as urbane and diverse; along with canonical texts of classical antiquity Russell uses modern travel writers and personal correspondence. The modern writers come from a diversity of backgrounds and nationalities, religious and non-religious travellers, those on pilgrimages or more 'open-ended' journeys,[104] and this is reflective of Russell's deliberate policy of inclusivity:

In the description which I am about to give of the principal towns, the buildings, the antiquities, the manners, the opinions, and the religious forms which meet the observation of the intelligent tourist in the land of Canaan, I shall select the most striking facts from writers of all nations and sects; making no distinction but such as shall be dictated by a due estimation of the learning, candour, and talents which appear in their several volumes.[105]

Russell's method of determining the scholarly merit of his sources has already been dealt with above, and it is reinforced by him, as he sets out his additional criterion of close geographical examination by primary writers –

The reader, who has pursued with attention some of the more recent works on Palestine, must have been struck with the diversity, and even the apparent contradiction, which prevail in their descriptions of Jerusalem ... The greater number, it must be acknowledged, have drawn from their own imagination the tints in which they have been pleased to exhibit the metropolis of Judea; trusting more to the impressions conveyed by the brilliant delineations of poetry, than to a minute inspection of what they might have seen with their own eyes.[106]

While Russell is keen to point out that others' geographical conceptions of Jerusalem are imagined, he apparently lacks an awareness that his own is as well. Russell, while never having been to the Holy Land at all nonetheless problematically claims for himself a privileged authority. The citationary structure of a Saidian Orientalist discourse is also to be seen at work here. Orientalism is a discourse, in Foucauldian terms, and here that discourse can be seen in the process of self-construction; a circular, self-referential discursive regime is constituting itself around the scholarship of self and others. An application of Foucault's archaeological methodology can allow us to see the true significance of Russell's use of particular sources by exploring the practice/knowledge axis, rather than the consciousness/knowledge axis,[107] so that we can see that this is high Orientalist scholarship, which erases the Eastern view of the East, and even rejoices in its triumph in doing so:

In our own days the number of works on these important subjects has increased greatly; presenting to the historian of the Turkish provinces in Asia a nearer and more minute view of society than could be obtained by the earlier travellers, who, instead of yielding to the characteristic bigotry of the Moslem, usually opposed it to a prejudice no less determined and uncharitable.[108]

The erasure of the active role of the populace of the Orient from literature about the population of the Orient is seen as a progressive step, an example of the Western progress that must be imposed on a chronologically static society. Billie Melman's analysis that, in texts like this, 'Real Orientals are denied humanity, history, and the authority to speak about and represent themselves' rings true here.[109]

The use of such concepts and modes of representation continues throughout Russell's book. At the beginning he discusses the availability of sources written by the inhabitants of the Holy Land in melancholic terms:

> The chapter on the Literature and Religion of the Hebrews cannot boast of a great variety of materials, because what of the subject is not known to the youngest reader of the Bible must be sought in the writings of the Rabbinical authors, who have unfortunately directed the largest share of their attention to the minutest parts of their Law, and expended the labour of elucidation on those points which are least interesting to the rest of the world.[110]

This discounting of the current activities of Eastern peoples is continued in Russell's conception of their mode of government: after considering how great the Holy Land once was, he bemoans 'The present aspect of Palestine, under an administration where everything decays and nothing is renewed...'[111] and reminds the reader of the opinion that 'Galilee, says a learned writer, would be a paradise were it inhabited by an industrious people under an enlightened government'.[112] Russell complains further that 'For some years this fine country has groaned and bled under the malignant genius of Turkish despotism. The fields are left without cultivation, and the towns and villages are reduced to beggary' however:

the latest accounts from the Holy Land encourage us to entertain the hope, that a milder administration will soon change this aspect of affairs, and bestow upon the Syrian provinces at large some part of the benefits which the more liberal policy of Mohammed Ali has conferred upon the pashalic of Egypt.[113]

Russell again, as in his work on Egypt, demonstrates his belief that becoming Westernized is the best thing for the East, as the present guardians of the sacred landscape are spoiling it for the purposes of Scriptural Geography, allowing it to decay and crumble, as in the example of Jericho, one of many which he uses:

> Jericho, which is at present a miserable village inhabited by half-naked Arabs, derives all its importance from its history... Of all its magnificent buildings there remain only the part of one tower, supposed to be the dwelling of Zaccheus the publican, and a quantity of rubbish, which is understood to mark the line of its ancient walls.[114]

The importance of places like Jericho is in their past. So little now remains that might interest the Western traveller. The walls of Jericho and the house of Zaccheus, the only architectural features of the town mentioned in the Bible, are the only things worthy of note, and it is criminal that they have been neglected, reminding us of Goren's assertion that: 'Throughout the nineteenth century and into the early twentieth, the significance of Palestine rested solely on its religious tradition'.[115]

The surface physicality of the land is just as important as the archaeological remains, as Russell believes that an 'outline of the geographical limits and physical characters of the Holy Land, may prove sufficient as an introduction to its ancient history'.[116] And so Russell makes an enthusiastic analysis of the geology of the Holy Land, and he seems almost at pains to see the entire land as a petrified entity, frozen in time and without animation or alteration. He laments that 'The miserable condition of ignorance and neglect into which every thing connected with industry has fallen under the Turkish government, prevents us from obtaining any information in regard to the mineral stores of that country'.[117] Russell's scientific analysis of the land is hampered by the fact that 'Every one who writes on the Holy Land has occasion to regret that travellers in general have paid so little attention to its geological structure and natural productions'.[118] In addition to limited studies of the geology and physical geography, Russell provides an outline of the natural history of the land, warning, however, that –

> The chapter on Natural History has no pretensions to scientific arrangement or technical precision in its details. It is calculated solely for the use of the common reader, who would soon be fatigued by the formal notation of the Botanist, and could not understand the learned terms in which the student of zoology too often finds the knowledge of animal nature concealed. Its main object is to illustrate the Scriptures, by giving an account of the Quadrupeds, Birds, Serpents, Plants, and Fruits, which are mentioned from time to time by the inspired writers of either Testament.[119]

Russell's concern for scientific and geographical accuracy is not overwhelming, but it does feature from time to time. He allows science and religion to interact briefly in his work:

> The reports of the latest travellers confirm the accuracy of the picture drawn by this divine legislator ... Moses might justly say that Canaan abounded in milk and honey. The flocks of the Arab still find in it a luxuriant pasture, while the bees deposit [sic] in the holes of the rocks their delicious stores, which are sometimes seen flowing down the surface.[120]

Yet this gives no indication of Russell needing to prove the truth of Scripture in the face of a threatening, field-based science. The biblical passage quoted is not one likely to be disputed, and the evidence in its support is not marshalled in a scientific fashion; Russell's project is simply to inform the reader of actual conditions in the Holy Land.

However, as might be expected, Russell used the biblical text to answer questions about geography, rather than the other way around: 'Dr Clarke ... maintains that the words of [Luke's Gospel] are most explicit, and prove the situation of the ancient city to have been precisely that which is occupied by the modern town'.[121] Russell's conception of scriptural authority along with Clarke's, is so strong, that Russell allows the text to determine the interpretation of the present day geography. This sort of project is that considered by Ben-Arieh, when he notes that 'Exploring the Holy Land was unlike the penetration of Africa or the discovery of the unknown regions. Here even the unknown was somehow familiar'.[122]

Russell's climatology, such as it was, also provided a link between Scripture and contemporary events: 'The phenomenon alluded to by the prophet Elijah is still found to diversify the aspect of the eastern sky, Volney remarks, that clouds are sometimes seen to dissolve and disperse like smoke...'[123]

To similarly link the Scriptures with everyday life among his readers and everyday life in the contemporary Holy Land, through the medium of that Land's geography, is Russell's constant project, and that of the whole didactic Scriptural Geography project. In the first instance a common aspiration is outlined: 'The account which is given of the Feasts and Fasts of the Jews, both before and after the Babylonian Captivity, will, it is hoped, prove useful to the reader, more especially by pointing out to him appropriate subjects of reflection when perusing the Sacred Records'.[124] Similarly, it is Russell's opinion that 'The reader of the sacred history will have his curiosity excited with regard to the time, place, and the manner of religious worship',[125] which curiosity Russell attempts to satisfy with detailed descriptions. The often dry prose of these descriptions filled the reader in on such spots of interest as Bethlehem:

> Bethlehem, where the divine Messias was born, is a large village inhabited promiscuously by Christians and Mussulmans, who agree in nothing but their detestation of the tyranny by which they are both unmercifully impressed. The locality of the sacred manger is occupied by an elegant Church, ornamented by the pious offerings of all the nations of Europe.[126]

So thorough are Russell's illustrative endeavours that he also covers some of the most obscure points of biblical reference:

The margin of the [Jordan], however, continues as of old to be closely covered with a natural forest of tamarisk, willows, oleanders, and similar trees, and to afford a retreat to several species of wild beasts. Hence the fine metaphor of the prophet Jeremiah, who assimilates an enraged enemy to a lion coming up 'from the swellings of Jordan', driven from his lair by the annual flood, and compelled to seek shelter in the surrounding desert.[127]

The phrase 'as of old' reminds us how Russell's project is to create a link between the reader and the biblical Holy Land rather than just the contemporary Holy Land. However, though the material may often be obscure the bulk of it is intended for a very general audience and in terms of broad interest, it is noted that 'The road from Jericho to Jerusalem presents some historical reminiscences of the most interesting nature'.[128] This road is one of those traversed by Holy Land pilgrims and pilgrimage is a topic close to the centre of Russell's project. It seems that one of his aims for his volume is that it might take the reader on a pseudo-pilgrimage; such an activity is deemed suitable since

[the pious Christian's] affections are bound to Palestine by the strongest associations; and every portion of its varied territory, it mountains, its lakes, – and even its deserts, – are consecrated in his eyes as the scene of some mighty occurrence. His fancy clothes with qualities almost celestial that holy land...[129]

The holiness of this 'consecrated' space can be understood in the terms of Graber, whose conception is of the way in which 'Sacred power is apprehensible through the medium of concrete objects, events, persons and places'.[130] Russell's view of the landscape transforms the material into the spiritual. Russell also shows insight as he uses the term 'fancy' in discussing the imagined geography that Christians in Britain have of the Holy Land. This link is strong enough to inspire pilgrimage of an exacting nature:

The connexion which Christianity acknowledges with the people and soil of Judea, has, from the earliest times, given a deep interest to travels in the Holy Land. The curiosity natural to man with respect to things which have obtained celebrity, joined to the conviction, hardly less natural, that there is a certain meri[t] in enduring privation and fatigue for the sake of religion, has in every age induced pilgrims to visit the scenes where our Divine Faith was originally established, and to communicate to their contemporaries the result of their investigations.[131]

It is indeed Russell's firmly held belief that '...no length of time can wear out the impression of deep reverence and respect, which are excited by an actual examination of those interesting spots that witnessed the stupendous occurrences recorded in the inspired volume'.[132] This notion of 'reverence' inspired by the landscape can be tied in to the ideas of Yi-Fu Tuan on geopiety.[133] Tuan reminds us that '"Geopiety" covers a broad range of emotional bonds between man and his terrestrial home ... Reverence is the essence of the emotion',[134] and Russell's geopious sentiments are strong. Furthermore, it is the case that

> The Christian traveller is, indeed, delighted when he obtains the first glance of Carmel, of Tabor, of Libanus, and of Olivet; his heart opens to many touching recollections at the moment when the Jordan, the Lake of Tiberias, and even the waters of the Dead Sea spread themselves out before his eyes...[135]

It is notable that this was written by a scholar who had never travelled to the Holy Land at all, and most probably had never left Great Britain, and yet, while his writings lack the existential immediacy of his travelling counterparts, they often describe scenes in prose less prosaic and more vivid. Russell has a cultivated immediacy, a strong imagined geography. For example, it is not only the physical features of the landscape that offer to the pilgrim material for their devotions, but the cultural practices of the people do so as well:

> It is not without pleasure that the traveller contemplates these unaltered tokens of the simple life which prevailed in Palestine at the time when our Saviour abode in the house of Mary his mother; and more especially as he cannot fail to contrast them with the precious mummery which now disgraces the more artificial monuments of Christian zeal.[136]

Russell's thoughts on the matter led him to roundly condemn the developing pilgrim industry, particularly the building of grottoes and churches at every possible sacred site:

> Dr Clarke, in a fit of spleen with which we cannot altogether refuse to sympathize, remarks, that had the Sea of Tiberias been capable of annihilation by [human] means, it would have been dried up, paved, covered with churches and altars, or converted into monasteries and markets of indulgences, until every feature of the original had disappeared; and all this by way of rendering it more particularly holy.[137]

It is not only the building of the chapels covering the sites of special events, but their locations that often raised Russell's ire: 'The mere circumstance that almost all the events which attended the close of our Saviour's ministry are crowded in to one scene, covered by the roof of a single church, might excite a very justifiable doubt as to the exactness of the topography maintained by the friars of Mount Moriah'.[138] Indeed:

> The scepticism with which such doubtful remains cannot fail to be examined is turned into positive disgust, when the guardians of the grotto at Bethlehem undertake to show the water wherein the infant Messiah was washed, the milk of the blessed Virgin his mother, the swaddling-clothes, the manger and other particulars neither less minute nor less improbable.[139]

However, Russell's faith in the authority of the divine record was not shaken, as

> ...it is of no consequence to the Christian faith in what way these questions [of site authenticity] shall be determined. The great facts on which the history of the gospel is founded are not so closely connected with particular spots of earth, or sacred buildings, as to be rendered doubtful by any mistake in the choice of locality.[140]

Consequently, Russell feels that the Christian traveller cannot fail to be impressed by the Holy Sepulchre, where the mind ... is not withdrawn from the important concerns of the hallowed spot by any florid decorations or brilliant display of architecture in its plan or in its walls; but the religion of the place is allowed to take full possession of the soul, and the visiter [sic] feels as if he were passing in to the presence of the great Jehovah.[141]

Like so many others, Russell displays a 'proper Protestant aesthetic' in regard to his taste in monuments and their decoration,[142] and, in spite of his cynicism, he advises that: 'It is, in fact, with the Bible as his guide that a traveller ought to visit the Holy Land. If we are determined to carry with us a spirit of cavil and contradiction, Judea is not worth our going so far to examine it'.[143]

As Russell did not go so far to examine it himself it should not be entirely unexpected that *Palestine* created a certain controversy. This was entangled in the controversy, beginning to rage at this time, that his liberal theological ideas created. His points of Scripture Interpretation, which had been published in 1830, and cast doubt on such things as the literal truth of the Bible, now came back to haunt him. Many members of the evangelical party of the Scottish Episcopal Church were displeased with Russell's theological ideas, and saw this as a time to strike. The *Christian Observer* carried a 'profound attack' upon *Palestine*.[144] Russell himself gave the details in a letter of 19 May 1832, to Bishop Terrot:

An attempt has been made to confirm this unfavourable impression [a reference to the Scripture interpretation debacle] by a review of my little work on Palestine. This small work has met with so great approbation that about 10,000 copies have been printed from first to last; and I have seen about sixty critiques of it, all very laudatory ... But at length an article appeared in the Christian Observer, evidently written in Edinburgh ... The number of the Christian Observer was sedulously handed about [in Edinburgh], and sent, among others, to the bishop.[145]

Russell in the end triumphed over his accusers and, as we will see, the incident did not slow his rise through the ranks of his church.

Russell's theology was indeed 'mildly liberal' and occasionally caused slight concern to some of his High Church colleagues.[146] However, it has been convincingly argued that:

If in any matter of higher importance Russell differed from his clerical brethren it was in his greater adaptability or his readiness to make changes required by changed times and circumstances – to encourage any step for rousing the Church from its lethargy, drawing forth its energies and developing its resources by united and corporate action.[147]

An example of such adaptability was Russell's interest in the science of phrenology. Russell corresponded with George Combe, an advocate of phrenology,[148] between March 1832 and February 1833. During a lecture Russell had evidently poured scorn on the findings of phrenologists. Combe wrote to Russell to suggest that his comments on phrenology, 'laughing at it', are merely indicative of how little he knows about the subject.[149] Russell quickly countered by stating that he would develop an interest in phrenology only insofar as it could be shown to be related to education.[150] After further correspondence, by 24 March 1832, Russell was then able to say 'although I am not a phrenologist to the fullest extent I can see the basis on which its main principles rest'.[151] By the following February Russell had evidently written to inquire about Combe's classes in phrenology, and Combe answered, warningly, that 'with a disposition to judge my doctrines only by their conformity to the standards of philosophy already existing in your mind, you will find the lectures only incongruous absurdities'.[152] And yet Russell had evidently shifted his position significantly since the previous March. His was a mind open to new possibilities and ready to grasp new ideas once their bases has been properly explored.

In extension from his theology, Russell's use of Scripture was very much in the High Church liberal tradition of the early nineteenth century. It has been said that, theologically, 'he was a man of his age and of his diocese',[153] and Russell's use of the Bible in his theology was contextual and situated. In one of his early sermons he shows how he feels Scripture should be interpreted:

...we are really ignorant of the exact boundaries which separate the natural from the supernatural, we are very incompetent judges of what, in an ancient narrative, ought to be regarded as miraculous and what not. As knowledge increases among men, miracles are always found to diminish in number; for that which is above nature, in one age, is discovered to be within its limits in the very next. Measuring everything by his own ignorance, man, in a rude state of society, is constantly surrounded by wonders and prodigies; for which reason, when we read the early history of pagan nations, we pass over their miracles either as matters of mere childishness – as the inventions of the fraudulent or the devices of the superstitious – but cannot be induced to consider them as a fair interpretation of nature, and far less a proof of divine interposition.[154]

Russell therefore can be seen to be free-thinking in his understanding of biblical narratives. It can also be seen that he does not view science as a threat to religion; he sees scientific inquiry as the ally of theology, in purifying our knowledge of the spiritual realm: 'It is, in short, the effect of experience, and of an enlarged knowledge of nature, to weaken the confidence of speculative minds in physical signs and wonders'.[155] Russell sees rather that Scripture interpretation should proceed on the grounds of: 'sound argument, profound knowledge, rational doctrines, and a beneficent morality joined to wisdom, zeal, pureness of living [and] piety'.[156]

Russell also contributed articles to the *Encyclopaedia Metropolitana*. Among these were biographical entries for many personages from classical antiquity, and a series of chapters on the Annals of Britain.[157] Most notably he wrote an entry on the history of Egypt.[158] This article, published in 1833, adds little to our knowledge of Russell. From it we can glean that he continued to use the same sources as in his book on Egypt, and that he continued to praise the role of science in explaining the world, praising the Egyptian '...love of Literature and Science, which are the most lasting basis of national glory'.[159] Unfortunately, in Russell's Western conception, 'The objects of moral science were not indeed wisely selected...'[160] which is further evidence of his Orientalist attitude toward the different values and emphases of Eastern thought.

In 1833 Russell published a further volume in the Edinburgh Cabinet Library, this time on *Nubia and Abyssinia*, not a work of particular interest to our present studies other than in the context of the remark of one of Russell's colleagues:

> A well known clerical brother in [Scotland] said to a friend of [Russell]: 'I suppose Dr Russell would write a book on any subject whatever if his bookseller asked him, whether he knew anything about the subject or not. He is publishing at present a work on Nubia and Abyssinia. Now what does *he* know about Nubia and Abyssinia?'[161]

Walker defended Russell on the grounds that though 'This was a plausible objection ... there was no real force in it. Dr Russell knew about Nubia and Abyssinia all that books could tell him'.[162] Again the issues of sources and the value of an existentially immediate experience of the subject of a geographically based work come under scrutiny. We can see the authority granted to textual sources, and the apparently unproblematic reliance on them. Among Russell's interests was education and in 1836 he published a pamphlet on *The Advantages of Classical Learning*.[163] In this essay Russell laid out what he felt were the uses of classical sources in education, and, more interestingly for our investigations in this work, the relative merits of classical literary knowledge and scientific knowledge. While Russell urged an education system based on classical literature entirely, with no reference to science, this is not because science was deemed dangerous by him, or a threat to religion, rather scientific knowledge was thought 'useless or unimportant'.[164] Perhaps this is an indication as to why Russell's Scriptural Geographies have the literature of classical antiquity as an important source.

In 1841 Oxford University admitted Russell to the degree of DCL *honoris causa*, having found problems in granting an LLD to a cleric of a non-established church. Russell was not naive about the honour and wrote to the Primus that

> I should have been better pleased if the bigwigs had thought of some other way of showing their kindness to our Communion. I am not vain enough to consider it personal, but that I have been

selected as the scapegoat to bear the load for the others – that is, to pay £100.[165]

However, the degree was an evidence of the esteem in which Russell was held in England: '...it is not as an administrator that Bishop Russell will be remembered in the Church, but as a learned and literary prelate. By nature and early habit he was a student, and living so long at Leith he had every encouragement and facility for the prosecution of literature'.[166]

In 1842 Russell contributed his last volume to The Edinburgh Cabinet Library.[167] Polynesia seems a subject far removed from the previous writings of Russell, but, the volume consists largely of accounts of the activities of missionaries in the islands, who are also the chief source of his information. Russell indeed sorrows over the situation that there is a '...great deficiency of information, owing ... to the fact that the missionaries, having in view much more important objects, do not devote any particular attention to the zoology, the flora, or the silva of the respective islands'.[168] A hint may be gathered from this statement that Russell perhaps viewed exploration to be equally as important as missionary endeavour.

RUSSELL'S WRITINGS IN RETROSPECT

Russell's huge and varied output marks him as a key contributor to the intellectual world of the first half of the nineteenth century. His footnotes indicate that he was an exceptionally widely read scholar, both in terms of the range of topics that his reading covered and the nationality of the writers whose works he perused. His writings, in their sheer scope and detail, have made an immense contribution to Scriptural Geography, as well as many other fields of inquiry.

Russell was unquestionably a didactic Scriptural Geographer. His use of the geography of the Bible lands to explain the biblical text, uncomplicated by the issues of apologetics, and prior to the widespread turn to modern science and modern theology, mark him as such.

The didactic Scriptural Geography enterprise, as conducted by Russell is marked by a number of key traits. First, his entire reliance on texts means that the Holy Land, and indeed the world, for Russell is a textual construction. In the same way that Barnes has argued for the construction of the world in a scientist's laboratory, saying that 'scientific theories are socially constructed', it can also be argued that, just like a scientific theories, textually constructed geographies like Russell's 'are not the precipitate of some universal, ineluctable, rational method'.[169] This deconstruction of Russell's intellectual world, with the methodology of Mayhew and the insights of the sociology of science, allows us to see that Russell's methodology is problematic.

Second, Russell evidently selected the texts on which his imaginary is based under the guidance of a moral framework. As we have noted, he seemed cautious of using works by non-Westerners, and he seemed to be averse to the writings of those Westerners who integrated themselves too fully with the East. This is linked to the moral discourse in which so many of his descriptions of the East are based. So often in Russell's work the East is degenerate, morally inferior, behind the times, regressing and every day losing its usefulness to the Western scholar.

Third, Russell built the texts he selected into a classic Saidian archive of Oriental knowledge. Russell can be seen as a part of the metropolitan section of the Orientalist 'machine'. He was handling the knowledge which 'is processed by the machine, then converted into more power'.[170] Particularly Russell may be implicated in the representation of Egypt from a distance. Timothy Mitchell argues that such was the value placed on pictorial representations and exhibitions in the nineteenth century West that many writers 'set about trying to describe the Orient as though it were an exhibition, a dilapidated mismanaged one of course, indeed an exhibition of its own dilapidation and mismanagement'.[171] Russell's sentiments which we have explored about, for example, the treatment of holy sites, illustrate Mitchell's arguments vividly. Furthermore, Mitchell notes that the power of this sort of analysis is to see without being seen. Russell views the East, therefore from an ultimately powerful position, in the metropole.

Russell's scholarship, particularly his theological work, fitted him well to make contributions to Scriptural Geography. His work connecting religious and secular history demonstrated that he was interested in situating Scripture records. His life of study equipped him to write geographies of places he had never been to, which, in his own terms, seemed satisfactorily experiential. His theology, of the mildly liberal variety, also furnished him with the necessary outlook to think of foreign lands as material for illustration, rather than simply as mission fields. However, his theology did have a practical turn as well, and as a bishop Russell had instigated slum ministries in some of the most deprived areas of Scotland, and had attended to their maintenance zealously.[172]

Russell died at his home in Leith on 2 April 1848. His life had contributed much to his church, scholarship in general and the didactic Scriptural Geography enterprise in particular. As a pastor Russell was remembered as 'ever the same – in all grades of office – gentle, moderate, tolerant, and conciliatory. Yet he was never deficient in zeal, energy or enterprise, though the enterprise took more readily the literary than the pastoral line'.[173]

In a fitting summary Russell's biographer declared that:

In every leading lineament of character the aged bishop ... recalled the youthful tutor and deacon. There was the same mildness and gentleness of disposition and manner, the same amiability of character, the same love of learning, and steady application to study, and faithful discharge of duty. To the last he continued *qualis ab incepto*.[174]

4 The Polemical Order: Josias Leslie Porter

I have visited these scenes with an object in view far different from that of a mere traveller or groping antiquary...[1]

JOSIAS LESLIE PORTER

Not many Irish Presbyterian ministers of the nineteenth century could tell the story of being kidnapped by warriors of the El-Misrâb tribe in the Syrian desert and Rev J.L. Porter, no doubt aware of this fact, told his story in a certain light-hearted, debonair tone:

> We all at once stopped, in the full consciousness that something serious was impending. Another horseman now galloped up, and, after speaking a few words to the former, rode off at speed across the plain. His companion, without uttering a word, turned and walked away slowly after him, and we calmly and silently followed him. 'What is this?' said I to my companion; 'where are we going now?' 'I fear', he said, 'that we are going just wherever that cavalier may lead us'... At last ... there appeared to our dismay some thirty horsemen, armed with spears and matchlocks, bearing down upon us with the swiftness of eagles. They were a wild and savage-looking group as ever it was my lot to behold... A robust man, dressed in a silk robe and scarlet cloak ... rode, as I imagined, directly towards me, brandishing a spear of formidable length, and I felt that if I remained quiet I had a fair chance of being run through. With a quick motion therefore, I cast aside my abeih. I scarcely know whether it was my intention to defend my life or jump off my camel ... I found, when the immediate danger was

over, that my right hand grasped firmly the only serviceable weapon amongst us... We assumed an air of perfect indifference and did not utter a word except when directly questioned.[2]

After the payment of sufficient ransom Porter and his party were released the following day. Scenes like this were not common in the lives of those who were to become Ireland's leading citizens in the Victorian era, and for this, among other reasons, Josias Leslie Porter is a figure of interest and significance in Irish history. While no biography exists, it is possible to reconstruct his illustrious and crowded life from archival and documentary sources.[3]

Josias Leslie Porter, the son of William Porter, a wealthy Presbyterian farmer and a leading figure of the Irish Rebellion of 1798, was born on 4 October 1823, in Burt, Co. Donegal, and died as President of Queen's College, Belfast on 16 March 1889. Porter had a long and distinguished career in the Presbyterian Church in Ireland, serving as a minister in Newcastle-upon-Tyne and as a missionary in the Church's Jewish Mission in Damascus, from 1849–1859. Upon his return to Belfast from Syria he was elected to the Chair of Biblical Criticism at Assembly's College and eighteen years later his administrative skills ensured his appointment as one of the government's two Assistant Commissioners for Intermediate Education in Ireland. After a year in this post he became President of Queen's College, Belfast, which position he held until his death. Porter returned on at least one occasion to the Holy Land, and also made tours of Egypt and Greece. He continued to rework his travel writings up until his death.

Porter was a prolific and well-read travel author, writing the *Handbook for Syria and Palestine* in the important Murray series,[4] of which 4,000 copies were sold in his editions.[5] He also wrote on topics such as the interface of science and religion and on biblical criticism,[6] he contributed geographical articles to the encyclopaedia of his day,[7] and he was the biographer of his famous father-in-law, Henry Cooke, a leading Irish Presbyterian cleric whose massive energies seemed to almost transform the denomination within a lifetime, and many of whose changes remain much-cherished parts of the structure and doctrine of the Presbyterian Church in Ireland to the present day.[8]

6: Josias Leslie Porter

Porter received his early education from the prodigious James Craig, who was himself just a teenager,[9] and by 1839 he was ready to commence his BA at Glasgow, graduating in 1841, and he received his MA at the same institution in 1842. He immediately left for Edin-burgh, where he was to study under Thomas Chalmers, as a can-didate for the Presbyterian ministry.[10] Porter's first congregational charge was in High Grove, Newcastle-upon-Tyne, where he spent three years before being appointed to the Jewish Mission.

The Irish Presbyterian Church's Jewish Mission has been called 'One of the most colourful chapters in the history of Irish Presby-terianism',[11] and it is easy to get the feeling that an eccentric Porter would have fitted nicely into this black sheep of the Church's mis-sions. We will discover that Porter was well informed about con-temporary intellectual currents in geography, geology and archae-ology, and he was evidently keen to try his geoscientific prowess fur-ther afield than Britain and so he set out for Syria in October 1849, willed on his way by the *Missionary Herald*, whose commentator noted the news and added a blessing:

> Mr Porter sailed from Belfast for Liverpool on the 9th of last month [October], to proceed to Damascus. May the God of Abra-ham take him and his wife safely to their field of labour, and grant them all the needful gifts and graces for the work to which they have devoted themselves, and abundantly bless them in it! ... Mr Robinson has learned with great satisfaction that the [Church's General] Assembly have resolved to sustain and strengthen the Mission in Damascus, and that he rejoices in the hope of being joined by a missionary from his native land. At no previous time were the prospects of the Mission in Damascus so encouraging.[12]

Porter reached Syria on 12 December of the same year, and the of-ficial report of his activities noted that 'Since his arrival he has been diligently engaged in the study of the language in which his mission is hereafter to be exercised'.[13] And yet, as we will see subsequently, Porter was a missionary whose primary goal was geographical field-work, as much as evangelism; his telling statement that 'I was hin-dered in part by the calls of duty'[14] reveals him bemoaning the fact that his evangelistic duties consumed fieldwork time. He also said:

> I determined to lose no opportunity which my travels might afford me of investigating the topography and antiquities, or elucidating

the geography and history, of this interesting region ... And if these researches should enable me to solve some difficulties in Scripture Geography, or to correct errors into which others have fallen, it will not be considered that I go beyond my proper sphere of labour...[15]

Therein we can see Porter's conception of himself as a theologically-inspired practitioner of science, a religiously-motivated conduit of geographical knowledge.

Porter was an important figure outside the Church, not only because of his travel writings, but he was also a respected academic, being an honorary graduate of Glasgow and Edinburgh Universities, prior to his appointment as President of Queen's College, Belfast and thereafter an honorary graduate of The Royal University of Ireland. It was during his time as President of Queen's College that he wrote up many of his travels, and repackaged many of his earlier writings for wider public consumption. Despite his role as a popularizer, Porter was, contextually, a serious contributor to the cutting edge of scholarly geographical knowledge, evidenced by his election to Fellowship of the Royal Geographical Society by 1856.

PUBLICATIONS

Porter began his publishing career with his semi-autobiographical *Five Years in Damascus*, published by John Murray in 1855.[16] This two volume work deals in depth with his travels and enquiries in Palestine from 1849–1854. The book employs a conversational style, and the scientific travel narrative is punctuated by stories of personal interest and undisguised opinion. Throughout the text biblical quotations are common, and Porter is always at pains to use his experience of everyday events in Palestine – greetings on the journey, mealtime customs – to help explain the oddities of Scripture: 'Milk is of two kinds – fresh, called *halîb*; and curdled, called *leben*. The latter is a common kind of refreshment. It is evidently the חמאה *hemah* which Abraham gave to the angels, and which Jael gave to Sisera (Judg. v.

25)'.[17] He also does not fail to grasp the opportunity to explain a Bible passage as he spots a mirage when out travelling:

> The name of the mirage in Arabic is *serâb* ... which corresponds to the Hebrew שׁרב. This illustrates Isa. xxxv. 7, where we may read 'the mirage shall become a lake'. A more remarkable manifestation of the Divine blessing bestowed on a land could not be conceived than the changing of such a plain as this into a lake.[18]

This first work remains the Porter *pièce de résistance*, and he never really rose to the same heights of textual elegance again.

Porter soon followed with the Murray *Handbook*, which is a necessarily less personal account, but just as biblical, beginning as it does with the assertion that 'The Bible is the best Handbook for Palestine; the present work is only intended to be a companion to it'.[19] The work is heavily referential, and urbane passages of historical background and allusions to the works of geographers who have gone before, including Arab, Frank and neither, like Ptolemy and Robinson, demonstrate Porter's scholarly approach. The main section of interest is the very lengthy introduction; the rest of the work comprises simple journey itineraries and ideas about what to see and where to go and practical details ranging from the length of a given trip on horseback in hours and minutes, to how the Western tourists may ensure that they are not slyly provided with a 'broken-down camel'.[20] The introduction gives a general overview of the country's history and geography which intimately blends physical geography and religious sentiment:

> Of the rivers of Syria the most important, whether we consider its physical peculiarities, or its sacred and historic interest, is the JORDAN. The fact of its running, throughout its whole course, beneath the level of the sea, renders it a natural wonder; and the fact of its having been the baptismal font of the Son of God Incarnate, for ever enshrines it in the heart and memory of Universal Christendom. Its highest source, or rather the source of its highest tributary...[21]

In Porter's narrative the Holy Land is constantly viewed through a religious lens, and it is the particular biblical events that took place at a certain spot that give significance to that place.

After his return from Palestine Porter published some minor journal and reference work articles, of which the most interesting and relevant to the Scriptural Geography project is the entry for 'Geography' in Alexander's 1864 *Cyclopaedia of Biblical Literature*, where Porter argues for the importance of geography to theologians, and makes a geographically-based apologetic argument:

> Many statements are incidentally made in Scripture which appear to indicate that the authors were acquainted with the leading facts of geographical science, both physical and political ... It must be further borne in mind that the Bible is from God, and that every sentence of it, *when rightly interpreted*, must be in absolute accordance with fact.[22]

This is a typical piece of polemical Scriptural Geography. Earlier didactic Scriptural Geographers would not have felt the need to make an apologetic argument like this, and later contextual Scriptural Geographers would have tended to question the absolute accordance of the Bible with fact. The entry comes to a close with a call which Porter would spend much of his life trying to answer – 'A systematic and thorough treatise on Biblical geography is still a great desideratum in our country's literature'.[23]

The next year, in 1865, Porter published a major work of just such a nature in his *Giant Cities of Bashan*, which appeared on both sides of the Atlantic, in substantially different editions.[24] The preface opens with an acknowledgement of the importance of geography: 'Bible stories are grafted upon local scenes'; he wrote 'and, as is always the case in real history, these scenes have moulded and regulated, to a greater or less extent, the course of events...'[25] The designation of the Bible's history as 'real' shows the polemical Scriptural Geography project getting underway at the book's very beginning. Porter's cry is that 'The topography of Palestine can never be detailed with too great minuteness...'[26] and he is quick to assert that 'the book is not a simple diary of travel; nor is it a disquisition on history or geography'[27] and to note that 'During all my journeys the BIBLE was my constant

companion'.[28] Perhaps these statements can be read as indicative of a
changing intellectual situation, and the need to verify Scripture more
ostensibly than previously: perhaps the need for the polemic of
polemical Scriptural Geography was increasing, and, in contrast to
the subtleties of 1855, by 1865 one needed to write one's apologetic
unapologetically. Increasingly, great emphasis was laid on the direct
experience of having been to the sites, of having witnessed the scenes
for oneself and communicating the findings of a self-professedly unprejudiced mind. Note how the personal pronoun dominates the
following gobbet:

> I have seen the plough at work on [Zion], and with the hand that
> writes these lines I have plucked ears of corn in the fields of Zion. I
> have pitched my tent on the site of ancient Tyre, and searched, in
> vain, for a single trace of its ruins. Then, but not till then, did I
> realize the full force and Truth of the prophetic denunciation upon
> it: 'Thou shalt be sought for, yet shalt thou never be found again'
> (Ezek. xxvi. 21).[29]

This is a sentiment which Porter believed to be creditable, because:

> This is no vague statement made at random or penned for effect.
> God forbid that I should ever pen a single line rashly or thought-
> lessly on such a topic. It is the result of years of study and years of
> travel. It is the result of a calm and thorough comparison of each
> prophecy of Scripture regarding Palestine's history and doom with
> its fulfilment, upon the spot. I had no preconceived theory of pro-
> phetic interpretation to defend. My mind was not biased by a false
> faith in literality on one side, nor by a fatal skepticism on the
> other. Opportunities were afforded to me of examining evidence,
> of testing witnesses, of seeing with my own eyes the truth or the
> falsehood of Bible predictions.[30]

The apparent truth of these predictions meant that Porter was able to,

> thank God that, with the fullest and deepest conviction – con-
> viction that all the plausibility of modern scientific skepticism can
> never overthrow, could never shake – I can take up and re-echo the
> grand, the cheering statement of our blessed Lord, and proclaim

my belief before the world, that 'Till heaven and earth pass, one jot or one tittle shall in no wise pass from the law till all be fulfilled'.[31]

Porter felt that his fieldwork 'upon the spot' and his investigations with his own eyes enhanced the credibility of his findings, and this scientific practice, in the field, is characteristic of much polemical Scriptural Geography. The volume is filled with just such passages, and numerous visitations of the sites of prophecy and evidence of its fulfilment, and Porter feels that 'these are only a few, a very few of multitudes of similar predictions ... special, graphic, and detailed'.[32]

In 1871 Porter's biography of Henry Cooke appeared, and this work, highly successful in capturing the attention and hearts of the 'Protestant people of Ulster',[33] just like its subject, ran to four editions and was a best-seller in each. Cooke was a noted conservative, and the production of a laudatory biography by Porter (who was also Cooke's son-in-law) indicated Porter's conservative theological bent.

In 1874 Porter published a pamphlet, *Science and Revelation*, which formed an important part of the Irish Presbyterian response to the threat to religion from science, a new theology and the collapse of the British Victorian social structure.[34] In it he attempted to clarify what he felt were appropriate fields of inquiry for scientists, and to discredit the speculations of scientific inquiries concerning the events of the earth's origin and the processes by which it had reached its present condition, coming down to what he felt was the irreducible truth, that 'God's truth, as revealed, can never be at variance with the phenomena of God's world'.[35]

In 1883 Porter returned to writing about the Orient, with his *Travels in Palestine*, following his most recent excursion there in the spring of 1874. The book is intended as a supplement to the *Giant Cities of Bashan*, and while this journey took in parts of Egypt and Greece as well, Porter limited his writing to the familiar territory of Palestine. The work has a more anthropological, analytical and reflective tone than the rest of his Palestine-based material, with a feel for the influence of geography on the inhabitants of the land and their customs. Porter once more reached the conclusion that 'Evidences of the truth, and of the divine origin, of the Bible are thus impressed, as we have seen, upon every district of Palestine...'[36]

In 1885 Porter was invited to address the Victoria Institute's annual meeting in London, and he gave a paper on Egypt. He was probably invited to give a talk on this topic as Egypt was then a matter of topical interest, given the Mahdist uprising of that year in the Sudan. Porter spoke of his detailed knowledge of Egypt and his enthusiasm for Egyptology: 'The history and antiquities of Egypt have had for me, during many years, a singular fascination...'[37] His address was thoroughly grounded in the Orientalist tradition, and he described Egypt as 'a grand storehouse of antiquarian lore – a museum of primeval art, revealing the origin and development of letters, science, and useful inventions'.[38]

By 1887 a major change can be sensed in the nature of Porter's work. He was by then a popularizer, producing Scriptural Geographies of a perhaps less scholarly (but no less effective) genre. They no longer have quite so intense a polemical aspect, and this is quite probably a reflection of the changing intellectual climate. A pair of companion volumes were produced. One dealing principally with *Jerusalem, Bethany and Bethlehem,* and one which travels in the footsteps of Jesus, *Through Samaria to Galilee and the Jordan.*[39] A more typical phrase was by then one which said 'I shall try to take my readers there in spirit...'[40] Porter was able to say: 'What I aim at in this volume is to place before the minds of my readers the same instructive pictures that flashed vividly before my own mind when I read my Bible in the Holy Land'.[41] This work, his final publication, was produced in the last year of Porter's life.

Three dominant themes knit together the threads of Porter's writings: topological apologetics, science and religion, and a popularization of Holy Land geography.

PORTER AS ORIENTALIST

Numerous scholars have considered the construction of the Orient as a particular space in the Western imagination, and an analysis of Porter's work helps to illustrate the particular role of polemical Scriptural Geography in Orientalist discourse.

Porter was, in some senses a poorly developed, but nevertheless emblematic, contributor to Orientalist discourses. His Orientalism is often direct and uncomplicated; for example, when visiting what he describes as a typical Muslim house in Damascus, he said –

It resembles, in fact, some scene in fairyland; and one feels, on beholding it, that the glowing descriptions in the 'Arabian Nights' were not mere pictures of the fancy. But it is only when the 'bright-eyed houris' of this sunny clime assemble in such a *salon*, decked out in their gay and picturesque costumes, and blazing with gold and diamonds, and when numerous lamps of every form and colour pour a rich and variegated flood of light all round, to be reflected from polished mirrors, and countless gems, and flashing eyes, that we can fully comprehend the *splendour* of Oriental life, and the perfect adaptation of the gorgeous decorations of the mansions to the brilliant costumes of those that inhabit them.[42]

This was Porter's take on the Orient, what he elsewhere referred to as the 'land of sacred romance'.[43] To quote again: 'Both the land and the people remain thoroughly Oriental. Nowhere else is patriarchal life so fully or so strikingly exemplified. The social state of the country and the habits of the people are just what they were in the days of Abraham or Job'.[44] We can see that Porter's particular imaginative understanding of the Holy Land's geography is as a setting for Biblical events. Derek Gregory's understanding of Orientalist scholars viewing the East as a series of tableaux is obviously relevant here.[45] Porter's view of the landscape, continually through the historical lens of Scripture, was as the stage on which past events can be played out, on which the stories of his religion can be re-enacted in his imagination, to impart to that space a spiritual significance. This emphasis on the spiritual significance of Oriental space was continued in the preface to the Murray *Handbook* which was couched in similarly celestial terms:

Something more than a book of roads has been aimed at. This country is the stage on which the most wondrous events of the world's history were enacted. Every nook and corner of it is 'holy ground' ... I think no known Scripture locality has been overlooked, and no incident of Scripture history, which would tend to enhance its interest has been forgotten. It is the *religio loci* which gives such a charm to the cities and villages of Palestine.[46]

The holy landscape is projected in such a way as to make it a fitting scene for the activities of the Patriarchs and Apostles – a sanitization project. In a classic Orientalist strategy, the holy landscape is also represented as unchanging and timeless. In his lecture to the Victoria Institute, while seeking to explain the biblical story of Joseph, Porter noted that 'It was quite characteristic of the strange transition of life and authority in the East that the slave became viceroy, and introduced his brethren to Pharaoh', and he then used this example to help illustrate his take on the whole of the history and politics of Egypt, as though the social state of Egypt was immutable.[47] This bears out the assertions of Makdisi that the Orient 'became the locus of a literature ... that relegated the empire to an abode of decadence, indolence, and, above all, an Islamic fanaticism that progress had left behind'.[48]

In just such a way the holy landscape of the present is subservient to holy landscape's biblical past. The contemporary, largely Muslim, inhabitants of the Holy Land are viewed as inferior to the population as imagined in the past: Porter refers to many places as 'dirty'. and 'backward'. Also he reports his thoughts with observations like: 'vice is spread over the nation like a flood, corrupting every dwelling, making wanton every thought and look, and polluting the very language which is the medium of social intercourse'.[49] This is the result of reading the contemporary landscape with eyes that had been trained to think of the Holy Land as a place of biblical epic and this gave Porter's gaze on that landscape a superior, colonial, colouring. John Urry's ideas about the nature of the tourist gaze are helpful here. In dissecting and analysing just how tourists gaze on a landscape, Urry notes that 'There is then a "romantic" form of the tourist gaze, in which the emphasis is upon solitude, privacy and a personal, semi-spiritual relationship with the object of the gaze'.[50] It may perhaps be the contemporary population of the Holy Land which disturbed Porter's solitude with his imaginary of his own Holy Land, and this interruption of solitude rouses Porter to an ill feeling against the current inhabitants, evident in such statements as 'It is a peculiar feature of Islam that traffic and religion, cheating and praying, lying and devotion, can be blended together without the least discord'.[51] Similarly he evidently considers the present population of the Holy Land to be entirely incapable of anything that he might consider to be, in Western terms, useful industry:

> Will not the hope of advantageously investing capital in the construction of railways, or in commercial enterprise, or in the cultivation of cotton, call the attention of England's merchant princes to a survey of this country, and a full examination of its resources? Syria has still, in its soil and in its people, the elements of greatness and prosperity waiting to be developed.[52]

It requires the English, Western, colonial mind to set the landscape to work again in a way that Western minds will understand, appreciate and benefit from.

However, Porter is a well versed student of Oriental aesthetics and an appreciator of Muslim architecture and poetry, music and costume. He is not shy of talking about the splendour of mosques, '...fine specimens of Saracenic architecture ... far superior in effect to the noblest specimens of the Gothic in our English cathedrals...'[53] or of praising the variety given to the cityscape by mosques, 'rich in the minute details of Saracenic architecture'.[54] While acknowledging the now largely unkempt state of these buildings, Porter romanticizes about the

> different impression ... left upon the mind when the attention is directed to the detail of these buildings. One cannot but admire the chaste patterns of the marble mosaics on the walls, the curious interlacing of the stones over doors and windows, and the fine proportions and delicate fretwork of the tapering minarets. But it is in the magnificence of its gateways that Saracenic architecture excels all other styles. The beautiful symmetry of the arch, the deep mouldings of the sides and the rich sculpture on the top ... The interior courts too are filled up with great elegance, even splendour. They are covered with a tesselated [sic] pavement: the large fountains are or marble, often inlaid with mother-of-pearl and porphyry; and the lower part of the walls are either cased with marble wrought in chaste patterns or with tiles finely glazed and ornamented with figures in brilliant colours...[55]

Despite the apparently stereotypical portrayal of the Orient, Porter's work thus also discloses a certain appreciation of and reverence for a world so different from his own. His always was an ambivalent Orientalism.

I want to argue that it was Porter's obvious fascination with and love for Oriental places of worship, splendid architecture, and interior beauty brought about by colour, propagated in Palestine, that landed him in trouble with Irish Presbyterians.

Places of Worship

The story requires a brief contextual sketch of the atmosphere of the Irish Presbyterian Church at the time, and the opinions then prevalent in the Church's courts and among its politically active members. In the second half of the nineteenth century, The Purity of Worship (Defence) Association, and the closely linked Church Purity Party, had been 'formed ... to advocate the maintenance of the worship of God in our Presbyterian church pure and entire, and defend it against all unauthorised and unscriptural innovations'.[56] The Association organized lectures, meetings and special sermons and distributed literature to further its cause. The Association's existence and considerable size is an indicator that the design of places of worship and the character of the activities carried out within them were burning issues for many Presbyterians at this time; constructing a church building in those heady days was therefore a perilous business. The Association was a witness to then prevalent feelings – the Presbyterian Church in Ireland was at that time deeply engrossed in the ritualistic controversy in the Church of England, and was within itself debating the ethics of issues like instrumental music in worship, informed by organizations like the Purity of Worship Association and Church Purity Party.[57] The weekly Presbyterian newspaper, *The Witness*, followed the ritualistic controversy closely, publishing the views of both sides – those who felt that a catholic ritual was helpful, and those who did not – over the course of several months, and the ugly head of Irish politics can be seen raising itself as the paper published 'Shame Lists' of those Anglican ritualists who had converted to Catholicism.[58] This combined with the broader currents of an unusually dynamic period in Irish politics, a period that saw the beginnings of the questions of Home Rule and Irish sovereignty, and a time of self-redefinition for Irish Protestants, meant that 'There was a deep suspicion of the introduction of anything unusual into Church services'.[59]

By 1878 the Presbyterian College in Belfast was in a stable financial and academic position, and expansion of the existing buildings was required, to include a Faculty Room, further student and staff accommodation, and, most pertinently for this story, a chapel.[60] An anonymous benefactor supplied almost the whole cost of the construction of the chapel and adjoining buildings.[61] Porter, at that time the Secretary to the Faculty, had a major influence on the design, and he was key in influencing the pattern of the stained glass windows for the chapel. On 17 October, 1878, the foundation stone was ceremonially laid, by a major College benefactor, Mrs Gamble, in the presence of a 'large and representative assemblage'.[62] Porter rose to address the company. There is no record of immediate disquiet in the crowd; however, Porter's speech may be viewed as an important incident in revealing how metropolitan places of worship could be shaped by travel experiences in the colonial periphery. Porter's words on this occasion were perhaps poorly suited to the broader historical context. His speech resonated with poetic imagery, and is worth quoting at some length:

> The College chapel will be a sanctuary of light, and love, and peace... It will show the Church and the world how sound is our theology, and how broad are our sympathies. The windows of our chapel – mainly the gift of the lady who has come to lay the foundation stone – will be emblematic; the designs which have been furnished will, I think, beautifully symbolise the truths preached from its pulpit. The pure light of heaven as it comes through these windows, will catch the glory of 'The Burning Bush', emblem of a God infinitely holy and just – emblem too of a church which has flourished even amid the fires of trial and persecution, and whose time honoured motto is *ardens sed virens*. The light as it enters will fall also across the open Gospels, showing the presence there of Jesus, IMMANUEL, 'God with us', and emblazoning the angelic proclamation, 'Glory to God in the highest, and on earth peace, and good-will toward men'.[63]

Porter's antagonists saw these words as a challenge to purity in worship, to the Second Commandment, and to the definitional identities of Irish Protestant places of worship: an introduction of the 'attractive novelties' so despised by the Purity of Worship Association.[64] This was an incident which recalls the words of one architectural historian: 'In Victorian Britain it was accepted that to build was to create meaning: architecture was "phonetic", it had "expressional character", and it exhibited "particular moral or political ideas"'.[65] Porter's windows evidently exhibited moral and political ideas, at least in the minds of his opponents.

Parts of the original windows still exist, and recent renovations at the College have brought to light four pairs of oriels (the chapel includes eight oriel windows altogether), which may be reasonably assumed to be original, but, importantly, not Porter's designs.[66] The designs are however rich and heavy with symbolism, incorporating brilliant colours and Latin script. The candlestick window, based on the emblem of the Waldensian Church, bearing the motif 'The light shines in the darkness' has a tangible Oriental feel to it.

In the late nineteenth century the Waldensian Church flourished in Germany and as Germany was one of the main mission fields of the Irish Presbyterian Church's Jewish Mission, perhaps some of Porter's influence can be seen here. Two of the other windows depict versions of the Scottish and Irish Presbyterian Burning Bushes, and the final pair of windows shows the Findlater family crest.

Stained Character

The Witness became the scene of a measured but powerful exchange between Porter and his accusers. The Purity of Worship Association produced its finest literati to deal with this undesirable intrusion of colour and strange theology at the heart of Irish Presbyterianism. The correspondents of the letters column, whose readers were already familiar with contention on the conduct of worship by Irish Presbyterians, saw Porter's speech as a challenge. Vitriolic adherents of purity in Presbyterian worship attacked Porter's words.[67]

7: The windows of the Presbyterian College Chapel

Porter's initial speech had been formed of poorly chosen words, and the application of a literalist hermeneutic to it proved unsettling for some Presbyterians. The problems of travelling ideas are highlighted as Porter's Orientalism became the victim of a parochialism based on Irish politics: some people saw only one way to read his speech – that it was direct from Rome.

James Maxwell Rodgers, a Londonderry correspondent of *The Witness*, wrote within the week to the editor to ask 'with the greatest of respect for Dr Porter ... are these words his, or are they the words of a Ritualistic Preacher (on the "Gospel of Glass", to use your own phrase), inadvertently misplaced by the printer?' Rodgers parodied

Porter: 'The windows of a Presbyterian house of worship (which has somehow become a "chapel") are "emblematic"; the "designs which have been furnished for them" "symbolise truths"; one of the designs is an "emblem of God!!!"'[68]

Early the following month the Belfast Presbytery was due to 'Visit' Sinclair Seamen's Presbyterian Church,[69] and at this 5 November meeting things were generally lively. Rev John Mcnaughtan was unable to attend due to illness, but had a motion moved on his behalf by Rev William Johnston, dealing with the College Chapel windows, suggesting that both the Faculty of the College and the College Committee be asked to commit an opinion on their design to writing, and that the plans for the windows be submitted to the Presbytery for examination. This motion was floored, despite the fact, as pointed out by a Rev Mr Meneely that 'Dr Porter had [already] intimated that he would abandon the idea'. The Presbytery minute book dryly records that 'Rev Mr Park said Mr Macnaughtan was quite aware of that fact when he framed his notice'. Others at the meeting expressed 'regret that they were not to have the windows'.[70]

Within a week of this Presbytery meeting Porter wrote to *The Witness*, to limit the damage, regretting 'exceedingly that the words I uttered regarding the proposed stained glass windows in the College Chapel have been so totally misunderstood by some of my Brethren'. Porter went on to assure that 'My words were figurative...' His letter begins to take on a more cosmopolitan, I argue Oriental, theme as he states his confession that 'I was desirous of making the College Chapel, as far as possible, a model of taste and beauty, and I thought windows of stained glass would greatly enrich it'. Porter however remained practical, and he closed his letter, hoping that 'those who have objected to the stained glass will get a kind friend to supply other glass, and thus save the college from additional expense'.[71]

Macnaughtan was still ill by the time of the December meeting of the Presbytery, and it was moved that his resolution should be removed from the books, as the College was not under the jurisdiction of the Presbytery, but that of the General Assembly. This motion was heavily defeated, but after the return of Macnaughtan, most of the January meeting was devoted to the chapel windows. Stained glass became a regular feature of Belfast Presbytery meetings thereafter, still consuming whole meetings three years later.[72]

Porter had already tendered his resignation to the General Assembly's College Committee in October 1878, to take up his new appointment as one of the two Assistant Commissioners for Intermediate Education in Ireland. However, in his resignation speech he told of 'his desire to remain a member of Faculty until he had completed the arrangements for the new buildings... The committee unanimously expressed their satisfaction with the statement made, and requested Dr Porter to continue to act as convener until the next Assembly'.[73]

Here is an example of Porter's mind, broadened by his Oriental experience, clashing with the minds of those who stayed at home. It is perhaps an irony that the same eastern experiences which allowed Porter to see the beauty of coloured light and intricate design were those which he was using to help uphold the orthodoxy at home, through the Scriptural Geography project.

PORTER AS EXPLORER AND CARTOGRAPHER

Has my reader ever remarked the accuracy of biblical topography, even in the minutest details?[74]

Porter travelled so widely that he claimed to have been to sites 'never before trodden by European travellers',[75] and boasted that, 'So far as I know, no other traveller has followed my route from Gerasa to Dera and Bostra'[76] and because of this originality his narratives are often striking as they convey his own sense of excitement and passion for the Holy Land –

> Along this route I have often ridden, alone and in the company of friends and strangers, by day amid unclouded splendour, and by night when the pale moon threw her silvery rays on crag and peak, and yet I have never wearied of the scene. I cannot promise my reader that he will not feel weary of my attempt to describe scenes familiar to me as the home of my youth; but I could safely assure him that, if I had him here on some balmy morning in spring,

mounted on a spirited Arab, his attention would not flag till we had reached the end of our proposed journey.[77]

We can sense how Porter privileged the existential experience of being in the Holy Land over simply reading about such an experience. We will discover that Porter based the authority of his geographical data on this experiential immediacy. But this direct experience of the data in the field is of a constructed field, as argued by Felix Driver: 'The field ... is not just "there"; it is always in the process of being constructed, both through physical movement – passage through a country – and other sorts of cultural work in other places'.[78]

Many scholars have noted the way in which the world a scientist engages with is constructed,[79] and so it is with the field for the traveller. Porter was exploring such a 'field', a field constructed both from his actual journeys in the Holy Land and from his imagined Holy Land geography, resourced by his reading of the Bible. Thus Porter was able to view his explorations with excitement. As he went about his investigation of Palmyra, for example, he says: 'During Monday the 7th, and the forenoon of Tuesday, we employed every moment in the examination of this interesting site. The whole space we divided into sections, and one after another we entered upon and explored in detail. We thus lost no time...'[80] Not only is Porter's fieldwork enthusiastic, it is conducted in a rigorous scientific style, with detailed measurements and written observations: 'Many years ago I visited that remote region of the Valley of Orontes where the Hittites had their chief stronghold and settlement, and I examined with care its topography and ruins. I made full notes on the spot...'[81]

Porter also considered the exploration of more mundane landscapes as discoveries, even if lesser ones: 'I did not expect to make any striking discoveries upon [this route]; but I did hope and expect to see the features of the country and the character of the soil'.[82] Porter's discoveries are not only of the topographic nature however, he is also quick to note the political, cultural, social, and obviously religious, differences of his potential converts, and make careful notes. He can thus be implicated in constructing an Other, in the terms of postcolonialist theorists, among them Said who reminds us that the Orient was always Europe's 'deepest and most recurring image of the Other'.[83] Porter's othering can be displayed blatantly and fervently:

> Dâma I knew was filled with Muslems ... Their fierce fanatical spirit, not disposed even in peaceful times to tolerate the presence of infidels, would now delight in avenging their wrongs in such unhappy stragglers as might fall in their way. Under present circumstances, and in such a place as Dâma, they would not be restrained by any feelings of fear as to the consequences; and even should they hesitate to make an open attack, unseen hands could deal deadly blows from behind inaccessible rocks.[84]

The people are constructed as wholly different from peace-loving Europeans, entirely hostile and capable of violence. These 'Others' are constructed as a collective, undifferentiated mass, best dealt with in the corporate. Makdisi's understanding of 'a European literary imagination bent on mapping out an exotic and erotic East' can be brought to bear here, as he notes further that 'In the process, the Orient was imbued with certain immutable qualities that made it radically and forever different from Europe...'[85]

As we have noted, Porter pursued a deliberate policy of visiting less frequented and lesser known sites, as his work sought to fill an increasingly small void in the growing genre of Middle East travel literature stating that 'My province is among less known, if less interesting sites and ruins'.[86] He can therefore be credited with much original archaeological research, most notably in his fastidious recording of the inscriptions on monuments he came across. However, his greatest work of exploration is probably cultural and intellectual, as his explorations are primarily triggered by intellectual problems of Scriptural credibility in the West. This exploration was an expression of the intellectual crisis of conservative Christian Britain. Porter was a small but significant part of the encounter between scientific and religious mindsets. That entanglement, which has been shown to be so complex,[87] had one particular outworking in the Holy Land, in the work of Porter and in his writings and cartography.

A map of the area around Damascus accompanies Porter's *Five Years*, and he states that:

The map accompanying this work has been constructed by myself, almost wholly from personal observations and surveys. My sextant and compass were my constant travelling companions on every excursion ... The great changes affected by my labours on this part of the map of Syria will be obvious to every student of geography...[88]

The obsession with scientific accuracy in capturing the Holy Land is evident in Porter's words, and is a key feature of polemical Scriptural Geography, and the search for truth. Porter can be considered as one of the more important Holy Land cartographers of the time. His map is interesting in that it lists places by their ancient names, more often than by their modern ones, and even locates some places of biblical antiquity which no longer have any topographic expression at all. It is part of an Orientalist attempt to encapsulate the East as a space in which time is of little importance and a space in which the development of society has stagnated. Matthew Edney notes of imperialist maps that they were a means of control. He argues that they 'constituted a technological fix for the Enlightenment's ... ideal of certainty and truth'[89] and John Keay's study of the Great Trigonometrical Survey of India notes that the certain and reliable representation of a landscape and its geographical relationships, portrayed 'in ink on paper, with or without the invisible chains of triangulation' would see India as 'engrossed, defined, and "enchained" as one. Critics would rightly see the "grid-iron" as a symbol of India's incarceration'.[90] Whatever his ambitions,[91] Porter did not construct base lines and he had no theodolite, and yet his survey can be seen as a similar, though contrasting project.

As a missionary, Porter journeyed around the Holy Land on preaching tours, and made his maps as he went. His cartographic inscription was a mirror of his theological inscription. Two sorts of colonial control were spreading across the Holy Land in tandem. Porter measured the distances on his maps largely by timing journeys on horse and camelback, assuming that his animals travelled on average at a uniform speed. This use of time, the concept that so many Orientalists saw as alien to the East, could be viewed as an entrapment of that space, in just the same way as the Great Trigonometrical Survey encased India. Porter's sketch maps no doubt had journeys marked in Western time: the time that a Westerner took to complete the journey to spread a Western religious message.

In connection with his cartographic activities, Porter had a real feel for landscape and this is prominent in his work. Typically he provided views of each city he visited, the more important ones from several angles, and he represented every ethnic group that he came across by a sketch of what he felt to be one of its prototypical members. It is interesting to note that, according to the prefatory remarks, many of the illustrations in the books are photographs which have been subsequently drawn, and probably altered in the process, possibly to depict the sacred landscape in an idealized form.

In his descriptions of the landscapes he traversed Porter allowed himself long flowing discourses of prose to capture the meaning of the landscape, and set it fully into its human, historical and geographical contexts:

When the stranger travels through the hill country, which separates the Judean range from the Philistine plain, his attention is arrested by many objects which seem strange and almost inexplicable. The rich plains are in a great measure deserted; yet the wildest recesses of these hills are studded with villages... Here are villages built amid labyrinths of rocks; there they are clinging like swallows' nests to the sides of precipices; while away yonder, they are perched like feudal castles on the tops of hills. Often, too, when riding through yawning ravines, between beetling cliffs ... Looking up we see, far overhead, vines hanging in festoons from the brows of jagged rocks, and miniature corn-fields on shelving hill-tops, round which the eagles sweep in graceful circles...[92]

The poetry of the phraseology of 'wildest recesses', 'labyrinths of rocks', 'like swallows' nests', 'yawning ravines' and 'beetling cliffs' is illustrative of the high order of Porter's writing, and the intensity of his experiences. Porter's Holy Land is represented as a land appropriate for poetic description, a land requiring the extremes of language and an intense set of literary metaphors. This is part of the literary project outlined by Said, when he argued that –

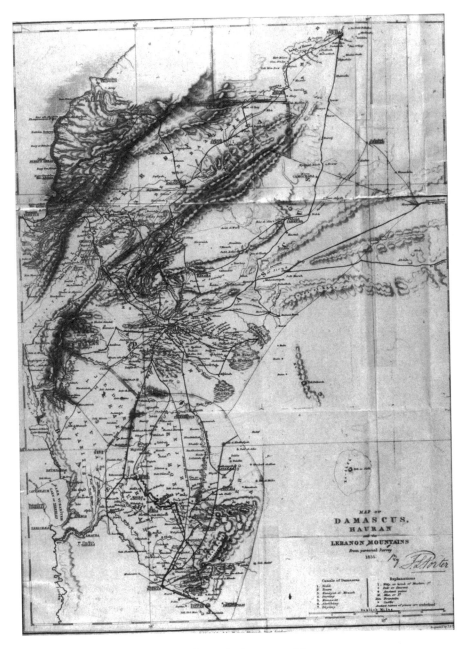

8: J.L. Porter's Damascus Map

9: Plates 10 (Egyptian Music-Girl, Joppa) and 51 (Sheikh of the Lepers, Jerusalem) from J.L. Porter's *Jerusalem, Bethany and Bethlehem.*

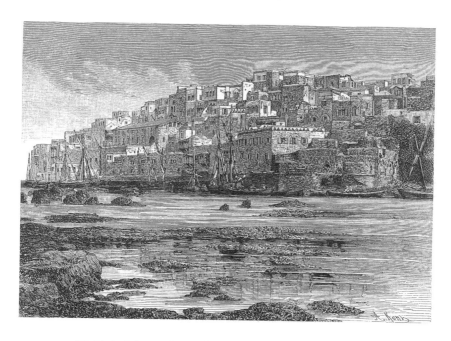

10: Plate 3 (Joppa from the South-west) from J.L. Porter's
Jerusalem, Bethany and Bethlehem

113

Everyone who writes about the Orient must locate himself vis-à-vis the Orient; translated into his text, this location includes the kind of narrative voice he adopts, the type of structure he builds, the kinds of images, themes, and motifs that circulate in his text – all of which add up to deliberate ways of addressing the reader, containing the Orient, and finally, representing it or speaking on its behalf.[93]

Porter's location of himself vis-à-vis the Orient, and the linguistic patterns which he felt appropriate for this position are evident through his employment of the language of romance and piety in his texts. When Porter first arrived in Syria, and had his first experience of the Land he had waited so long to see his language was suitably expansive –

...the first sight of Syrian shores, and of the mountains of Israel, is not soon forgotten. There is a magic power in the living reality which neither poet's pen nor painter's pencil can ever appropriate. The descriptions of others, however graphic, and even the sketch of the artist, however faithful, only place before the mind's eye an ideal scene, which we can contemplate, it is true, with unmingled pleasure, and even with satisfaction; but when the eye wanders over the plain and mountain, or the foot touches 'holy ground', the superiority of the real over the ideal is at once felt and acknowledged. Such, at least, has been my experience... a single glance at the magnificent panorama of Lebanon gave rise to emotions I had never before experienced...[94]

Porter's strength of emotion at the sight of the holy landscape is indicative of just how strong his previous imaginative geography of it had been: 'Often had I pictured the beauty of Syria's landscapes and the grandeur of its ruins, and often had I thought of the holy associations that would crowd upon the mind as the eye rested on spots celebrated in history or sanctified by Holy Writ...'[95] Porter had a keen sense of geography, of the value of personal, immediate experience of places and of the power of place in shaping human emotions and selfhood. Such concerns have been dealt with by numerous theorists, including Robert Sack. Sack argues that the human condition is intimately bound up with space and place, in a mutually constitutive relationship. Sack's exploration of this interchange distils to the statement that: 'The structural similarities between self and place – the fact that they both interweave elements of nature, meaning, and social relations – are the key to their interconnection'.[96] This is a useful insight for our understanding of Porter's geography, particularly when linked with Sack's analysis that 'Places can become linked to meaning in a stronger sense, as when meanings are preserved through places'.[97] For Porter, the Holy Land and its holy sites, are spatial preservers of meanings, in the sense of geographical storehouses of religious tradition. His relationship with these places can be seen as a mutually constitutive one, whereby his identity was negotiated through the geographical expression of his religious faith, and the identity of the holy sites was negotiated through the meanings attached to these places by Porter's geographical imaginary of the Holy Land.

As a practitioner of geography himself, Porter excelled in invoking the *genius loci* of the Holy Land, and had a real sense of place. Locality was important for Porter's work, and his feeling on the subject was that: 'Bible stories are grafted upon local scenes; and, as is always the case in real history, these scenes have moulded and regulated, to a greater or less extent, the course of events; consequently, the more full and graphic the descriptions of the scenes, the more vivid and life-like the stories will become. The imagery of Scripture is eminently Eastern: it is a reflection of the country...'[98]

As a participant in the discourses of geographical science Porter recognized that 'there are some in [Damascus] who ... possess a considerable knowledge of the state of science in Europe',[99] but excursions to more rural areas find him fascinating locals with stories of railways and telegraphs, locals who are still keen to learn of Western science – '[A local] was not satisfied with a mere utterance of "Wullah!" or "Mashullah!" [invocations of the Islamic deity] in doubting astonishment, but he questioned us until he got a full explanation of the principles of locomotion and electricity'.[100] It is evident that Porter brought considerable knowledge of the world, of contemporary geography and of enlightenment principles with him to Palestine, and very often this knowledge is displayed in these 'power encounters',[101] as he, often inadvertently, conducts conversations and demonstrations that he considered educated the indigenous peoples in the ways of Western knowledge. However, from an evangelistic point of view, Porter does not seem to have capitalized on the fetishistic power of railways or electricity or compasses in the way in which many missionaries used their superior knowledge and power to win converts.[102] Porter did however have a concern for what he considered to be promoting the intellectual achievement of the indigenous peoples and his complaint against the mission schools of Damascus is that 'In none of these schools ... is any attempt made to give any instruction in arithmetic, geography, history, or indeed in any of the branches of an ordinary education...'[103] The only saving grace being 'instructions in ... geography', given in the school which is particularly associated with his own church's mission.[104]

Porter's explorations admitted the practice of some ethnography, and in a memoir to a statistics section, Porter talked at length about the various ethnic groups to be found in Damascus, and his opinions are interesting. He wrote of the lack of positive influence that Western civilization and education have given to the Arabs, and shows an, albeit unsympathetic, understanding of how truth and even morality are differently constructed in different places. To take an instance of a breakfast invitation:

We were ere long comfortably seated in a capacious tent, with a monster dish before us, filled with delicious dates, and having in the centre a large cake of snowy butter... Before leaving Damascus we had heard that the Baghdad caravan had been plundered, and now here were we seated, partaking of the spoil, the invited guests of the robbers. The affair looked bad enough in *theory*, but then we had ridden nearly four hours without breakfast, and our entertainers thought moreover that they had a perfect right to the contents of the caravan. It was scarcely a suitable time for us to enter on a discussion of abstruse questions in moral philosophy. Trespassers are often severely punished in England, and why may not the Bedawîn borrow a leaf from the English code? The laws of the desert, it is true, are somewhat severe, and their execution summary. All goods found within the borders of a tribe are confiscated. But these laws are of great antiquity and universally known; all therefore who despise them must just bear the consequences when caught.[105]

However, it is how Porter constructed his truth in the scientific approach he took to making his maps and observations that we will look at now, as we examine another aspect of his work.

A FRANK TRAVELLER AND SCOTTISH COMMON SENSE PHILOSOPHY

'What is mind? No matter. What is matter? Never mind!'[106]

Porter employed scientific methodology in his work – in his cartography, his fossil classification, his geology, his ethnography and his statistical analysis. His particular brand of scientific practice is something, I argue, that he carried with him from his Irish background. The influence of Scottish common sense philosophy can be traced throughout Porter's work, and this section will attempt to show how it influenced his particular brand of polemical Scriptural Geography.

The Anatomy and Habitat of an Idea

Scottish common sense philosophy can be traced to Francis Hutcheson, an Ulster-Scots Presbyterian philosopher.[107] It had widespread currency in Scotland during the eighteenth century and from there it travelled around the world, via Belfast.

The philosophy owed much to the Baconian and Newtonian traditions of the philosophy of science and the epistemology of classical foundationalism. Common sense philosophy was based upon the foundation that there are certain 'fundamental certitudes' which 'did not need to be held on the basis of any other beliefs that one held. They could be taken for granted without demonstration'.[108] These included states of consciousness, things evident to the senses, and self-evidently necessary truths. These beliefs we are compelled to hold, they are not the result of reasoning, rather they are based on intuition.[109] To accommodate these intuitions, common sense philosophers argued 'that all humans possessed, by nature, a common set of capacities – both epistemological and ethical – through which they could grasp the basic realities of nature and morality. Moreover, these human capacities could be studied as scientifically as Newton studied the physical world'.[110] Three points of focus can be distinguished within common sense. These have been characterized as epistemological, ethical and, probably most pertinently for analysis of the works of Porter, methodological common sense.[111] These emphases combine to produce a theory of a mind which engages with a world revealed directly to it, and which has the ability to 'know by [its] own being certain foundational principles of morality'.[112]

Thomas Reid was a key figure in the development of the philosophy, in his mistrust of speculation and his anathema for advancing materialism.[113] These tenets of the philosophy are a direct product of the theological tradition which initially conceived it and nurtured it in both Scotland and Belfast, within the work of figures like James McCosh. This 'thoroughly empirical turn' argue Livingstone and Wells, 'was intimately bound up with McCosh's moral perspective' as was his adoption of Francis Hutcheson's original moral sense theory.[114] Reid invoked belief in a human faculty devoted to morality, necessary to 'direct the individual towards that course of action which will promote the common good'.[115] This was considered a suitable way for later Victorian philosophers to engage with the crumbling nineteenth century social structure, and explain the deprivation and poverty by appeals to the obvious moral vacuum of both materialism and idealism. As we consider the epistemological goals of polemical Scriptural Geography it is natural to argue that polemical Scriptural Geography is one particular application of common sense philosophy, as both emanate to some extent from a particular type of evangelical Christian response to a failed Christian society and both seek to restore and reinforce the certainties that had disintegrated.

Scottish common sense is a philosophy characterized by maintaining a balance between 'a loose and airy idealism and a shallow materialism' in the construction of its epistemology and through it 'The Scottish thinkers intended to discipline the unearthly qualities of one [idealism] by an appeal to the real world and to common sense; they would check the deadening naturalism of the other [materialism] by upholding an independent spiritual reality, in man and in the universe at large'.[116] An inductive method was employed, grounded in the works of Bacon, who was hailed as a latter day Moses, having 'led us forth' out of the 'barren wilderness'.[117] The philosophy essentially wanted to ground an understanding of the world in the terms of 'what was obvious to the general sense of mankind'[118] while scorning the abuses of genius of which it considered idealism guilty, when it found 'intelligent minds asserting that there is no heat in fire, or no color in the rainbow'.[119] Thus the Scottish philosophers attempted to recast philosophical understanding of the world by combining elements of both cosmothetic and absolute idealism, while fully espousing neither.

Among the problems offered by Scottish common sense is its reliance on consciousness as dictating all beliefs about an external world. Philosophical consistency, admitted Hamilton, a leading Scottish common sense philosopher, was sacrificed by common sense's evasion of absolute idealism, however, the Scottish philosophers' belief was that such an idealist position was 'profoundly wrong'.[120] The moral discourse is equally as important as the philosophical in constructing common sense, and it was probably this that made it so attractive to figures like Porter. A world in which humankind can be argued to have a common sensibility for the spiritual is one in which common moral and ethical codes can be applied and upheld.

Common sense philosophy encouraged a particular approach to systematic theology, especially in evangelical circles. To those already feeling the force of the claims of the new scientific cosmology, a school of thought which could impart a similar type of truth to the Bible was a welcome panacea to Christianity's credibility problems, as 'the influence of common sense appears ... in the way evangelicals have constructed the nature of the Bible's truthfulness'.[121] The Bible was employed as a collection of data which could be worked upon according to 'The example of Newton [which] encouraged evangelicals to believe that the end product of theology was a system of certain truths, grounded on careful induction from simple facts, eschewing hypothetical flights of fancy, and providing a universal picture of God and his ways'.[122] So, it has been argued that 'the common sense tradition has not so much provided American evangelicals with theological principles as it has given distinctive shape to the style, the apologetics and the biblical shape of an already existing faith'.[123] So theology sought the ostensible universality and credibility of science by the application of Baconian scientific method to the analysis of the Bible and Christian experience.

The Idea in Space

One of the most honed adherents of such Scottish philosophy was, as mentioned previously, Prof James McCosh. McCosh was educated at Glasgow and Edinburgh Universities, and his training in the common sense school was thorough. McCosh himself however was not a common sense philosopher per se; he rather used major elements of common sense as he 'looked to a flexible stance that could adopt from the new while protecting the best of older ways'.[124]

McCosh carried his philosophy with him when he left Glasgow for Belfast in 1856. When he arrived in Belfast he began a religiously-inspired intellectual crusade, as his unique biographical position at the 'juncture of ... Scottish philosophy and nineteenth-century evangelicalism'[125] well suggested that he might. This campaign he pursued with great vigour, until higher callings (which he had privately expected for quite some time) saw him leave Belfast to become President of the College of New Jersey, subsequently Princeton University. However, he never wrote quite so enthusiastically after his time in Belfast, and it was during his time at Queen's that all but one of his major philosophical works were published.[126] It is effectively argued, I think, that 'McCosh did make Queen's Belfast a bastion of strength for the Scottish philosophy',[127] bearing out the remark that 'Ulster Presbyterians were not only beneficiaries of the Scottish Enlightenment, but also participants in it'.[128]

One of McCosh's biographers, Sloane, ebulliently states that

> a consideration of [McCosh's] output, amazing as it is, will give no just idea of the extent to which Dr McCosh's writings were read ... His books were part of the apparatus to be found in every divinity school, and on the shelves of many working ministers. They were literally read around the world.[129]

Our concern here is less with the world and more with one who was closer to the author's intellectual home than most. Porter was undoubtedly a reader of McCosh. Their times at the closely-linked Queen's College and the Presbyterian College overlapped by eight years, and they were both protagonists in many of the contemporary theological and intellectual debates on issues like creationism and morality, even though their positions might not always have been in complete agreement.[130] The Presbyterian College's historian views the intellectual context of common sense in Belfast as one of change, as 'new currents of thought were affecting the church's outlook', particularly on issues of Biblical inerrancy, which, when coinciding with 'the publication of such works as Darwin's *Origin of Species,* and Lyell's *Principles of Geology* gave rise to doubts regarding the Biblical account of the creation...'[131] It has been shown that Belfast was one of the places where this situation provoked a response characterized by an appeal to the inerrancy of Scripture and a rejection of evolutionary theory and its cohort of ideas.[132]

Porter, as a practitioner of science and as a figure involved with the British Association for the Advancement of Science, had an axe to grind here. In his regional geographies of the Holy Land Porter frequently had recourse to the methods and interests of science as he attempted to understand the physical features of the landscape around him. He constantly worked with his compass, sextant and chronometer,[133] and he noted and described the rock and soil types and landforms,[134] he identified fossils,[135] and he recorded the wildlife around him.[136] Porter was unquestionably a scientist, but one who put certain limits on what science can tell about the natural world, and severe strictures on what it can tell about those aspects of the world which interact with issues of faith.

Porter wrote very much in the vein of Scottish common sense as he tried to stave off the influence of speculative science on his theology. Drawing on tradition, he identified a division of knowledge, based on the distinct 'Provinces' of science and theology, and warned against the interference of each with the affairs of the other. It is after all, surely obvious that 'minds trained to scientific research alone, and habitually occupied with the severe and exact demonstrations of geometry, or with the palpable forms of matter, encounter an almost insuperable difficulty when they attempt to enter the world of abstract thought'.[137] But, argued Porter, 'As a theologian I have no desire to fetter science. I willingly accord it the utmost freedom, and bid it "Godspeed" in its own field'. After all, science is 'friendly territory, where [God's] footsteps can be traced by every unprejudiced philosophic mind'.[138] A separation of what can be discovered by the senses and what is presented directly to the mind was required. Things revealed to the mind must not be compromised by science, yet no 'theological dogma can annul a fact of science'.[139] Science, if conducted inductively, was thought a perfectly acceptable means of deciphering the words of the Book of Creation.[140] However, should science attempt to deduce knowledge about the world, then it would be in error, its 'conclusions so arrived at are no more worthy of belief than the splendid creations of a poet's fancy'.[141] Hence comments by scientists on events like creation, which can no longer be experienced, or like evolution, which cannot be experienced inside a single lifetime, and have left at best only tenuous evidence of their occurrence, cannot be believed. The truth of such occurrences can only be got at by revelation, and 'Revelation does not give a scientific cosmology'.[142]

When the same methodology is applied to the study of Scripture, it is possible to induce the accuracy of the whole Bible from the scientifically proven correctness of those passages which deal with descriptions of specific places in the story – its geography. Porter's Scriptural Geography can therefore be seen as an instance of his application of science, in the common sense tradition, as an apologetic in the form of a topological hermeneutic, and as a textual hermeneutic. Porter used a science tempered by common sense to read the landscape of the Holy Land and to read the biblical texts, the analysis of one in support of the other.

George Macloskie's writings on the relationship between science and religion, at around the same time as Porter was writing, echo Porter's thoughts. Macloskie's understanding of apologetic projects operating in the face of scientific knowledge was that: 'The aim of the believer in the Divine origin of the Bible must always be ultimately to effect a reconciliation; to show that science, rightly understood, and the Bible when fairly interpreted agree, or at least in no way disagree'.[143] Macloskie further noted the methodology employed in the process, in a passage resonant with the surety and optimism that common sense philosophy permitted:

Nature, like Scripture is an infallible teacher, if we can skill to know it. Men may misunderstand them both, but progress is being made in their exegesis. The employment of science for the eluci- dation of Scripture rests on the same principle as the employment of one part of Scripture to elucidate another, though written by a different hand and in a distant age. We employ Scripture to ex- plain Scripture in matters of doctrine, and science to explain Scrip- ture in matters of science.[144]

In our analyses we will see that Porter's use of common sense phil- osophy is a prevalent feature of his work and the medium through which his geographical knowledge is largely negotiated.

POLEMICAL SCRIPTURAL GEOGRAPHY

By publishing seven volumes, Porter was established as a major figure in polemical Scriptural Geography and the content of his works can be understood from theological and geographical perspectives.

Theological Basis

As we have seen Porter's particular brand of Scriptural Geography was rooted in the conservative Irish Presbyterian theology of his day, and in the concepts of Scottish common sense philosophy. Porter had a solid set of ideas about scriptural inspiration, and these were made clear in his critique of Bishop Colenso's theological writings. Porter decried Colenso's practice of placing more trust in some sections of the Bible than others and built an argument on the basis of which

> We are thus bound, in common honesty, to reject the dogma of Bishop Colenso, and to accept the Bible *as a whole*, or, *as a whole*, to reject it. We must not attempt to divide it into sections, to clas- sify it into Divine and human, to arrange its narratives under the headings of 'True' and 'False'.[145]

In further support of his argument for accepting the Bible as an entirely divinely inspired piece of literature, Porter quoted a 'few out of multitudes of passages that might be produced to prove that all the sacred writers claim for themselves divine inspiration'.[146] And, more specifically, Porter's firm set of beliefs concerning the nature of biblical prophecy was laid down in one of his later works, *Illustrations of Bible History and Prophecy From Personal Travels in Palestine*, where he set out the criteria for the sort of prophecy whose accuracy he wanted to establish. In a definition of prophecy the work exhibits a key tenet of Porter's argument – 'Biblical prophecy is prediction, but it is something more. It always embodies a moral element. It is part of God's great providential government of the Church and the world'.[147] It is through the appeal of this conviction that we can see how the polemical Scriptural Geography enterprise is forcing a dialectical exchange between the geographical space of Palestine and the ideological space of contemporary social, religious, cultural and intellectual trends in Britain. The argument was stated more fully, as Porter rose to his life's work's apogaeic song – 'The special object of prophecy was to testify to the omnipotent personal rule of God, in, and over, the Church and the world, and to prove that the Bible is His revelation to man'.[148] Such aims, he insisted, were easily achieved, because, 'in a word, THE WHOLE OF BASHAN AND MOAB IS ONE GREAT FULFILLED PROPHECY',[149] and the evidence can be seen in the field, as we will discover below. It was commonplace for the author to become emotionally involved – 'I cannot tell with what mingled feelings of sorrow and of joy, of mourning and of thanksgiving, of fear and of faith, I reflected on the history of that land...'[150] The notion of a place arousing particular, deep emotions is one which, as we saw earlier, geographers have considered: Porter's words here can be interpreted as exemplifying the discourses of Geopiety, as discussed by Wright and Tuan.[151] For Porter the holy sites existed not just in the material world, but also in an eschatological landscape of prophetic discourse and religious sentiment. This constructed landscape has its own topography, the outlines of which can be sensed in Porter's writing through the application of the methodology of science studies and the invocation of Knorr-Cetina's concept of processed nature.[152] For Porter, the holy landscape's geography was a processed phenomenon: Porter constantly interpreted the geography around him by reference to an established set of rules found in his understanding of the biblical text.

Hence, in polemical Scriptural Geography between Biblical prophecy and witnessed geography the 'harmony is complete'[153] and the features of the geography of Palestine stand as 'testimony to the truth and accuracy of Moses, and monumental protests against the poetical interpretations of modern rationalists'.[154] Porter grinds his axe against liberal biblical interpretation as well as the ideas of the materialistic, skeptical scientist. Having established the witnessed warrant for the geographical assertions of the Bible, and thus establishing the authority of a biblical morality as a panacea for the Victorian social and moral condition, he made the clarion call of his polemical Scriptural Geography: 'Let us all – all sects, all churches, all classes – unite in upholding Bible truth, in propagating Bible Christianity, and in practising Bible morality'.[155]

Geographical Content

The abundance of geographical data within Porter's polemical Scriptural Geographies means that they are rich funds of spatial data and geographical awareness. However, in this sense, it is geography written not in a descriptive or analytical mode, it is rather constantly employed as a vehicle for apologetics. Porter outlined the results of his geographical project in a straightforward manner: 'One is deeply impressed, when travelling through Bible lands, with the graphic descriptions of scenery, the minuteness of topographical details, and the vivid sketches of Eastern life, character, and costume, given by the sacred writers'.[156] This demonstration of the accuracy of Scriptural truth is what Porter was attempting and his fieldwork was always conducted expressly for this purpose. He remarked of one expedition that 'We had halted for some time on the top of a mound to get a wider view of the country and a clearer idea of the destruction impending over it'.[157] His phraseology indicates that it was almost as if he expected the prophets' denunciations to take place before him. On another occasion he noted the reason for visiting a certain spot: 'Our object here was to verify an inscription, on the reading of which a delicate theory in biblical criticism has been grounded by some commentators'.[158] Continually when on expedition Porter had his apologetic project before him:

> While wandering through Bible Lands my chief object has been to illustrate Bible truths; and the result of extensive travel, and no little research has been to impress upon my mind the fact that the more we extend our labours in Palestine, whether as antiquarians, geographers, or politicians, the more strongly we are convinced of the literal fulfilment of prophecy, and of the minute accuracy of the topographical and statistical sketches contained in the Word of God.[159]

The confidence which such, apparently unshakeable, evidence gave Porter allowed him to make bold assertions, like the grand concluding statement to one of his Scriptural Geographies –

> Evidences of the truth, and of the divine origin, of the Bible are thus impressed, as we have seen, upon every district of Palestine ... irresistible proofs of the ... inspiration of the Bible... Let no speculations of philosophy, no theories of science, no assertions of learning, however bold, succeed in weakening our faith in its divine origin, or shaking our confidence in its grand achievements and regenerating power...[160]

Porter also used place in religious narratives. When talking of holy places, he was keenly aware of the effect of place upon pilgrims to Jerusalem, as he comments on their Easter devotions, he remarks that: 'Place was the object of worship, and not God... I was then glad to think that the real place of our Lord's passion was not dishonoured'.[161] Porter warned against too great an attachment to geography, as 'the whole spirit of the gospel, the whole writings and teachings of our Lord and his apostles, tend to withdraw men's minds from attachments to places...'[162] This however did not stop Porter writing a book exclusively on Christian holy places, and endeavouring to 'take my readers there in spirit'.[163] Space and place have an ambivalent role in Porter's Scriptural Geography – the placelessness of God is acknowledged, but places are still viewed as fundamental aids to the religious imagination.

Porter's geography is however more than places: his interpretation of the census data of Damascus and his site-analysis of Damascus are of a character which would have fully satisfied many later human geographers. Also, his collection of data is constantly done within a spatial framework, and he is fully aware of the geographically-embedded nature of the information he gathers.

As he journeyed through the landscape, Porter provided work that is rich for analysis. Porter's output can be seen to contain examples of the sites/sights construction of Gregory's analysis.[164] However, the Scriptural Geography project provides a very specialized instance of this feature. Porter visits the sites and the sights he sees there are informed by the sites of the pages of Scripture:

> When I read this most striking and instructive [biblical] narrative on the spot, with Jacob's Well beside me, and the ruins of the Samaritan temple on the top of Gerizim in full view overhead, it seemed almost a new revelation. It assumed the vividness of reality, and I realized, as I had never done before...[165]

Porter's use of sites in his project was primarily because of their history. He was enabled to use the sites to form sights in his imagination: 'The place, unlike most of those in Palestine, is not less remarkable for the natural beauty of its situation than for its classic and sacred associations'.[166] His imagination was deeply inspired by Jacob's Well in particular: 'I seemed to see advancing before me a group of travellers; their leader in mien and face singularly attractive ... His followers press closely round him ... It is Jesus of Nazareth, THE GREAT TEACHER'.[167]

Also an expression of the relationship between routes and roots, is present in Porter.[168] It is through a contextual understanding of Porter's roots in Christian thought that we can see what so often determined the routes of his travels – 'Not only do we follow the footsteps of Jesus in that remarkable journey described in the fourth chapter of St John's Gospel, but at every footstep we have around us scenes framed in Bible history'.[169] As these routes were negotiated they became part of a process of inscription.[170] Porter's map was his chief inscriptory contribution, and, as we have noted, is a singular form of cartographic representation.

Again in Gregory's terms, Porter conducted his travels in a very literary way. He was well read in Holy Land geographers and made frequent reference to them:

> A perusal of Burckhardt's valuable notes, and of the rough sketches of Buckingham, had given me some idea of the general features of the country ... While a study of the Sacred Scriptures, of the writings of Josephus, and of the erudite geography of Reland had ... prepared me for profiting by a tour...[171]

However, Porter's chief literary companion was always his Bible, again an aspect of travelogue peculiar to Scriptural Geography.

The significance of these scripted and spatially and literarily inscribed journeys is the way in which Porter, through their performance, introduced new perspectives to the understanding of the Orient: those of the apologetics of an intellectual controversy in the West.[172] Porter's writings transplanted the engagement of Western minds into an Eastern space, and the Western intellectual posturing on this holy stage reinforced the importance of Holy Land geography for polemical Scriptural Geographers and added another layer to the eschatological topography of the holy landscape.

CONCLUSION: APOLOGETICS AND DIALECTICS
ON THE DAMASCUS ROAD

J.L. Porter was a geographer as well as a traveller, and as he journeyed along routes determined by his roots he took in the sites/sights, which he documented in the fashion of the travellers of the time, with copies of inscriptions and pencil sketches; he also visited and sketched many of the Roman ruins of once-great cities like Palmyra; he conducted some ethnographic enquiries and was always keen to describe the habits and costumes of those he came across on his journeys; he described his interest in local poetry and music,[173] and was keen to relate this to the wider cultural formations of Palestine as it then was. Porter was at the same time a physical geographer, and he noted the morphological and geological features of the landscapes that he traversed, identifying rocks, soils and fossils and sketching even the smallest flora and fauna of the natural world. Herein we begin to see the problematic dialectic of polemical Scriptural Geography, of competing truths in space. Porter is a practitioner of science – geographical science – yet he was also a strong critic of the viability of some of the knowledge that science produces and so a dialectic develops between common sense science and speculative science. Porter, like so many polemical Scriptural Geographers, fought speculative science with common sense science, against a backdrop of divine revelation. His pamphlet, *Science and Revelation: their Distinctive Provinces*, is where he argued most forcibly against science's interference with Scripture, in a work prompted by John Tyndall's address to the meeting of the British Association for the Advancement of Science at Belfast in 1874. When geology attempted to cast light on the origins and age of the earth Porter warned: 'I shall ... feel it my duty to warn the public that [the] conclusions so arrived at are no more worthy of belief than the splendid creations of a poet's fancy'.[174] Yet the same Porter, when in Palestine, could identify the same fossils which gave the geologists of the day their clues to the age of the earth. Porter was unquestionably a scientist himself, and displayed a scientific obsession with accuracy in fieldwork. He constantly carried his compass, sextant, chronometer and notebook, and he was often disparaging of the lack of accuracy among his contemporaries; for example, he noted the mistakes of other workers, and said: 'I could not have made such mistakes, as my description was written not from memory or from short notes, but *fully, while sitting in the chamber itself*, and my friend Mitbah sleeping across the door to keep out a crowd of Arabs'.[175] Of another scientific travel account's claims he asserted that – 'Statements like these may be pardoned, on the plea of poetical licence ... but in a professedly scientific work, they are altogether inexcusable'.[176] Porter attempted to strike a very delicate balance between wholly discrediting geographical science and applying it for his own ends: a balance founded both on the geography of where the science is practised, and the thought of the common sense school. Porter's particular feeling about the role of science in the curriculum for matriculation at Queen's College is evident in his response to a query of 1883, when he had been President of the College for more than twenty years. Porter was never an opponent of science per se and stated his opinion that, to be of use, a scientific education must be of a high standard:

> I am opposed to an examination merely upon the nature and use of simple instruments, and upon experiments made by them. All this can be got from a primer, or by a week or two of 'Cram'. Instead of, or rather along with, this the pupil should be grounded in the first principles of physics; he should be taught to think about them, and to apply them. Thus only, in my opinion, can he acquire that elementary knowledge of the Material World, its phenomena, and laws, which prepares for, and leads to, the study of Natural Philosophy.[177]

Porter was happy to encourage science as an enterprise explaining the workings of the natural world, however, he remained suspicious of science which attempted to explain the origins of the natural world and determine the place of humankind in it. Porter was deeply involved in the broader intellectual dilemma of the Victorian crisis of scriptural authority that we thought about earlier; the problem created by the loss of confidence in the Bible and the ascendancy of a godless science was as outlined by Greene, that – 'Either mankind could have no knowledge whatever concerning values and the meaning of human existence, or science itself would have to derive meaning and value from the processes of nature-history'.[178] In answering such questions as the meaning of human existence Porter was unwilling to let scriptural authority slide, and so in a changed intellectual climate, he found it necessary to conduct scientific research in its support himself: to go to the Holy Land and carry out fieldwork. Why did Porter and his contemporary polemical Scriptural Geographers consider the Holy Land a suitable field site? Livingstone notes that 'the field is constituted by academic projects and narratives. Its existence as a scientific site depends on the stories scientists tell about it'.[179] The stories of Scripture made the particular field site of the Holy Land a fitting location for a project to augment Scripture's claim to contain reliable knowledge. The stories told by the polemical Scriptural Geographers on their return reinforced the status of the Holy Sites as a vital location in religion's struggle for intellectual and social superiority, and inspired others to perpetuate the project.

Furthermore, Livingstone's question about field spaces, as to the kind of relationships which 'pertained between the private and the public in those spaces, and indeed between the specialist space of the investigator and the outer world of intellectual commerce',[180] has obvious resonance within our understanding of the polemical Scriptural Geography project. The importance of the Holy Land as both a knowledge repository and as a space of knowledge creation is a factor at both personal and international levels, because of the special circumstances of the religious status of the knowledge within polemical Scriptural Geography: religion is in some sense a personal matter of faith, and yet established religion in much of the Western world in the nineteenth century exerted a hugely powerful control on society. In these contexts we can understand more fully Porter's relationship with scientific fieldwork.

The influence of Scottish common sense philosophy is also an important context in which to locate Porter's output. We have seen how Porter, when asking and answering questions of origins, meaning and authority leant upon the fundamental certitudes of his religious faith, and that his writings did the same. As we have noted, he was a proponent of a society based on biblical morality and he saw this as the way to deal with the Victorian social crisis. Porter's polemical Scriptural Geography sought to engage directly with this crisis, on the basis of the facts of geography combined with and supporting the revelation of Scripture, thereby bolstering the authority of a biblically based moral code. Porter's abhorrence of the Victorian ideas of materialism and pure idealism, so evident in his engagement with Tyndall, reinforced his commitment to common sense ideas and strongly coloured Porter's scientific practice in the particular methodology of Scottish common sense.

Treating these points together, this, I argue, diagnostic dialectic within polemical Scriptural Geography, of types science that are practised in different spaces and that try to answer different sorts of questions of moral importance, does not reach a synthesis in Porter's work and remains the methodological weakness of the polemical project.

Polemics and Hermeneutics

So, what can be said about the polemical Scriptural Geography enterprise, as exemplified by Porter's work? Said would see intellectual investment in the Orient, a use of that space's genius loci, to justify Occidental notions. Using Said's ideas I want to argue that Porter's time in Palestine was a crucial influence for the rest of his life, on his theology, on his cosmography and on his views on sacred spaces, particularly spaces of worship. The special circumstances of Porter's missionary activity meant that he was exposed to both the intellectual and religious aspects of the Oriental world and this exposure created in him the desire to make the sacred landscape manageable by means of science. The landscape already had for Porter a palimpsestic overlay of eschatological meaning, and he added to this a further scientific mantle. Said would surely note Porter trying to control and encapsulate the Eastern landscape in terms of his own manufacture.

An important perspective is also the geography of scientific ideas, and I hope I have highlighted the importance for Porter of the spatial context within which science is practised. Polemical Scriptural Geographers had tremendous problems with science when it was practised 'at home', where it strayed from its proper province, by engaging with the truth claims of Holy Scripture. However, once on the ground in the Middle East, science of course became the proper tool for elucidating the same sacred texts. The geography of that sacramental space provided a holy context for the application of a scientific cosmology. So, I want to argue for the importance of geography in modifying perceptions of science.

Finally, using the insights of this contextual and biographical understanding of Porter's work I hope that we have traced the genealogy of the Scriptural Geography project through its polemical phase, noting the changing relationship with science, the need to engage with changing social and intellectual structures, the importance of individual biography in understanding science and the continuing widespread public interest in the geography of the Holy Land.

5   The Contextual Order: George Adam Smith

Never a day passed without his careful readings of temperature and barometric pressure, and never an evening ... without his minute recording of everything done, seen and heard...[1]

GEORGE ADAM SMITH

An official of the 1881 Census checking forms in Aberdeen was growing more and more bewildered: 'Born in Calcutta! Hebrew professor! Is he black?'[2] The landlady who put up Rev (transiently Prof) George Adam Smith had an awkward task in explaining her extraordinary tenant. Quite how the temporary Professor of Hebrew and Old Testament Exegesis at the Free Church College in Aberdeen came to be a 25 year old from Calcutta, of unlikely disposition, unlikely prospects, and with an unlikely future ahead, and quite how the geography of the Holy Land and the spatial biography of his life were crucial elements in determining that future, are our concerns here. George Adam Smith had ahead of him a future that would see him a best-selling author for two generations, a cleric deep in theological controversy, an honorary graduate of more than a dozen universities on both sides of the Atlantic,[3] the holder of the highest office in his church, Principal of one of Britain's oldest universities and the recipient of a knighthood from George V, whom he would also serve as Scottish Chaplain. George Adam Smith was, in every way, a person to stimulate remark and demand superlatives; his extraordinary life of scholarship, travel and reflection was one which has left its mark deep upon Scottish Christianity and Holy Land geography. He was truly 'an outstanding personality'.[4] Smith was always a popular public speaker and made four lecture tours of the United States of America, to lecture on both theology and politics,[5] as well as numerous addresses to organizations such as the British Academy,[6] the British Association for the Advancement of Science, the Royal Scottish Geographical Society, and many universities at home and abroad. Particularly he spoke on his own fields of expertise: the Old Testament and the Holy Land. He was also a member of the Palestine Exploration Fund and a regular contributor to its journal, *The Palestine Exploration Fund Quarterly Statement.*

Background and Early Career

George Adam Smith's family might have been designed to produce a scholar of unusual inclination and merit. He was the firstborn of ten in his family, on 19 October 1856 in India, to a Raj couple, and his father, George Smith, was the principal of a school, Doveton College, in Calcutta. Subsequently his father was employed as a journalist, for *The Calcutta Review*, *The Spectator*, and *The Friend of India*, he also served both of the latter as editor and part owner, and eventually he was employed as the India correspondent of *The Times*. (George Adam himself was employed as a journalist for a short time after his first graduation, reporting on the Berlin Congress of 1878, for *Mayfair*.) George Smith Senior continued to work as a journalist in one way or another after his return to Britain in 1875 and until his retirement. He was also the author of numerous works, including *The Geography of British India*.[7] However George Smith's main work after returning home was in the Foreign Mission Office of the United Free Church of Scotland, where he served as Assistant Secretary and then Associate Secretary.

Following a period of poor health in 1858 George Adam Smith's mother had to return to Britain from Calcutta, and brought the young George back with her to her native Scotland. Eventually she regained her strength and went back to India, however, George Adam Smith remained in Scotland, in the care of his older sister and cousin,

Mary and Hannah, at Leith where he enjoyed a very happy upbringing, with much scope for self-expression.

As a child he was encouraged to act out Bible stories with his siblings:

> These stories were chiefly from the Old Testament, and Aunt Mary would give graphic descriptions of places and people ... Who can doubt but that the seeds were sown which bore fruition in the books that have helped to make the Old Testament a reality and living force to many?[8]

From his earliest days he wanted to be a minister. His favourite reading as an adolescent was the writings of the Jewish classical historian Josephus.[9]

Smith attended the Royal High School in Edinburgh and was a notably enthusiastic and successful scholar there. In time he went to Edinburgh University in 1871 and graduated with an MA at the age of eighteen, consisting of arts, Greek, Latin, English literature and philosophy. In his free time he also attended classes in political economy, and this economic knowledge is much in evidence in his work on *Jerusalem*.[10] Immediately after taking his degree he offered himself for ministry in the Free Church of Scotland, and commenced theological studies at New College in Edinburgh in 1875.

During this time he had the opportunity to travel to Germany in his summer vacations. He twice visited German universities to study – Tübingen (from 21 April to 6 August 1876) and Leipzig (in 1878)[11] – and I shall want to argue that these visits were crucial in determining the direction of his life at various subsequent points. During his time in Leipzig he demonstrated the keen spatial awareness of one who would become a geographer, drawing a sketch map of the part of the city in which he lived and worked, and sending this home for the benefit of his family.[12]

His studies at New College disclosed his bent for theology. In his illustrious academic career, George Adam Smith was principally a theologian and yet it is difficult to assess his theology. Primarily this is because, as Riesen observes: '(a) he does not say enough and (b) he almost never treats matters theologically'.[13] Smith shied away from publicity and even during his near-trial for heresy at the United Free

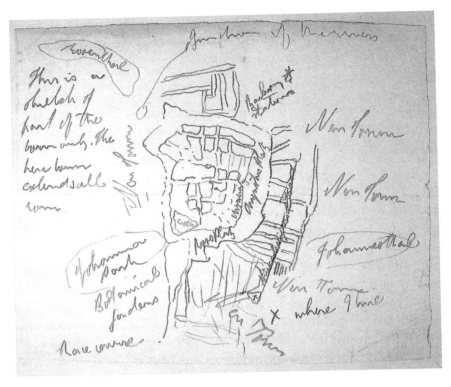

11: George Adam Smith's
sketch map of his residence in Leipzig

Church General Assembly of 1902, we will see below that he only entered the debate 'With the very greatest reluctance'.[14] However, an examination of what Smith was prepared to say about his theology can assist us in our understanding of his approach to Scriptural Geography, his use of texts and topography in the negotiation of his faith and his position within the Scottish theological tradition.

Smith's geographical location during his student days was an essential factor in the development of his theology: he visited Germany to study during summer vacations and it was here, in the particular academic atmosphere of nineteenth century Protestant Germany, that he was first exposed to higher criticism and its entourage of scholarly connotations in a direct way.[15] Higher criticism is the practice of asking questions concerning the authorship and authority of biblical texts, using contemporaneous historical sources and modern linguistic analysis. It often provides different answers concerning, for example, the authorship of the Scriptures, than the Scriptures do themselves. Smith began reading such German theology and studying the Pentateuch in depth. In a summary of his domestic expenses he recorded that he bought a Hebrew Pentateuch, a German bible and German dictionary at this time.[16] His study of German works is detailed in a letter to his father – 'I am getting on well with my reading – I have finished W. Fell and have almost done with Schillers Jung from New Orleans. On Tuesday I mean to commence "Faust" and read it very carefully...'[17] The reference to W. Fell is evidently Winand Fell, a German theologian (1837–1908), who was a church historian working in Leipzig, and who published his doctoral thesis at Leipzig in 1871.[18] But the young Smith evidently read and listened to a wide range of scholars engaged in biblical higher criticism.

Higher criticism was one of the major developments in biblical study in the post-Enlightenment period and its impact on Christian theology, one way or another, is hard to overestimate. The reasons for its impact on Smith are obvious: in Leipzig the young Smith would have come across Keil and Delitzsch, and he certainly sat in the classes of Diestel and Roth (and von Harnack)[19] at Tübingen.[20] Smith remained a lifelong friend of the famed theologian Budde.[21] However, while it is acknowledged that these scholars were largely conservative, orthodox figures, and members of the Confessionalist School of modern biblical critics,[22] it must be noted that Smith was still dealing with creative and free thinkers. Delitzsch 'had embraced significant aspects of the German speculative and idealist philosophy of his day, and sought to combine these insights with confessional theology and with biblical exegesis'.[23] This was George Adam Smith's experience, and it is instructive to realize that it was not a unique one. The movement of higher criticism from its native Germany to an often stormy reception in Britain has been well documented and Riesen argues that 'Biblical criticism was originally ... an almost exclusively German phenomenon ... The picture is of theory and practice spreading from Berlin, Tübingen, Bonn and other centers to the uttermost parts of the earth'.[24] Riesen attributes this movement of ideas to 'the trend in the late eighteen hundreds for the better divinity students from Britain and America to visit German universities during their summer vacations to imbibe the most recent advances in biblical scholarship'.[25]

Thomas Howard also demonstrates how higher criticism is a largely Teutonic enterprise, with roots deep in the German Enlightenment; his analysis situates biblical criticism within the mood of crisis generated by German historians in the eighteenth century, and he argues that the rise of historical consciousness was traditionally thought to be coupled with the emancipation of historical awareness from 'traditional, religious patterns of thought'.[26] However, in contrast to other scholars, Howard does not feel that modernity necessarily gave rise to a post-theological world and that this liberated history, which in turn influenced the intellectual currents in theology. Howard does not see the modernity born of intellectual enlightenment as a necessarily anti-theological undertaking, rather: 'The German Enlightenment is distinguished by its profoundly religious character ... Might then a secular historical outlook, born in the wake of the German Enlightenment, retain traces, revealing elisions, hereditary marks that betray significant continuities between premodern-theological and modern-historical ways of thinking?'[27] Howard wants to suggest that the problems created by theological study itself required new historical methods, and that biblical criticism was the cradle in which a new historicism was born. Theologians themselves created the new ideas to cope with the problems they were increasingly encountering in the pursuit of a hopefully clearer theological truth. This, argues Howard, was a particular outworking of the Reformation project of attempting to refine Christianity: 'Like many Protestant critics, de Wette [a famous critical scholar of the time] believed that he was continuing the work of the Reformation, using historical-critical exegesis to discover the true religious kernel of Christianity while discarding accumulated ecclesiastical and cultural dross'.[28] This project, in Howard's telling, is what overtures the intellectual history of Europe right up to the present. Howard feels that it is one of the most 'important and perplexing aspects of modern European intellectual history'.[29]

This is the context in which I want to situate Smith's work. His theological writings, limited though they are, provide us with an important window on the influence of geography on theology; of space on historiography; of location and the import of geographical immediacy for biography. Below I will argue that the ideas of higher criticism employed in Smith's work, including radical ideas about the authorship and authority of Old Testament books and their use in contemporary theology, and the role that this type of use played within the church and his 'Revolutionary opinions'[30] have their roots in his time in Germany and in his existential experiences of the biblical spaces of the Holy Land.

1879–1898

The first of those experiences was when Smith went to help with the United Presbyterian Church of America's Mission in Cairo, in 1879–80, and the journeys following this work fulfilled what had been for him a long-held dream – 'From his earliest days he had longed to go to Palestine'.[31] He was able to tour the Holy Land on foot, with nothing more than the bare essentials for the journey. His wife's account of this journey gives a feeling for how it was undertaken:

> With the money he had acquired and the language he had learned, he started on his travels in that country – his only companion an Arab muleteer ... He tramped the country on foot (the mule behind with his baggage, chiefly books), going from place to place as the spirit moved him.[32]

This was a journey which was, in Duncan and Gregory's terms,[33] thoroughly inscribed on the spaces of Palestine: '[Smith] talked to the people he met, the workers in the fields, the fellaheen in the villages, the local sheikhs, and he came to understand their ways of thought and expression'.[34] And his was a truly existentially immediate experience of the country: 'At nights he slept in a mud-walled village, or a lonely khan, or, more often, the Syrian stars looked down upon him as he slept in the open with his mule tethered nearby'.[35] His wife could therefore argue that on this journey –

12: George Adam Smith as a young minister

the land unfolded itself to him in all its many aspects. His eyes were opened to see the reasons and the meanings of words and events which, until then, he had only partly understood, and there is no doubt that the idea of writing a book upon the country was born in his mind from that first solitary journey.[36]

His letters home, written on the spot, from such locations as 'On board the Scamandre'[37] and 'Our Camp, the plains of Jericho, by Judah'[38] bear out this feeling of immediacy and the spatial embeddedness of experience. These letters reveal a traveller who was a careful observer, full of learning ('I diligently read *Josephus* all morning')[39] and eager to fully experience a place which he had waited so long to go to, and was at pains to record. A very rich passage of thick description shows Smith getting to grips with the diverse and cosmopolitan nature of Jerusalem –

> Filth and refuse lie everywhere. The bazaars are horrible places, full of filthy, flea-infested crowds. There are Oriental German watchmakers and carpenters, Polish shoe-makers, Spanish merchants of the better sort – these all Jews – Russian tea-sellers, exactly as your photo's make them, Armenians in all sorts of dresses, often with the large circular sheepskin caps of central Asia. Greeks and the various subjects of the Sultan, give the town a very cosmopolitan appearance. The impressions left upon you far exceed those of Leipzig fair.[40]

Here we encounter a Western traveller unable to determine the indigenous order of an unfamiliar society, and seeing only disorder in what must have been, to a local observer, an expediently laid out trading place. Smith's recourse to the chaotic geography of Leipzig fair helps to locate the experience in terms of a comparable phenomenon for those whose routes had remained closer to their Scottish roots: it is an attempt to bring the defiant Otherness of the Oriental spatial order within the arc of European familiarity.

13: Letter from George Adam Smith, en route to the Holy Land, to his Mother

In the course of this trip Smith visited all the usual holy sites as his pilgrimage demanded, and paid them suitable attentions, but the young Smith also noted that:

> For their own ends the churches have crowded the chief scenes of Scripture history within the walls [of the Holy Sepulchre complex] and when they seemed to fail they have not hesitated to invent others. The visitor to Jerusalem is offered a choice of sites of the closing events of Christ's life ... The Chapel of Scourging and Crowning With Thorns lies a few feet from the holes in which they declare the three crosses stood. These holes are absurdly near each other ... In fact the whole thread of Bible history has been rugged and tugged at by the different sects till it lies before you knotted and twisted and torn and almost unrecognisable.[41]

Perhaps this is why later Smith decried the practice of trying too precisely to locate too many of the events of the Bible:

> I have felt that just at present the geographer of Palestine is more usefully employed in the reducing than adding to the identification of sites. In Britain our surveyors have been tempted to serious over-identification, perhaps by the zeal of a portion of the religious public, which subscribes to exploration according to the number of immediate results.[42]

This view on one aspect of the Scriptural Geography project shapes Smith's whole contribution to it: Smith did not wish to prosecute his Scriptural Geography on the bases of public acclaim, popular subscription, or the wide appeal of an apologetic project.

However, he did seem to be affected in a real way by his encounter with the religious practice of many Holy Land pilgrims:

> I went off to the Jews' wailing place, on the inside wall of the temple. |[43] I did not – I could not stay more than a minute there. People have said that the descriptions of this wailing are very much exaggerated. They must have gone at a wrong hour. I witnessed a most impressive scene – a scene, which although I saw it only for a minute I shall never forget ... They kissed the old stones!! They laid their heads upon them and sobbed as if their

hearts would break! With what broken voices did they chant the responses, to a ritual that their leader stammered out with difficulty, and which it almost brings tears to the eyes to read. After that you will not wonder that I stayed only a minute.[44]

And again – 'I must pay tribute to the warmth and sincerity of the devotions I witnessed in the churches'[45] – a phrase showing an admiration of the zeal of the other pilgrims which puts him at odds with many travellers to Jerusalem, starkly in contrast indeed to the vast majority of his Protestant colleagues, who decry such appeals to emotionalism among their Catholic and Orthodox Christian brethren.[46] Nevertheless he was not willing to glaze sentimentally over his feeling of disappointment with some of what he sees: 'Olivet – bare and stoney with scarcely a sufficient number of trees to merit its name'.[47] Also, 'Without doubt the whole aspect of the immediate surroundings of Jerusalem is disappointing. The hillsides are stripped and sterile'.[48] For George Adam Smith the sites of Palestine are apparently quite often disheartening sights when compared to the imagined geographies that he has had since his childhood pastime of acting out Bible stories at Leith, the letters home show signs of dissatisfaction with the landscape and its inhabitants at various points. Smith's writing demonstrates an often profound disjunction between the aspirational geography of a young actor and the experiential geography of a Holy Land pilgrim. However, Smith's enthusiasm for the project of visiting the Holy Land cannot be doubted:

> I rose yesterday morning at half-past four and rushed up the Mount of Olives in the soft warm dawn to see the sun rise over the Mountains of Moab on the other side of the Jordan Valley. Under the light above them the hills looked clear bluer than before, and gradually the valley and hills between us and them rose from haze into a light that they do not enjoy later in the day. After this the sun rose high enough to touch the city and I waited till the light spread over the Mount of Olives into the deepest recesses of Kidron.[49]

In coping with the bible land scenes, the ploy of domestication is evident, as he writes: 'Dear Father, | When I awoke yesterday morning it was raining and blowing heavily, and a preliminary walk through some of the "closes", for there are no streets in Jerusalem, brought stormy days in Edinburgh very vividly into my memory'.[50] The scenery in rural areas too 'recalls the highlands of the Border Counties [of England and Scotland]'.[51] So that it is then natural, in this landscape, portrayed by devices designed to compare it to home, to begin reminding himself of Bible texts learned at home: 'it recalled more than one text to see the herdboys separate them carefully at the gates and take goats in one direction and sheep in the other'.[52]

Importantly for Smith, as a contextual Scriptural Geographer, the evidence of his own fieldwork allowed him to challenge prevailing traditions on the location of Scripture events: 'It is not likely that Christ in a triumphal procession and riding, would choose a mere mountain path, which is so steep that he would have to dismount at many parts of it. It is more probable therefore that he took the main road from Jericho'.[53] As we can see, Smith had no difficulty in discrediting the sentimentality of the faith of popular appeal.

When writing from the desert camp, away from the bustle of the city and its obvious fabrications of holy sites, and able to take perspective over the land,[54] his mind was focussed even more strongly on how the land illustrates Scripture. He wrote:

> You may understand how much I enjoyed that quiet Sunday afternoon in the fields, and the animals wild and tame in them, and the men who cultivated them, gave me at nearly every step I took some clear illustration of Christ's parables, or the different manners and customs mentioned [in] the Bible.[55]

Not only did Smith evidently find pleasure in seeing the Bible illustrated for him, he also enjoyed undergoing the same experiences as biblical characters, as he was quick to point out the parablesque scene in which he participates:

> The Bedouin escorts that were to accompany us and defend us from the fate of the other man who went down to Jericho and fell among thieves were swaggering up and down a side street in all the splendour of silk head-dresses and [?][56] robes, sabre and guns. Everything was in picturesque comparison...[57]

'Swaggering', here, can be viewed as a powerful word: it awakens a sense of Western superiority and patronage towards the presumed less psychologically self-aware inhabitants of the Holy Land. Here is the arrogance of the detached Western observer, viewing the people of the land from what Lock describes as the 'proper aesthetic distance'[58] As Smith journeyed in this 'picturesque procession' he tells how he 'had adopted the native headdress – a splendid protection from the sun' such was his desire to participate fully.[59] A geography of performativity is embedded in these passages. The same Smith is, ambivalently, the avid pilgrim participant, and the detached Western observer at different times; when taking part in the event he is an actor, and, later, when writing his account of it he is an observer. These different roles are played out in the letter, as the account of the event shows the eager player, while the role of detached Western observer is actually performatively created by the act of writing the words in the letter. This is an example of how a tableau *vivant*, in this case scripted by Smith's prior knowledge of, and reference to, the victim in the biblical story of the Good Samaritan, is performed to create an extension of Orientalist discourses.[60]

Church Work

After Smith returned from his first visit to the Holy Land he immediately entered parish ministry in the United Free Church of Scotland. Smith's ministry saw him serve in three parishes. His initial term was as an Assistant Minister from 1880, in Brechin, near Dundee, from which post he was called in the same year to temporarily take on the teaching of Hebrew and Old Testament Studies, at the Free Church College in Aberdeen. His precocious appointment as a temporary professor at the college in Aberdeen was the result of a dispute. His predecessor in the post, Prof William Robertson Smith, had written an influential article, 'Bible', for the *Encyclopaedia Britannica*'s ninth edition of 1875, and the content was, for many Scottish Presbyterians, disturbing;[61] the article appeared to be phrased in such a way as to shed doubt on the inerrancy of the Bible and the status of the Old Testament prophets; it employed the methods of higher criticism, and Robertson Smith was tried for heresy by his church with considerable fervour; after all, the Free Church was a church which was 'proud to be orthodox. An unquestioned article of its creed was the supreme authority of the Bible'.[62] In a long and tediously drawn-out series of engagements 'proceeding from one church court to another, with varying and ambiguous fortunes',[63] culminating in 1881, the case made its appearance for the third time at the Church's highest court, the General Assembly, which finally deposed William Robertson Smith from his chair at the Church's New College in Aberdeen. It has been said that 'despite his defeat at the hands of the guardians of the Free Church's sacred flame, Smith's influence was both deep and lasting',[64] and William Robertson Smith became one of those whom Riesen refers to as 'martyrs for religious truth and academic freedom – heroes, in other words, as well as heretics'.[65]

Such trials were an indicator that traditional faith in the broader Scottish church was under attack from theologians in one of the most conservative parts of that church, and, interestingly, as we have seen in the thinking of Howard, the problems were not generated by theology narrowly conceived, but by what Riesen calls the 'seemingly harmless and arcane province of historiography'.[66] Riesen argues that the 'growth of a feeling for history'[67] was the key intellectual development of the nineteenth century, and that this new hunger for historical detail and completeness seemed sacrilegious when it caused scientific-sounding, probing questions to be asked about the context of the lives of the biblical writers and the development of Scripture, and in consideration of the connotations of whatever the answers to those questions might be for the Christian faith. Concisely put by Riesen –

The thing that intimidated and infuriated ordinary Christians about this modern science was not simply that it was modern or scientific, but that in its scouring of the sacred text it often came up with theories concerning dates and authorship ... that were different from those that the Church had always held, and in some cases different from the Bible itself ... As a consequence higher criticism ... was seen by many not as an aid to understanding the Bible, but as a questioning of its inspiration and authority...[68]

George Adam Smith would have observed this trial closely. Recently returned from his visits to Germany, and full of the questions of higher criticism himself, he must have watched the fate of Prof Smith with considerable interest. As he perhaps observed the trial, and maybe even voted in its outcome, he didn't then know that he was to become the next Professor; and the next-but-one United Free Church minister to have a brush with heresy.

And so one of the net results of the William Robertson Smith heresy case was that a young George Adam Smith was called temporarily to the Chair of Hebrew and Old Testament Exegesis at the Free Church College in Aberdeen. As we shall see below, George Adam Smith's own work was later also a cause of suspicion, and he found that his theological ideas, while not much different from those of William Robertson Smith, were only slightly more palatable to the commissioners of the General Assembly: it has been argued that this was more the result of his different personality than any doctrinal shift in the Free Church,[69] and George Adam Smith can certainly be seen as a less abrasive personality.

George Adam Smith was not only a successor to, but a friend of, William Robertson Smith. They had met initially in Port Said, in 1879, and Campbell is not slow to point out that 'The significance of the meeting, far away from ecclesiastical and theological controversies in Scotland cannot be overlooked, for it offered a unique opportunity to discuss events in which their lives were both involved'.[70] Again, the importance of spatial biography becomes apparent: the space between the Glasgow Assembly Hall and the Egyptian seaport allowed for a more expansive and freer discussion of the details of the problems wracking the Kirk at home; the two scholars, at almost opposing points in their careers, had much to discuss that interested them both deeply; they had much to discuss that would bear upon both of their futures; they had much to discuss that would bear upon the future of Christian theology.[71]

In 1881, when George Adam Smith went to Aberdeen to take up his temporary post at the behest of the General Assembly, he met William Robertson Smith again and as his wife later recalled:

The fiery little man seemed not too well pleased to see him, which was scarcely surprising. 'What would you do', he demanded fiercely, 'if I should refuse to obtemper the decision of the Assembly and insist on taking the class myself?' 'Then', said George, 'I would be proud to go and sit among your students'. After that they became good friends.[72]

So it was that a lifelong relationship began, and the continuity of critical scholarship in the Free Church began to be assured. As Campbell observes: '[George Adam Smith's] respect for the Professor was great, and his meeting with him was one of the most important experiences of his own life, confirming in his mind the necessity of remaining in the Free Church in order to continue the work of critical scholarship'.[73]

Smith carried out his duties at Aberdeen effectively, until the newly-founded congregation of Queen's Cross in Aberdeen called him to be their first minister, and he was ordained by the Presbytery of Aberdeen in April 1882. Frequent preaching visits around local congregations and a prominent role in the intellectual and cultural life of Aberdeen meant that 'his influence was felt throughout the city'.[74] The power and clarity of his preaching is evidenced by the large crowds who came specifically to hear him,[75] and the fact that he had at least one complete volume of sermons published,[76] and various single sermons published in literary journals.[77] He was affectionately remembered long after he had left Queen's Cross, and some of its members had him marry them, or baptize their children in the Chapel at King's College, when he was later Principal at Aberdeen University.[78]

Smith was noted as a compassionate and proficient pastor, and was heavily involved in social concerns beyond the work his incumbency required of him. Additionally, while in Aberdeen he was Secretary of the Royal Scottish Geographical Society from 1885,[79] and his geographical leanings were much in evidence in his theology lectures when he had been at Aberdeen as 'a former student ... wrote to Smith's widow ... "I can picture [Smith] round that raised contour map, where he so often gathered us, enthusiastically explaining why such-and-such an expedition went this way and not that. It was all so infectious and so natural. And it made preachers"'.[80]

In 1885 when the British Association for the Advancement of Science met in Aberdeen George Adam Smith acted as secretary to the

Geographical Section.[81] Also in addition to his ministerial duties, he enjoyed frequent holidays to Switzerland for the purposes of pursuing his chief recreation – mountaineering. He was an accomplished member of the Alpine Club, and his feats astounded many fellow mountaineers.[82] It was on such a trip in 1889 that he met his wife, Lilian.

14: George Adam Smith's camp, the Holy Land, 1891

Writings

George Adam Smith was a prolific publisher, and has been labelled as 'enviably productive'.[83] His output included theology, historical geography, archaeology and much review work. He began his publishing career during his time in parish ministry in Queen's Cross in Aberdeen, and his first major work was the first of two volumes of commentary on Isaiah, in the important Expositor's series. This work contains an important insight into Smith's ideas about the Bible and its relation to the evidence of field studies: 'Signs of a development [within the text] like these may be fairly used to correct or support the evidence which Assyriology affords for determining the chronological order of the chapters [of Isaiah]'.[84] This is evidence of how Smith viewed the relationship of higher criticism, used to distinguish the developments within the text, and the field evidence of archaeological studies in more fully understanding Isaiah's prophetic utterances, and the problematization which, for Smith, surrounds the relationship between biblical and scientific sources of information.

Smith visited the Holy Land again in 1891, funded by his Queen's Cross congregation, and notebooks kept by him on this trip are preserved.[85] They show a scholarly interest in all seen and done and are peppered with references to contemporary literature on the Holy Land as well as biblical quotations and allusions. Much of the material is obviously destined for *The Historical Geography of the Holy Land*.

In 1891 he also reviewed the new edition of Baedeker's *Palestine* for *The Expositor*, and, while quite probably in the process of writing his own book about Palestine, opined that 'A guide-book to Palestine is far more than a guide-book. Numbers buy it who never intend to use it for a tour'.[86] This is very much the vein in which his own book was written. He continued, discreetly outlining his own project in the guise of reviewing another's –

[A guide-book] ought to be the most accurate and vivid manual of sacred geography within reach of the student – such assistance as he can get nowhere else so well for determining the distances and difficulties of biblical journeys, the lines of the ancient campaigns, and generally all the perspective of the Holy Land, as well as the latest results of biblical archaeology and geography. One cannot conceive of a better preparation for teachers of the Bible-classes than to have made their own way, in the spirit, through Palestine with the help of a modern guide-book and a good map. Never afterwards will they feel from home in the scenes of sacred history.[87]

This was very much the set of premises on which his own works were based.

He remained in Aberdeen for ten happy and productive years until eventually he took up the position of Professor of Hebrew and Old

Testament Exegesis at the Free Church College in Glasgow, and it was during his time in this job that much of his output was written. In Glasgow, Smith continued his work of social concern and carried out projects as diverse as a campaign against sweated labour, the organization of the Boys' Brigade for the city and the establishment of a play centre.[88]

In the year of his arrival in Glasgow he reviewed an Isaiah commentary and we see an overture of what were to be some of the great concerns of his own life of scholarship: '[this commentary] contains the usual reasons for the appearance of such a work – the progress of Comparative Religion, the recent discoveries in the East, the revolution within the interpretation of the Old Testament itself...'[89]

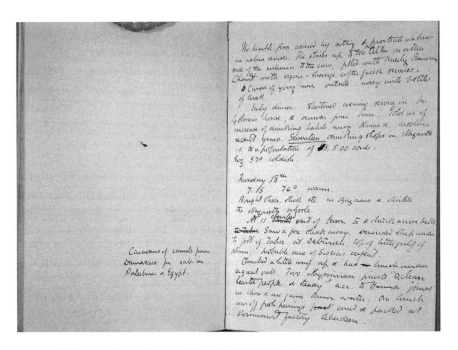

15: A page from George Adam Smith's Holy Land notebook, 1891

By 1893, now a permanent Professor, Smith was considered a scholar of merit, and the content of his *The Preaching of the Old Testament to the Age* confirms this. This is the published version of his inaugural lecture at Glasgow, and in it he attempted to show the benefits of higher critical analysis of the Old Testament. He acknowledged that 'For a long time past, every relevant science, every possible school of belief, have shot across the Old Testament their opposing lights',[90] and he attempted to describe what those lights had revealed, and what the modern preacher was left with. He quieted the fears of his audience by reminding them that 'the new criticism is not necessarily connected with the rationalism which cuts the sinews of the preacher...'[91] and in consolation offered an argument that would later feature in his address to the General Assembly of 1902: 'more than one critic has offered in corroboration of the truth of the new theories, the conviction that they are of greater apologetic value than were the traditional'.[92]

In 1894 Smith produced his best known work. This book was where Smith packaged his life of Oriental scholarship and travel for the religious benefit of a wide audience. *The Historical Geography of the Holy Land* was first published by Hodder & Stoughton, and immediately received the highest acclaim from reviewers.[93] Phrases like 'the author has a special gift of vivid representation ... The book is an extremely valuable means of aid to the understanding of the history, especially of the Old Testament' and 'careful attention has been paid to details ... The author proves himself a thoroughly informed craftsman'[94] and

The book is too rich to summarise ... Few pages are without some telling phrase ... The wealth of imagery would be excessive for prose if it were not that it is chosen with such appropriateness and scientific truth ... [The] maps alone are more suggestive and enlightening than many treatises, and they are destined, we trust, to enliven many a sermon, and turn the monotony of the records of Israelitish wars into a thrilling romance...[95]

were common in reviews. Recent commentators have commended the work as 'a pioneer book, written by a powerful communicator and preacher'.[96] C.J. Robertson has remarked that:

Smith integrated his material in a way that transformed it into geography ... he was able to describe and interpret the landscapes of Palestine from his extensive personal observations and from a wide acquaintance with the archaeology, ethnography and history of the country and particularly his intensive scholarship in Biblical literature.[97]

The book ran to twenty-six editions, with the first four arriving inside two years, and a progression of one each year for the next twenty years. The work quickly became the definitive treatise on the topic and remained in print until 1976, the rights having passed through different publishing houses. It still enjoys a healthy second-hand circulation and apparently a wide readership, and has also recently been published in Hebrew.[98]

Smith quickly found himself the recipient of a huge quantity of correspondence about the book, much of which is preserved. Overwhelmingly his correspondents were full of praise and encouragement, with the occasional one of correction of some minor detail. One especially pedantic letter, about the site of some particularly obscure event, asking for a reply to a challenge enclosed a stamped addressed envelope for reply, which is still unused.[99] One of the most interesting letters indicates that within a year of its publication the book had become almost the sole constituent of the syllabus for religious education in a boys' school in Kent.[100]

The Historical Geography of the Holy Land is truly monumental, encompassing a huge range of theological, geographical and archaeological field sources. The book is thinly illustrated, with only four maps of the land and, as one reviewer puts it, appears like a military hand book,[101] until we engage with the poetic text. The sparseness and simplicity may be symptomatic of what Lock sees as the Protestant 'plainness' in interpreting the Holy Landscape.[102] It is perhaps not inappropriate that the book had a military appearance, as Allenby used it as his handbook in the Palestine Campaign of the Great War.[103] The book is poetically written, as may be expected of a scholar of many languages, and much thick description, strongly suggestive of compilation from notes written on the spot, permeates the pages.

The *Historical Geography* treats the Holy Land first systematically, looking at the climate, soils, geology and landscape as a whole, and then regionally, taking each region and thoroughly describing it, while relating it to the scholarly and biblical literature. The 'dense web of textual associations' sensed in so much Victorian travel litera-

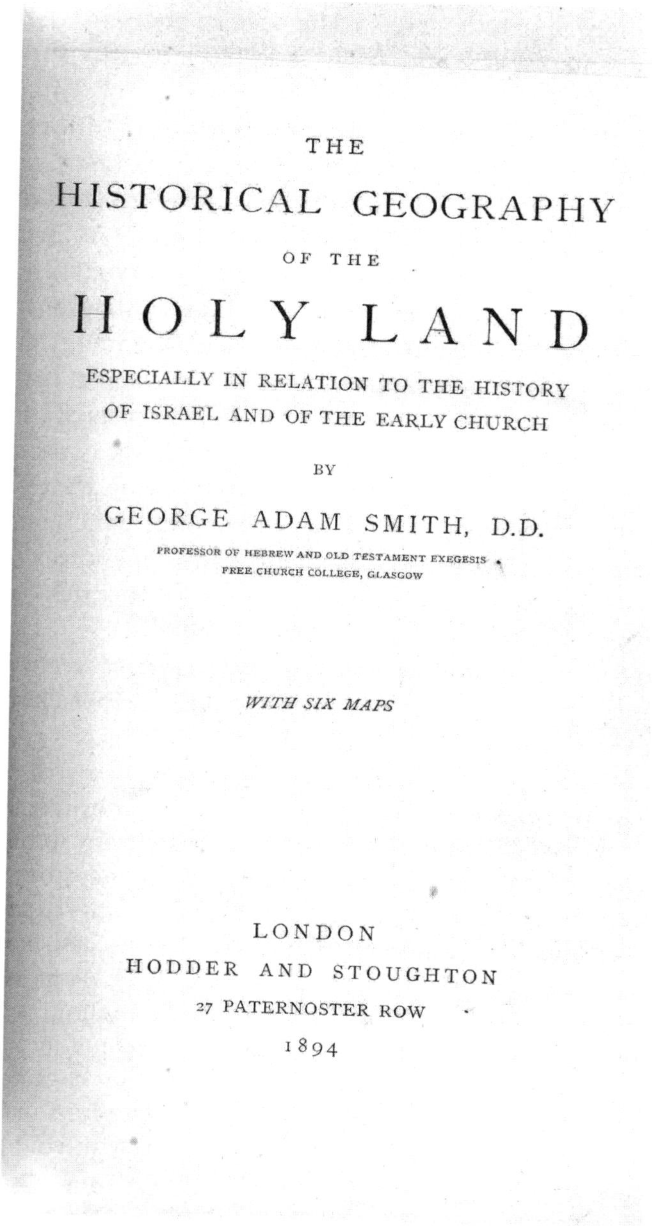

THE

HISTORICAL GEOGRAPHY

OF THE

HOLY LAND

ESPECIALLY IN RELATION TO THE HISTORY
OF ISRAEL AND OF THE EARLY CHURCH

BY

GEORGE ADAM SMITH, D.D.

PROFESSOR OF HEBREW AND OLD TESTAMENT EXEGESIS
FREE CHURCH COLLEGE, GLASGOW

WITH SIX MAPS

LONDON

HODDER AND STOUGHTON

27 PATERNOSTER ROW

1894

Illustration 16: The title page of *The Historical Geography of the Holy Land* (1894)

ture is strongly apparent here.[104] The text of the book is peppered with biblical and classical quotations, and has a healthy sprinkling of references to more modern works on the region.[105] The initial section, which presents a broad view of Syria's place in world history forms an overture to all that Smith later says about the influence of such a small province on the world. This chapter forms the introduction to the first Book of Smith's work. Another four chapters in this Book deal with the interconnections between Syrian topography and history, the interconnections between the land's climate and religion, the links between Holy Land scenery and Old Testament poetry and the uses of Holy Land geography in textual criticism. A fifth chapter closes the Book, with a description of the view over most of the land, from the summit of Mount Ebal. The second Book contains seventeen chapters, which deal, regionally, with Palestine west of the Jordan and a third and final Book has seven chapters which perform the same function for Palestine east of the Jordan. Appendices of biblical passages using geographical terms and historical theories concerning Israel's development complete the work.

The text is artistic and poetic in style. Dry representation never serves Smith's purpose. He opens the section on Holy Land scenery by noting that:

The land has been stripped and starved, its bones protrude, in parts it is very bald – a carcase of a land, if you like, from some lower points of view... Yet, even as it lies to-day, there are, in the Holy Land, some prospects as bold and rich as any you will see in countries famed for their picturesqueness. There is the coast-line from the headland of Carmel – northwards the Gulf of Haifa, with its yellow sands and palms, across them brown, crumbling Acre, and in the haze the white Ladder of Tyre: southwards Sharon with her scattered forest, her coast of sand and grass, and the haggard ruins of Athlit ... westwards the green sea and the wonderful shadows of the clouds upon it – grey when you look at them with your face to the sun, but, with the sun behind you, purple, and more like Homer's 'wine coloured water' than anything I have seen in the Mediterranean. There is the *excellency of Carmel* itself: wheat-fields climbing from Esdraelon to the first bare rocks, then thick bush and scrub, young ilex, wild olives and pines, with undergrowth of large purple thistles, mallows with blossoms like pelargoniums,

stocks of hollyhock, golden broom, honeysuckle and convol-
vulus...[106]

This romantic language, with so much openly subjective content, is
the stuff of which Smith's work is composed. Smith was deeply affected by this landscape, and when viewing the Holy Land from Mount
Ebal, noted 'How the heart throbs when the eye sweeps that long and
steadfast skyline'.[107] Smith also demonstrates a keen awareness of the
power of eloquent narrative in setting the context for the histories
that he tells. His chapter on Damascus is opened with a pen picture
of a journey into the city:

> It is best to enter Damascus in summer, because then everything
> predisposes you for her charms. You come down off the barren
> flanks of Anti-Lebanon. You cross the plateau of Sahra-ed-Dimas,
> six shadeless miles that stretch themselves, with the elasticity of all
> Syrian plains in haze, till you almost fancy you are upon some
> enchanted ground rolling out with you as you travel. But at last
> the road begins to sink ... The air is still, the rocks blistered, the
> road deep in dust, when suddenly a bank of foliage bursts into
> view, with a white verandah above it. The road turns a corner; you
> are in shadow, on a bridge, in a breeze. Another turn and you have
> streams on both sides, a burn gurgling through bushes on the left,
> on the right not one stream but one banked over the other, and
> the wind in the poplars above... You pass between orchards of figs
> and apricots. For hedges there are the briar rose, and for a canopy
> the walnut. Pomegranate blossoms glow through the shade; vine-
> boughs trail across the briar; a little waterfall breaks on the edge of
> the road... And all this water and leafage are so lavish that the
> broken mud-walls and slovenly houses have no power to vex the
> eye, exulting in the contrast of the valley with the bare brown hills
> that shut it in.[108]

A geographer of the style of Smith must travel over 'enchanted
ground', the foliage must 'burst', the blossoms must 'glow', not simply grow, and the wind does not need to be classified in terms of
origin, direction or strength, its only feature of note is that it is 'in
the poplars above'. This is the witchery of Oriental geography. And
yet the superiority of the Frank traveller is here as well: Smith must

talk of 'slovenly houses', and note that they are made bearable only by the beauty of the sacred landscape. Smith began his description at the edge of the Damascus valley, and yet noted that one must traverse 'two miles more' between trees and 'a mile more orchards' before coming in sight of the city itself.[109] Once in the city he highlights the bazaars, and his pen enthused similarly about them: 'if anyone confesses the bazaars dull, he has neither eye for colour nor wit to read the city's destiny in the faces she has gathered to them from Nubia to the Caucasus'.[110] Smith's geography can be darker as well, but no less exalted, as he described the Dead Sea shore in terms that he felt fitting: 'In this awful hollow, this bit of the infernal regions come up to the surface, this hell with the sun shining into it, primitive man laid the scene of God's most terrible judgment on human sin'.[111]

As well as being a poetic discourse, the text exhibits the way in which Smith's experience of the Holy Land was a direct and immediate one. He showed how his familiarity with the landscape's features was negotiated on the spot, as he quoted 'The following extracts from our diary in 1891, [which] will give some impression of what these hot sandy winds make of the atmosphere'.[112] And he relates every place to his own experience of it – 'More famous than the tilth of Eastern Palestine is her pasture. We passed through at the height of the shepherd's year...'[113]

Smith skilfully blends this feeling for masterly descriptive narrative and existential immediacy to create a real feeling for historical geography:

[Syria] has been not only the highroad of civilization and the battle-field of empires, but the pasture and school of innumerable little tribes. She has not been merely an open channel of war and commerce for nearly the whole world, but the vantage-ground and opportunity of the world's highest religions. In this strange mingling of bridge and harbour, of highroad and field, of battleground and sanctuary, of seclusion and opportunity – rendered possible through the striking division of her surface into mountain and plain – lies all the secret of Syria's history, under the religion which has lifted her fame to glory.[114]

Smith's geographical sensibility for historical events helped him to not only situate the happenings, but to begin to understand why it was that various events happened in various places. His writing about the Shephelah district is particularly potent:

> Altogether, this is a rough, happy land, with its glens and moors, its mingled brushwood and barley-fields; frequently under cultivation, but for the most part broken and thirsty, with few wells and many hiding places; just the home for strong border-men like Samson, and just the theatre for that guerilla warfare, varied occasionally by pitched battles, which Israel and Philisitia, the Maccabees and the Syrians, Saladin and Richard waged with each other.[115]

Perhaps no geographer but Smith could speak of a physical landscape as 'happy'.

Smith was able to bring a blend of his ideas gathered from a direct experience of geography, classical and biblical literature and his lyrical style to bear on illuminating the Bible:

> On the plateaus east of Jordan snow lies regularly for some days every winter, and on the top of Hermon there are fields of it through the summer... This explains the feat of Benaiah, who *went down and slew a lion in the midst of a cistern in the day of the snow.* The beast had strayed up the Judaean hills from Jordan, and had been caught in a sudden snowstorm. Where else in Palestine could lions and snow thus come together?[116]

In Smith's understanding of the biblical account of the vision of St Peter at Joppa, Smith's experience of the place allowed him to fully understand the passage. In the biblical account Peter saw a four cornered sheet come down from heaven, full of food that it was unlawful for him, as a strict Jew, to eat, and had it revealed to him that the Jewish food laws had been superseded by Christianity's freedom. On Smith's visit to Jaffa, modern day Joppa, he noted that this is one of few trading ports on the Holy Land coast, and one of the very few that trade in Western goods, as it did in Peter's time. And 'we can understand as [Peter] moved about its narrow lanes, leading to the sea, where his scrupulous countrymen were jostled by foreign sailors and foreign wares, he grew more concerned than ever about the ceremonial law...'[117] and Peter was thus, according to Smith, in a mood to receive a vision concerning it. The four cornered sheet full of forbidden food Smith can see in the square sails of gentile ships approaching from the west, full of gentile goods. But Smith also notes, more subtly, that while Peter had the vision here, at the very edges of Jewish territory, it was when he was on the gentile soil of Caesarea, and in a freer atmosphere, that Peter declared what he understood the vision to mean.

To subject the book to Duncan and Gregory's terms of analysis for travel writing,[118] it is indeed a multi-vocal product and we can see passages not only created by the inhabitants of the land, but involveing them – 'Bring up man and animals on the scene, and you see the landscapes described by Old Testament writers exactly as you will see them to-day – the valleys covered with corn, the pastures above clothed with flocks, shepherds and husbandmen calling to each other through the shimmering air...'[119] Here we see the performative practice of life being enacted in the Holy Land as illustrative of Smith's imagined understanding of Holy Land life, gleaned from a hermeneutic engagement with the biblical text, while he was still a youthful Bible reader in Scotland. Here we also see Smith moving in what Rajchman has described as a 'space of constructed visibility',[120] one full of sites and sights,[121] where Smith's sights are things that are relevant to contextualizing the Scriptures. His sight was blinkered by the task in hand. When he said 'In all this the Palestine of to-day is much more a museum of church history than of the Bible – a museum full of living as well as ancient specimens of its subject'[122] even the two options he allowed himself show a blindness to what must have been much of the landscape of everyday Palestine. It is a space whose visibility is constructed in a particular way, as when he directs us to '...see those details which are so characteristic of every Eastern landscape, the chaff and the rolling thorns blown before the wind ... we shall surely feel ourselves in the atmosphere and scenery in which David fought, and Elisha went to and fro, and Malachi saw the Sun of Righteousness arise with healing in his wings'.[123] This is, in the terms of Timothy Mitchell, a 'museumified' Palestine, in which the present landscape only exists as a vestige of the past.[124] And in the terms of Lock, the Holy Land has become 'a relic (albeit on a vast and nonportable scale) ... the Holy Land itself is holy only because it has been, like a portable relic, in contact with the Divine'.[125]

Yet the same Smith, at times speaking of the divine nature of the landscape, was, at other times, not shy of showing the more contemporary, less holy, more profane, influences of life in the Holy Land, as he described his mixed feelings about the site of Jacob's Well:

> It is on Ebal too ... that the old wonder comes strongly upon us of the influence of so small a province on the history of the whole world. But the explanation is also within sight. Down below us at the mouth of the glen [a delightfully Scottish term] lies a little heap of brown stones. The road comes up to it by which the patriarchs first entered the land, and the shadow of a telegraph post falls upon it.[126]

The term 'wonder' shows a transportation of the imagined geography of a wondrous Holy Land from Scotland to the land itself: a wonder had been felt in Scotland, the wonder remained in Palestine, even when telegraph posts overshadowed the landscape.

While the book is not in its intention an Orientalist *project*, it is, in Saidian terms, an Orientalist *product* and Smith exemplified the particular sort of Orientalist product that it is by noting of Palestine that '[The racial diversity] which is so perplexing to the student, [is] in such thorough harmony with the natural conditions of the country and with the rest of history'.[127] This phrase combines both Orientalist ideas and another characteristic of Smith's major geographical works: obvious evidence of the idea of environmental determinism, mediated through German geographical scholarship, which is a key feature of Smith's take on geography. His footnotes demonstrate familiarity with geographers such as Ritter and his environmental determinism goes further – 'To such a climate, then, is partly due Israel's doctrine of Providence'[128] and indeed further still to suggest that 'The natural fertility of Syria ... intoxicated her immigrants with nature-worship...'[129]

Smith's use of the deterministic concept rose to the familiar poetic heights as he opined that: 'volcanic extrusions ... dykes of basalt ... scatterings of lava ... hot sulphurous springs flow by Tiberias, and the whole province has been shaken by terrible earthquakes. The nature

161

of the people is also volcanic'.[130] Here Said would point to 'the nature of the people' being considered as a monolithic whole, an epistemologically undifferentiated, essentialized group.[131] The same idea of determinism is also displayed more subtly, in political terms, 'When we turn from the physical characteristics of this province of the subterranean fires and waters to her political geography we find influences as bold and inspiring as those we have noted [in the physical landscape]',[132] and indeed in religious terms:

> For myself, I can only say that all I have seen of the land, and read of its ancient history, drives me back to the belief that the monotheism which appeared upon it was ultimately due to the revelation of a character and a power which carried with them the evidence of their uniqueness and divine sovereignty.[133]

The same influences are also held to exist in anthropological and cultural worlds: '...the background and environment of this stage of our Lord's ministry was thronged and very gay – that it was Greek in all that name can bring up to us of busy life, imposing art and sensuous religion. The effect upon the Galilean temperament is obvious'.[134] And indeed in worlds of literature and warfare:

> In the deserts of Arabia, life is wonderfully tempered. Nature is monotonous, the distractions are few, the influence of things seen is as weak as it may be in this universe; the long fasts, necessary every year, purge the body of its grosser elements, the soul easily detaches itself, and the hunger lends the mind a curious passion, mixed of resignation and hot anger. The only talents are those of war and speech – the latter cultivated to a singular augustness of style by the silence of nature and the long leisure of life. It is the atmosphere in which seers, martyrs, and fanatics are bred. Conceive of a race subjected to its influences for thousands of years! To such a race give a creed, and it will be an apostolic and devoted race.[135]

Mitchell's understanding of essentialism is relevant here.[136] Smith speaks of a 'race', an imagined concept, and imparts to all members of this race the same set of responses to their environment. This classic Orientalist strategy, mingled with deterministic geography, is a diagnostic component of Smith's geography.

There is also an undoubted influence of German geography on Smith's work. His use and praise of Teutonic ideas permeates the work – 'The Germans' he says 'have also given what has been much lacking in Britain, a scientific treatment of the geography in the light of Biblical criticism: in this respect the work of Socin, Guthe, and their colleagues in the Deutsches Palästina-Verein, has been most thorough and full of examples to ourselves'.[137] And it is these German ideas which create a dialectic within Smith's work; where we see geographical, witnessed, authority in competition with that of biblical criticism, we can see him struggling to satisfy his readers' conservatism. Thus he wrote:

The relation of the geographical materials at our disposal, and the methods of historical reconstruction, have been wholly altered by Old Testament science ... That part of criticism which consists of the distinction and appreciation of the various documents, of which the Books of Scripture are composed, has especially contributed to elucidation and arrangement of geographical details in the history of Israel ... I heartily agree with most of what is said on the duty of regulating the literary criticism of the Bible by the archaeology of Syria ... But we must remember there is a converse duty as well. We have had too many instances of the embarrassment and confusion into which archaeology and geography lead us, apart from the new methods of Biblical criticism. And to those who are distrustful of the latter, I would venture to say that there is no sphere in which the helpfulness of recent criticism, in removing difficulties and explaining contradictions, has been more apparent than in the sphere of Biblical Geography.[138]

An atlas accompanied the *Historical Geography* and this is where the topographical science came in.[139] Smith's atlas differs little from many contemporary biblical atlases and it contains little of special note beyond Smith's introduction, which outlines how the project came to fruition, many years after it was first planned, how the selection of subjects for the maps was decided upon and how the progress of sacred geography has allowed many places to be identified, or more credibility to be lent to various identifications.

The main bulk of the atlas's letterpress contains simple outlines of the contents of each map, and a minimal amount of explanation of how the political and economic features displayed in the maps reached their state as shown. The maps themselves depict the Holy Land's relations with the whole of Western Asia, Africa and Europe, and its internal geography in political, topographical, and economic terms at various historical periods; these maps bring the geography of the land up to the time of Napoleon's 1799 invasion. Two ancient maps, that from the *Tabula Peutingeriana* of uncertain date, and that of *Marinus Sanutus*, of 1611, are reproduced, before a map of Palestine as it was immediately prior to the Great War, and one of Christian missionary interests in Palestine, which finishes the volume.

So much for *The Historical Geography of the Holy Land*. A work of travel, characterized by a particular view of the spaces involved, informed by a synthesis of German geography and theology; and rich with poetry and the voices of competing perspectives. By the time of Smith's death in 1942 the book had sold over 35,000 copies.[140]

Subsequent to the publication of *The Historical Geography* Smith's output continued to extend and his commendation of continental scholarship, particularly critical work was ongoing: 'Upon the Old Testament no more useful work has lately appeared than Professor Budde's translation of a number of Kuenen's treatises. Students of all lands will welcome the collection into one volume, in the classic language of criticism, of essays ... landmarks in the history of Old Testament science'.[141]

In 1896 Smith published again in the Expositor's series of biblical commentaries, this time a work on *The Book of the Twelve Prophets*, the second volume of which appeared in 1898.[142] Again Smith disclosed how he had moved with the contemporary intellectual currents: 'criticism of the prophetic books has now entered on a period of the same analysis and discrimination as in the case of the Pentateuch'.[143] Throughout Smith showed an intimate knowledge of the terrain over which the prophets and their contemporaries worked. For example:

the purple mountains, into which the wild sons of Esau clambered, run out from Syria upon the desert, some hundred miles by twenty of porphyry and red sandstone ... From Mount Hor, which is their summit, you look down upon a maze of mountains, cliffs, chasms, rocky shelves and strips of valley. On the east of the range is but the crested edge of a high, cold plateau, covered for the most part by stones...[144]

Smith laboured to set the geographical context of the life and work of the prophet Amos into vivid prose:

> Six miles south from Bethlehem... there rises on the edge of the Judaean plateau, towards the desert, a commanding hill, the ruins on which are still known by the name of Tekôa. In the time of Amos Tekoa was a place without sanctity and almost without tradition... The men of Tekoa looked out on a desolate and haggard world. South, west, and north the view is barred by a range of limestone hills, on one of which directly north the grey towers of Jerusalem are hardly to be discerned from the grey mountain lines. Eastward the prospect is still more desolate, but open; the land slopes for nearly eighteen miles to a depth of four thousand feet. Of this long descent, the first step, immediately below the hill of Tekoa, is a shelf of stony moorland with the ruins of vineyards. It is the lowest ledge of the settled life of Judaea. The eastern edge drops suddenly by broken rocks to slopes... From the foot of the slopes the land rolls away in a maze of low hills and shallow dales, that flush green in spring, but for the rest of the year are brown with withered grass and shrub.[145]

Smith's poetic pen ascended to romantic heights as he strove to communicate to the readers of this work his passion for the landscape of the Holy Land. This writing bears obvious evidence of a traveller to the land: one whose direct experience of the geography of the Holy Land has deeply impacted upon his understanding of the biblical text, and whose commentary is rich with details not available to scholars who had never been to the Holy Land. Smith indeed added detail far beyond what is normally required in a scholarly exposition of a text, filling in the romantic geography of a land that is holy:

> Beyond the rolling land is Jeshimon, or Devastation – a chaos of hills, none of whose ragged crests are tossed as high as the shelf of Tekoa, while their flanks shudder down some further thousands of

feet, by crumbling precipices and corries choked with debris, to the coast of the Dead Sea. The northern half of this is visible, bright blue against the red wall of Moab, and the level top of the wall, broken only by the valley of the Arnon, constitutes the horizon. Except for the blue water – which shines in its gap between the torn hills like a bit of sky through rifted clouds – it is a dreary world. Yet the sun breaks over it, perhaps the more gloriously; mists, rising from the sea shimmering in its great vat, drape the nakedness of the desert noon; and through the dry desert night the planets ride with a majesty that they cannot assume in our troubled atmospheres.[146]

Not only through picturesque language did Smith conjure up, from his direct experience, an imaginative geography of the land around Tekoa for his readers, he wanted to leave them in no doubt of the image that he wanted to promote: 'it is a very wild world'.[147] After thoroughly setting the context of the geographical world in which Amos worked, only then can Smith turn to the man himself:

Upon this wilderness, where life is full of poverty, and danger – where nature starves the imagination but excites the faculties of perception and curiosity; with the mountain tops and the sunrise in his face, and with Jerusalem so near – Amos did the work which made him a man, heard the voice of God calling him to be a prophet, and gathered those symbols and figures in which his prophet's message still reaches us with so fresh and so austere an air.[148]

This blend of geography and theology characterizes Smith's output: a contextual understanding of the biblical text informed by a thorough grounding in the geography and history of the land of the Bible.

The death of Smith's close friend Henry Drummond in 1897 occasioned the production of a biography of Drummond.[149] What is most interesting about the work is those aspects of the history surrounding Drummond's life to which Smith devotes much more space than they might have been thought to require. Most striking is the account of the trial of William Robertson Smith. George Adam Smith acknowledges that Drummond took no active part in the debates surrounding the case, because 'he himself was not equipped with the knowledge of the original languages of the Bible which could have enabled him to form conclusions of his own'[150] and yet he devotes a large section of Drummond's biography to the facts of the case, as he saw them. Essentially, it seems that Smith's presentation of his own views here was an outlet for the publication of these opinions, which may have otherwise been denied him. George Adam Smith's position was one of undoubted support for William Robertson Smith, as might be expected; his own liberal evangelical stance and his belief in an evolution of religious thought allowed him to understand and ac-knowledge William Robertson Smith's ideas; his own scholarly inclin-ations, as we have already seen and will see further below, carried his opinion to the extent of outright defence of Robertson Smith, whom he regarded as 'sacrificed'.[151]

Drummond's main work was as a scientist, at the Free Church College in Glasgow, and it was while teaching at the College that he and Smith came across each other, and Smith liked to think that his progressive influence had rubbed off on Drummond: 'Since coming to Glasgow Drummond's eyes had been opened to the great signs of evolution within Scripture itself'.[152]

1899–1908

In 1899 Smith was invited to Yale University to give a series of eight lectures and his theology was more to the fore, and I feel it shows the influences of both Germany and Palestine. While Smith rarely wrote explicit theology, what he said in many of his works obviously came from a particular theological standpoint. This lecture series was an attempt by Smith to draw together the trends in state of the art Old Testament criticism, and show how these might be applied by preachers and the laity in their use of the Bible, and what sort of au-thority they might want to invest it with. The lectures were published in an expanded form in 1901 (while Smith was on another Holy Land tour) as *Modern Criticism and the Preaching of the Old Testament*, and we now turn to this volume, to consider its significance for the trad-ition of Scriptural Geography.

Characteristically for the modest Smith, he never saw himself in any other role than as a presenter of others' ideas. He showed no consternation in openly discrediting the ideas of previous generations in these lectures – the ideas which many of his colleagues in the Church of Scotland and United Free Church still held dear, as a foundational tenet of their faith – 'It is often maintained' he began,

> that the accuracy of the topographical data of the book of Genesis is proof of the truthfulness of the narratives in which they appear. But ... that a story accurately reflects geography does not necessarily mean that it is a transcript of history ... Many legends are wonderful photographs of scenery, and therefore let us at once admit that ... we cannot prove [the historical truth of the patriarchal narratives] on the ground that their itineraries and place names are correct.[153]

Again we see Smith's dim view of the logic employed in the polemical Scriptural Geography enterprise. His methodology is clearly set apart, intentionally and deliberately.

His study of German theological methods is nowhere more apparent than in this book, on one page alone he quoted Graf, Wellhausen, Nöldeke, Dillman, Kautzsch, Stade, Budde and Holzinger;[154] with frequent references to de Wette and Hupfeld's documentary hypothesis throughout the lectures. He also cited the actual geography of the Holy Land in his arguments, as 'the geographical evidence, then, so far as it goes, does not contradict, but supports the critical analysis of the documents and the critical conclusions...'[155] Here we have the authority of directly-experienced geography being given an equal footing with the authority of the biblical text itself, in telling the story of Scripture.

But some of the content could almost have been designed to strike fear into the heart of his audience at home; for Smith to even ask his bold question: 'Can we still receive the Old Testament as the record of a Divine Revelation from God?'[156] would immediately set alarm bells ringing in the Kirk. Probably most disturbingly for the theological conservatives however, in the key sentence of this book, and certainly the most often quoted, an audacious Smith said 'Modern

Criticism has won its war against the traditional theories. It only remains to fix the amount of the indemnity'.[157]

When published and circulated back in Scotland these ideas were obviously going to cause problems for many orthodox members of the Kirk. Trouble began for George Adam Smith within a few months and as he approached the United Free Church General Assembly of May 1902, Smith knew that he had a stormy time ahead. Already a memorial to the General Assembly's College Committee, under the auspices of which Smith worked, had been produced by a meeting of elders the previous September, a memorial whose tone can be described as vitriolic. Already a Special Report had been produced by the Assembly's College Committee on *Modern Criticism and the Preaching of the Old Testament*. Already Smith had published a statement in response, but, in the highly-charged and litigious atmosphere of the Assembly Hall it seemed likely that a libel would be raised against him: a heresy trial, of the sort that the Kirk had a well-developed taste for, was on the cards.

Heresy trials for this sort of thing were not unprecedented, as we have seen William Robertson Smith underwent one, as did Marcus Dods and A.B. Davidson.[158] The Free Church was not shy in making martyrs of her freethinkers.

In George Adam Smith's case, the Memorial to the College Committee outlined the problems that some Scottish Presbyterians were having with his work:

> the publication of the volume referred to constitutes an emphatic challenge to the Church for the toleration or tacit approval of the revolutionary opinions therein set forth, which have awakened deep anxiety throughout the Church ... in particular ... Professor Smith's affirmations as to the polytheistic character of the religion of Israel until the age of the great prophets; as to the absence of history from the first nine chapters of Genesis...[159]

and further: 'Professor Smith's teaching in this book appears to be subversive of the historic truthfulness of considerable sections of Holy Scripture, and to be inconsistent with the Divine inspiration and authority of the Bible'.[160] Smith's reply, characteristically understated and self-effacing, began by suggesting how 'The Memorialists carefully ignore the general purpose of the book, and in particular its detailed argument for the Old Testament as containing the authentic revelation of God...'[161] and continued to simply rehearse the book's arguments in slightly less abrasive language, with the linchpin of the declaration being that –

> I endeavoured ... to show that a critical treatment of the facts presented by the Hebrew Scriptures, so far from compelling a thoughtful Christian to give up his faith, furnishes, for the main doctrines of religion, what ... are stronger grounds than those furnished by the former apologetic of the Church.[162]

In the run-up to the Assembly's meeting an anonymous opinion piece of in one of the Church's periodicals caught what turned out to be the mood of the Assembly neatly, while adopting an admonitory tone:

> It is to be hoped also that those 'spoiling' for a new heresy case will find their anticipations not realized. It is not 'processes' for heresy the Church needs at the present moment to give it increased vitality, but a stronger sense of its responsibilities, and a more determined resolve to give effect to them both towards God and man.[163]

A tongue-in-cheek account of the ordeal itself appeared in the July issue of *The Union Magazine*, where a journalist, under the pseudonym of Teka, noted that 'The hall was a wonderful sight on the Friday morning of the George Adam Smith debate... Dr Rainy ... pleaded for patience with his young Glasgow colleague...'[164] Unusually large crowds packed the hall and the atmosphere was boisterous. Towards the end of the debate,

> Dr Rainy was just about to reply when the audience unaccountably broke into thunderous applause. Dr Smith was making his way to the rostrum to pour out his soul in an apologetic that made it more difficult for many to put him again under the teeth of his namesake's sharp threshing instrument.[165]

'With the very greatest reluctance',[166] George Adam Smith spoke in his own defence, persuaded the Assembly commissioners to vote in favour of adopting the College Committee's Special Report anent the case, and thus prevent the debate from becoming a heresy trial. Pouring holy oil on the secular waters of turmoil, the Committee's Special Report to the Assembly, to which the commissioners agreed, stated quite anticlimactically that –

> the Committee did not find that [Dr Smith] had contradicted any part of the received doctrine of the Church ... they however think it right to say that they regard the remarks which Dr Smith has made in his Statement with reference to them as helpful toward a clearer apprehension of his position.[167]

So in the end no libel was raised against George Adam Smith. Primarily, I want to argue, this was because the intellectual climate of Scottish theology had begun to change, hinted at in the Committee's report, where

> the Committee are persuaded that it would be wrong to make Dr Smith personally responsible for a system of learned opinions which has for years been entertained by scholars of all the Churches; which is not uncontradicted indeed, but prevalent, and has to be dealt with in a spirit of faith and patience.[168]

Perhaps the war had not been won, but there was now, albeit in grudging terms, an acknowledgement that the proponents of historical biblical criticism had a legitimate reason to fight. German ideas had become more widespread, and I argue that the episode of George Adam Smith's near heresy trial was catalytic in bringing them to a wider audience in Scotland. A writer in *The Union Magazine* after the event noted perceptively that:

> The General Assembly, in adopting the report of the College Committee anent Professor Smith, came to the only possible conclusion in such a case. No one wished to prosecute Dr Smith for heresy. In other words, everyone admitted that he was asking legitimate questions about the Bible, though not everyone agreed with the answers he gave. But to grant the legitimacy of the questions is everything: in process of time the answers will be found by the

proper method, and when they are found we shall all accept them.[169]

After the formal proceedings of the Assembly further publicity was granted to Smith and his controversy. William Logie, a lay member of United Free Church of Scotland, published a *Reply* soon after Smith's appearance at the Assembly, which showed the very real reservations that many United Free Church of Scotland members still had with the critical methods employed by Smith.[170]

Smith's final visit to the Holy Land was in 1904, and was part of a journey to aid his recovery from typhoid, brought on, it is suggested, by the strain of his near-trial at the Assembly in 1902.[171] In the course of this trip he spent a long time in Jerusalem, no doubt collecting material for his book on the city to appear in 1907. Smith also wrote poetry during this trip and some of this direct and effective verse has survived:

> From distant angles of the Plain
> Wind to their junction rivers twain.
> Charged by the high, eternal snow
> With wealth for all the land below,
> Indifferently her walls they force
> And trace invasion's destined course.
> Their waves reflect the double star,
> Highways at once of life and war.[172]

This poetic geography indicates the extent to which Smith's engagement with the landscape influenced his understanding of its history. Smith wrote the poem while camped at Attock, near the confluence of the Indus and Kabul rivers, which historically has proven a key strategic site in many Eastern battle campaigns, both in biblical times and more recently.

In 1904 Smith had a volume of his sermons published, and it is obvious that in this text he was laying out what he saw as the important issues in contemporary theology. These sermons had originally been delivered during Smith's time at Queen's Cross Church in Aberdeen, and it is interesting to speculate why he chose to publish sermons, very popular with his hearers at the time, and making use of the insights of higher criticism, so soon after his experience at the Assembly of 1902. His concerns included the shifting intellectual opinions on the nature of Divine revelation in Scripture and the fact that 'the moral education of the race can only be a gradual and a slow process'[173] and that this meant that while much of the Bible can, with hindsight, be viewed as 'rudimentary',[174] it does still have one uniting feature: 'the unity of ethical purpose which it manifests from first to last'.[175]

The most important feature of these sermons is that they demonstrate that Smith thought deeply about his handling of Scripture, and his attempts to understand it and to contextualize it by means of literary scholarship and geographical inquiry, and that he considered this important enough not just to write about it, but also to preach about it.

Jerusalem, which can be considered Smith's second major work, was published in two volumes in 1907 and 1908, following his fourth visit to the Holy Land, however it is of lesser interest to our present study than the *Historical Geography* is. *Jerusalem* was designed to compensate for the lack of information on the holy city in the *Historical Geography*. *Jerusalem* received high praise from reviewers, and a writer in *The Times Literary Supplement* noted that – 'The author, we feel, has chosen his vocation well. He not only has the eye of a geographer to see at once the salient features in the scene that he is describing, but he also has the "visual" imagination to conjure up at will the picture of the past'.[176] The *Dundee Advertizer* opined that: 'As a piece of descriptive writing few things in recent literature equal the series of word pictures which Dr Smith provides in his "Introduction"'.[177] Smith's words are indeed eloquent and he devoted much space to poetic descriptions of the city which he refers to as 'bride of Kings and mother of Prophets'.[178]

17: The opening page of Chapter 19 of *Jerusalem* in
George Adam Smith's script

The book opens with an introduction titled, in grand terms, 'The Essential City', in which Smith gives a very full and detailed picture of the city and a sweeping account of the city's unique place in world history. Thereafter the work is divided into three Books. The first Book deals with the topography, climate and geology of Jerusalem, and the extent to which these interact. The second Book deals with the economics and politics of the city, and how the city's peculiar location affects these. The third and final Book – which forms the whole of the second volume on its own – deals with the history of Jerusalem.

This work, like the *Historical Geography*, has a large stock of sources, as Smith made use of biblical, classical and more contemporary writings on the city. In addition to a thorough grounding in literature, the work shows a diligent level of field work, and an amalgam of personal experience, fluent expression and historical feeling is often found in the text:

> He who would raise again the Essential City must wait for night, when Jerusalem hides her decay, throws off every modern intru-

sion, feels her valleys deepen about her, and rising to her proper outline, resumes something of her ancient spell... It was a night in June, when from a housetop I saw her thus. There was a black sky with extremely brilliant stars; the city, not yet fallen asleep, sparkled with tiny lights. I could scarcely discern the surrounding hills. Moab was invisible.[179]

It is notable however, that Smith constantly viewed the present city of Jerusalem as inferior when compared to his imaginary of how it was in biblical times.

This work is more heavily illustrated than the *Historical Geography*, and almost all of the plates are made from photographs taken by Smith himself. The text also retains the romantic style of the *Historical Geography* and the same motif of personal experience illustrating the Scriptures is expounded: 'The wind was chill and mournful, and brought up to one the keynote of the ancient dirge –

"When the Lord beclouds with his wrath
　　The daughter of Sion"'.[180]

The link with scientific understanding is strong, as Smith argues that 'To understand the Geology of the site of Jerusalem, and of the basin in which it lies, is necessary to the student of her history...'[181] However, to make the balance whole and the understanding more complete, another sort of knowledge is needed: 'I have been constrained by the Biblical evidence to conclude ... that the original Sion lay on the East Hill...'[182]

Smith continued with his employment of environmental determinism in *Jerusalem*, as he said of the settlement that:

Geographically considered, the City is the product of two opposite systems of climate and culture. She hangs on the watershed between East and West, between the Desert and the Sea...[183]

Jerusalem is a work which compares and contrasts neatly with the *Historical Geography*. Its style, fluency, attention to detail and wealth of sources is the same; however, the Jerusalem work's content is less relevant to the Scriptural Geography project, and less our concern here. Politics, economics, and the history of Jerusalem itself as a settlement need not detain us further.

University Administration

In 1909 Smith was offered the position of Principal of Aberdeen University and accepted enthusiastically, leaving his academic position in Glasgow.[184] He remained in this position until his retirement in 1935.

Smith's first key publication after moving back to Aberdeen came in 1912, when his Schweich Lectures delivered to the British Academy in 1910 were published. These mainly concern a very technical analysis of ancient Israelite poetry, and in them Smith discussed his incisive survey of how the people of Britain relate to Old Testament poetry, an analysis which has a surprisingly contemporary ring about it:

> In one aspect [Hebrew poetry] is the nearest poetry of all, the first which we learned; through the open windows of which we had our earliest visions of time, of space, of eternity, and of God. Its rhythms haunt our noblest prose; its lyrics are our most virile and enduring hymns. But in another perspective, which has only recently been cleared for us, Hebrew poetry lies very far away: the product of an alien race and of a stage of culture distant from our own.[185]

It is this distance which it was much of Smith's life's work to try to close. Yet it was Smith and his Orientalist contemporaries who also, unawares, made the distance. It was and is a created space, part of the externalism of Said's Orientalism.

During the Great War Smith made lecture tours of the United States of America. For the greater part these were to drum up support for the Anglo-French cause, and their content is of only marginal interest to us here; though an aside in one of these lectures shows a Smith trying to enthuse British and French Universities to a more thorough engagement with critical biblical scholarship 'to show that in this respect the German universities are not indispensable to us'.[186]

In his last major publication on the geography of the Holy Land, Smith considered the impact of the Great War (a section about which was added to later editions of the *Historical Geography*) and at one stage saw the conflict of his work close to resolution: 'there is close correspondence between the relevant data from the Bible and Talmud and the physical facts of today...'[187] However, this is unfortunately a case of Smith's superficiality and betrays a significant lapse, not progression, from his earlier struggles of balancing the competing sources of data.

In 1922 Smith was still firmly committed to the deterministic nature of the Syrian landscape on its people. In the published version of his Baird Lecture to the (Established) Church of Scotland in 1922 he spoke of the land thus:

> One of its influences on the spirit of its greatest son [the prophet Jeremiah] was its exposure to the East and the Desert. The fields of Anathoth face the sunrise and quickly merge into the falling wilderness of Benjamin. It is the same open, arid landscape as that on which several prophets were bred: Amos a few miles farther south at Tekoa, John Baptist, and during his temptation, our Lord Himself.[188]

It was Smith's belief that '...the waste and crumbling hills shimmering in the heat, the open heavens and far line of the Gilead highlands, the hungry wolves from the waste and lions from the jungles of Jordan are all reflected in Jeremiah's poems'.[189]

One of Smith's final publications was a sermon he delivered to the British Association for the Advancement of Science in Aberdeen. At the Association's 1885 Aberdeen meeting he had been Secretary to the Geography Section: at its 1934 Aberdeen meeting he seemed to be its chaplain, and his sermon was on the relationship between religion and science. His tone was characteristically optimistic and his treatment of the issues characteristically non-theological, perhaps vague and imprecise, and certainly unsatisfactory. Smith preached of an increasing closeness between the results of scientific research and religious revelation:

> With the development since Darwin of the theory of Evolution the assertion arose of new and alleged conclusive reasons for denying the faith in a Personal Creator and in consequence for fresh opposition between science and religion. It is remarkable that for the haste and bitterness of this revived antagonism between science

and religion theologians have been far more to blame than scientists. For theologians of all people should not have failed to see that their Scriptures ... present what is perhaps the most remarkable display of evolution which human history has to show us. From the first to last the Old Testament is a tale of gradual development, not only intellectual but moral, of the conception of God from being that of a mere national deity to that of the Father and Creator of mankind...[190]

Furthermore, Smith was of the belief that 'no longer is there any cause for those distressing controversies which embittered the tempers and warped the minds of our fathers a few years ago'.[191] This sums up Smith's method for dealing with the relationship between science and religion concisely.

Smith's conception of an evolving Scripture and his consistent belief that he was doing good by answering the questions which his method of research posed meant that he was able to see developments in Scripture interpretation, made possible by the fruits of archaeological fieldwork, as beneficial to theological understanding.

The evolution of the Jewish people's religion in the Bible, from the time of polytheistic animal tribes until monotheistic Judaism at the close of the prophetic era was a notion that made sense to George Adam Smith because,

The Bible, in Smith's conception, is not itself a revelation, but the records of a revelation, or more precisely, the records of the history of a revelation, for it is the essentially progressive character of the revelation ... which is paramount in his view of Scripture. Indeed the genius of the Bible is precisely in this, that it is a record of a history which overcomes itself.[192]

Smith also believed that the accuracy of the actual historical details in the Old Testament was fairly irrelevant, generally speaking, as this was not the goal of the sacred writers.[193] When these ideas were informed by the writings of Charles Darwin on evolution, and when Smith doubtless discussed matters with his lifelong friend Henry Drummond, 'he saw theory [evolution] and book [the Bible] together [and] recognized what for him was a harmonious and edifying combination. It was the opportunity to have science and religion, scholarship and belief, united in believing criticism'.[194]

And so George Adam Smith's biographer was able to say:

> It has been said that the greatest work George Adam Smith did was to reconcile the outlook of an advanced scientific scholar with the spirit of devout reverence. Hitherto the two positions had appeared to be incompatible. He showed that the critical and open-minded study of the Bible, instead of detracting from its authority and value, only confirmed it.[195]

Quite how well Smith was able to do this and with what degree of intellectual rigour he held this position has been debated,[196] but that is not of importance to this study, as Smith's theology is only of interest to us here insofar as it is related to his Scriptural Geography. Whether his theology was to the satisfaction of theologians or not is not my concern: how it influenced contextual Scriptural Geography's theological underpinnings in the work of George Adam Smith is.

Smith also believed that he was continuing the work of the Reformation in the evangelical purification of religion, and that this was a work begun by Christ and the Apostles:

> But while we look to Christ as the chief Authority for the Old Testament, we must never forget that he was also its first Critic. He came to a people, who lived under a strict and literal enforcement of the Law ... not only did Jesus reject these traditions, he equally rejected some parts of the Law himself, and directed his own conduct in sovereign indifference to many other parts.[197]

Argued even more generously, according to S.A. Cook, Smith's use of Scripture was characterized by his actions as: 'In the spirit of the Reformation he treated the Bible as the Book reflecting men's lives and thoughts, their failings and their victories, a book which had fresh meaning for every age'.[198] Also, in Smith's own terms: 'the treatment of the Old Testament by the Apostles, so far from silencing critical questions, raises these in a somewhat more aggravated form than the Old Testament by itself does'.[199] And so it can be seen that George Adam Smith himself saw the origins of his theology in New Testament times, and the handling of the Old Testament Scriptures by the figures of the New Testament. He saw no lack of moral integrity in the practices of higher criticism. He felt that it was for the good of the contemporary Christian Church. Throughout his life Smith defended this position and argued that –

> Those who, with Professor Robertson Smith, instigated [the critical study of the Scriptures in the Free Church] were some of the devoutest men in the Church ... These men believed that Christ's promise of the Holy Spirit for the education of His Church was being fulfilled not less in the critical than the experimental use of the Bible; they defended criticism on the highest grounds of faith in God and loyalty to Christ.[200]

This was George Adam Smith's contribution to what has been called the 'battle for the Bible'.[201] I want to argue that Smith's acceptance of these ideas in the face of so many who rejected them was a response to his travels; both to Germany and to Palestine. His spatially negotiated biography was what opened his understanding through existential experience to embrace the opinions of scholars who were willing to use geographical and archaeological data on an equal footing with textual sources.

CONCLUSION: A PROPHETIC VOICE IN SCOTTISH CULTURE

Rev Prof Sir George Adam Smith's career as a minister, theologian, traveller and geographer was surely remarkable. Having examined this career and the textual legacy of Smith what do I now want to say about what the geography of one individual's contextual Scriptural Geography can tell us about the influence of geography on our minds, our ideas and our lives? George Adam Smith's life's work could be considered prophetic in its own way: his struggle was as much about the placing of his own prophetic, theological voice as it was about the understanding of the Old Testament prophets to which he sought to contribute.

Smith's was an unusual contribution to the life of his church(/es),[202] remarkable both for its vivacity (his immense personal energy is something that most commentators remark on)[203] and the diversity of its functions. In recognition of his merit he was elected to the Moderatorship of the General Assembly, the highest office in his denomination, in 1916, the same year in which he was elected FBA, and received his knighthood: eventually he was accepted by his own church, as well as in broader academic circles.

The intellectual currents which made possible the eventual acceptance of the ideas held by George Adam Smith had their roots much earlier, in the Western Enlightenment of the eighteenth century. In the spaces of the Enlightenment, knowledge became a rationally induced phenomenon, not simply the accepted wisdom of canonical texts, and so Smith, as both a textual critic and conductor of fieldwork can be seen as an Enlightenment scholar. Smith's scholarly journey indeed, reversed the familiar situation of a text which explains a landscape, as on his travels he found a landscape which explained a text.

Travel and Theology

During his student days Smith twice during summer vacations spent considerable periods of time in Germany, absorbing German theology, and evidently geography too. He also visited the Holy Land four times, and seemed deeply affected by his visits to the sites of so many Bible events, as our analysis of his letters and published works has proven. The nature of the travelling experience provides us with some material: the sites of Palestine are sights for Smith in a way that they are not for many of his readers.[204] The parcels of knowledge produced at those sites, the books inspired by them and written at them, had a profoundly different meaning for Smith than for his stay-at-home readers. I want to argue that this is why Smith's take on the uses of the geography of the Holy Land and biblical criticism in Scripture contextualization is different from that of those whose theology was born in, and grew up exclusively in, Scotland.

Theological inquiry has a long and respectable pedigree in the history of humankind's endeavours to explain itself and the world.

Like scientific knowledge, the knowledge produced by theologians has been thought of as preternatural; as Livingstone would say, it has been thought of as having 'ubiquitous qualities ... both local and global ... particular and universal ... provincial and transcendental',[205] and yet unlike science, theology does not have any fixed, international, standards of measurement. When we consider theology and its place in the world, it can be argued to be much more a national, regional enterprise than science and so when we come to ask questions of how one set of doctrines can clash with another across space, we must look at where the knowledge that informed the creation of a theological doctrine was gathered, where it was created, and what places the author had been to. Gregory would want to argue that Smith visited particular, meaningful places, in the Cartesian space of the Holy Land.[206] Smith travelled around a set of places which meant something specific to him after his study of German theology and geography and his careful perusal of Jewish history, but meant something different to those who had not travelled, and this was what landed him in controversy with some members of his church.

Smith's travels to Palestine itself were significant in forming his theological ideas, as demonstrated by his writing. He wrote of how 'for our faith ... a study of the historical geography of Palestine is a necessary discipline...'[207] because he believed that the actual evidence of the geography of the Holy Land, which he was willing to use to critique Scripture, giving it equal authority to *both* Scripture's ideas about itself, *and* higher textual criticism's ideas, was a crucial part of coming to understand the context of the Bible's formation and therefore the nature of its inspiration and so its authority. Smith was therefore not only a believer in the effects of environmental determinism, he was prey to it himself.

Authority and Archaeology

The key dialectic, I want to argue, within Smith's work is that competition between the truths of scientific fieldwork and textual criticism on the one hand, and divine revelation on the other. Smith himself did not seem bothered by it, though he did include a section in *Modern Criticism and the Preaching of the Old Testament* which, in a way, dealt with the issue, but only on a superficial level.

From the opening sentences of a Smith contextual Scriptural Geography it is clear that an uneasy mood prevails. The work is founded on a strangely easy marriage of divinely revealed and scientifically induced truths. It is symptomatic of the genre that Smith chose to make as much use of science and scientifically produced knowledge as possible, while keeping the obvious question of the relationship of this knowledge to the inspired, biblical knowledge in a condition of uncertainty.

Smith noted that:

> our century has been one not only of biblical research, but of the discovery and examination of the histories and religions of the peoples who surrounded Palestine... there have been unearthed and deciphered a vast multitude of monuments which ... afford us the most ample material for testing the chronology of the Old Testament...[208]

Smith's concern to use these archaeological and palaeoecological data was much more pressing than his ideas about the usefulness of geographical data:

> ...it will be obvious that geography cannot be of much use in the support of the critical conclusions as to the dates of the documents. The only cases in which it can afford any evidence of these, are where documents, judged by critics to be late on other grounds, contain geographical names which are themselves of late origin.[209]

And yet, after dealing with the data gleaned by science's understanding of the Old Testament literature, Smith notes, almost with surprise, how so much of the best Old Testament preaching of the past has evidently been based on a form of fiction, and how preachers in his own day are now cautious of preaching about much of the Old Testament. Smith is not fearful however, he counsels fellow preachers that: 'In this somewhat disorderly retreat from the great sources of our art, the first thing to rally our minds is to remember how small a portion, after all, of the Old Testament has been affected'.[210] Perhaps not words well chosen to mollify the effects of the excesses of that generation's enthusiastic practitioners of higher criticism: Smith neatly avoided dealing with the issue, by pointing out how small it seemed. The dialectic created by the geographical and critical textual methods of analysis of the Bible does not reach any sort of satisfactory resolution in Smith's work.

The factors that might have influenced Smith's employment of geographical data in the development of his theological ideas can now be examined, and John Rajchman in his book *Philosophical Events* makes an observation on the work of the French philosopher Michel Foucault that resonates with this study of Smith's life and work: 'Foucault finds that the same organization a period assigns to inner or psychological processes recurs in external "public" ones such as making maps or illustrating scholarly works ... visibility is a matter of a positive, material, anonymous body of practice'.[211] Rajchman's distillation of Foucault's ideas is of course temporal – 'a period' – but I feel that many postmodern theorists, such as Edward Said, would want it to be spatial as well. For the spatial to operate on the individual's biography, the individual must be in the right place, not just the right time; the individual must form an existentially immediate relationship with the landscape about which they write, and thus have their ideas influenced by that space; and so the outer organization of ideas presented by a place's constructed visibility impacts upon the inner organization of ideas in an individual's mind. For Smith's contextual Scriptural Geography, writing from a distance just won't work: the individual must be and must be being in the right place. Smith's letters and books demonstrate that he had just this sort of relationship with the landscape of the Holy Land.

Therefore I want to argue that the practices of being on location are crucial to how travel writers, like Smith, come to communicate their experiences. The pseudo travellers of early times lack the immediacy of their later, travelling, counterparts. Yet I want to say more. The immediacy of the travelling experience doesn't just affect how we write our travel narratives, it affects how we present the rest of our lives too. If we are to follow Foucault's logic then our other writings will be affected as well. George Adam Smith is one traveller who has provided us with a case study: his theology was influenced by his experience of the landscape of Palestine.

Smith can be considered a much-misunderstood figure whose Scriptural Geography has been of lasting value and proven popularity, yet much of his work is still treated with caution and suspicion by some theologians today.[212] That continuing vibrancy of debate pays homage to the far-reaching nature of George Adam Smith's scholarship and says much about the enduring nature the contextual Scriptural Geography project.

In a long and illustrious career George Adam Smith occupied a full range of academic positions: from student through to Principal and Vice-Chancellor of one of Britain's oldest universities. His was a huge contribution to British and North American academia and he has left deep imprints upon Old Testament studies, to the extent that his work is not only still discussed, but is still cited today, in academic contexts.[213] He has influenced historical geography to the extent that his works are only recently out of print in English, readily available, and apparently still widely read, despite the dating of their content.

6   Conclusion: Learning From the Story

Palestine is desolate and unlovely. And why should it be otherwise? Can the curse of the Deity beautify a land? Palestine is no more of this work-day world. It is sacred to poetry and tradition – it is dream-land.[1]

CONCLUDING REMARKS

In attempting to follow the genealogy of the literary portrayal of the geography of the Holy Land we have traced the ideas and practices of Scriptural Geography through two millennia and three distinct phases. On the way we have stopped off at three particular instances, and have sampled the genre at each of these three moments, in the individual lives of three authors. We have engaged with texts, and, alert to the dictum that 'a text without a context is a pretext',[2] we have attempted to understand the writings of three Scriptural Geographers, while labouring to show the contexts of the works of Bishop Michael Russell, Josias Leslie Porter and George Adam Smith. Throughout it has been our concern to illustrate why these three figures thought and wrote about the Holy Land so differently, but within what I have argued is a discrete and coherent genre. Necessarily the story of Scriptural Geography told here is a partial one. It has been noted that 'there is no history on the mortuary table',[3] and we have been hampered not only by this consideration and the caution that it prescribes but also by the vast scope of this particular part of history. The three figures chosen represented three distinct orders of Scriptural Geography and as we have followed their lives and work we have come to understand something about the way in which each of the three orders of Scriptural Geography owed something to the context of the lives of its authors.

The Story of Scriptural Geography

In telling the story of Scriptural Geography the enormous circulation of Scriptural Geographies cannot be overemphasized: we have noted the widespread interest generated by the foundation of the Palestine Exploration Fund, and David Gange has revealed the populist nature of the activities surrounding the establishment of the Egypt Exploration Fund in 1882.[4] Such broad general enthusiasm was translated into large sales figures for books and large attendances at public meetings, all serving to remind us that 'Few lands can attract the attention of so many people with such a wide range of interests as does the land of Palestine. It is a land of history, of pious devotion, of religious and political tension'.[5] Such enthusiasm also serves to remind us that the texts of the Scriptural Geography project circulated far outside the academy. This wide circulation was important in creating an enormous number of imagined geographies of the Holy Land. These geographical imaginaries were constructed at a deep level, and were remarkably enduring. As Long has noted

> Biblical scholars continue to play a role in the old story. If not a model, then a photograph. If not a photo, then a map. If not a map then a painting. If not these then assemblages of Holy Land knowledge shaped for political relevance. All desire to convey a touch of the real, while all enable a fantasy of a real-imagined place of surrogate travel.[6]

This role, as geographical opinion-former, has been one of Scriptural Geography's most lasting legacies, feeding more and more information into the Orientalist archive, so that 'For many people in the West, the thought of the Southern Levant conjured up images of shepherds and olive trees, of dusty hills and donkeys...'[7] The scope of this geographical projection, brought to the public's attention by Scriptural Geography, surely demands treatment by historians of geography that it has so far not received, and it is within this context that this book has aimed to fill such a significant lacuna in geography's history.

More broadly, the story that has been told can be considered under four thematic perspectives. As has been observed, much intellectual history can be understood in terms of power and post-colonialism.[8] The three authors with whom this study has dealt in depth all practised their Scriptural Geography within a colonialist framework, and we are reminded that 'Victorian geographical practices [such] as exploration, cartographic survey ... can only be understood in the context of imperial manipulation, management and exploitation'.[9] Within this colonial context, we have noted how Russell, Porter and Smith all dealt with the holy landscape in different ways and emplaced colonial power in different ways in the texts of their geographies.

The notions of textual surfaces and hermeneutic engagements are vital parts of our understanding of the practices of writing a geography. It has been argued that the world's geography itself can be thought of as a textual surface,[10] and Scriptural Geography, we have discovered, is about both traversing the epigraphic landscape of the Holy Land and producing texts based on a reading of that landscape. These texts are both created from geographical imagination, and subsequently serve to help create geographical imaginaries in others: they are both products of and productive of geographical imaginaries. A variety of texts has permeated our discussion at all points, and this is perhaps because, as King opines, 'There is a clear literary bias within modern Western conceptions of religion',[11] and texts, readings and hermeneutic practices are the stuff of everyday life for clerical writers.

I have attempted to demonstrate how the genealogy of the Scriptural Geography tradition can be limned, at least in part, by pursuing the biographies of three Scriptural Geographers, and this understanding of the relationship between biography and writing has been espoused by writers, such as Livingstone, arguing that 'situating a life in its spatial circumstances might uncover the messiness of a "life as it is lived" more authentically than the remorselessly sequential biography'.[12] It is, on some level, this notion of spatiality's influence on human existence that has impacted all three of the Scriptural Geographers that we have dealt with. However, these broad gleanings are only emblematic of a part of the moment of the approach permitted by such contextual spatial biographical understanding: the smaller-scale spatial details of a person's life are crucial in determining their intellectual angle on any number of matters as well. What we can refer to as the micro-geographies of authors' lives are also significant details in helping us to understand their Scriptural Geography.

Furthermore, writing a geography is a scientific project, and in our reading of Scriptural Geographies we have noted how the lands through which the writers travelled and in which they practised their science, are constructed entities, just as samples and sets of scientific apparatus in the laboratory are constructions of reality. The negotiations between science, culture and theology have informed our analysis at many points: it is indeed from this triumvirate relationship that this study has drawn much analytical force. As long ago as 1899 Scriptural Geographers were aware that the writing of a Holy Land geography was an activity bound up with scientific practice as well as apologetics. One author considered how this conglomeration of intellectual concerns, unique to the Scriptural Geography project, was evolving: 'Nobody, not even the professed pleasure-seeker, is any longer satisfied with the mere allegation of authority in matters of belief';[13] and so he went on to counsel that the importance of the apologetic role of Scriptural Geographies was not to be underestimated: 'However passionately some may desire that it might not be so, Sacred History ... is so far from being exempt from the influence of these modern demands and tendencies, that it is precisely in this field of inquiry that men are most anxious to bring their opinions into harmony with fact'.[14] As our investigations have revealed this anxiety was a decisive dynamic in the evolution of Scriptural Geography.

We have categorized Scriptural Geographies on the basis of their relationship with modern Western scientific knowledge and practice, and the contrasts of how the three orders of Scriptural Geography employed science has been clear. The extent and character of the use of science in each case was, I have argued, determined by the theological beliefs of each individual. The intellectual culture in which each carried out their research and writing was different, and we have seen the influence that such differences had on the writers.

Orientalism

Michael Russell, a didactic Scriptural Geographer, wrote at a time of rapidly expanding colonial horizons, and his work had openly colonial aspirations. His use of the holy landscape was for the benefit of the Bible-reading public in a simple and uncomplicated way; yet he commandeered the geography of the Holy Land for his purpose while lamenting what he saw as its ruination by its present population; all in accordance with Said's ideas about how such texts operate. However, in another part of our investigations we have detected that geographical data concerning the Holy Land are often commandeered in other ways: frequently they were employed as weaponry in a wholly Western struggle over the human mind. Our studies have indicated that at least one of the intellectual crises of Victorian society was dealt with, in part, by J.L. Porter, on the soil of Syria. This particular type of colonial appropriation, the use of a colonized land's geography as a religious apologetic, is largely unstudied. There needs to be a greater appreciation that polemical Scriptural Geographies, as part of the Orientalist canon, represent a specific and specialized use of Oriental places as a battleground, as a space onto which a clash of Western mindsets was projected.

Meanwhile, Porter was at pains to establish a warrant for his theological assertions. On our excursions through his works, we have sensed how his writing is overtly polemical, often with a sense of urgency, and very much in the character of the apologetic of one who was under threat. Porter's writing is complex in its relationship with the land. His hermeneutic circle took him between his pre-imagined geography of the land, his direct engagement with the land, and those things in his actual experience which he decided to record and publish. The first category of conceptions was informed entirely by the biblical text, and was created in Ireland, before Porter left home. The second category was a more compromised set of data than might be imagined. Marten, whose work deals with Scottish Presbyterian missionaries, with whom the Irish Presbyterian Church's mission had a close working relationship, has argued that 'The missionaries generally came from a relatively exclusive middle-class oriented background that determined how they understood the environment they were going to...'[15] Porter's background, in particular his theological background, influenced the third category of what he considered to be sights among the sites of Palestine, and which parts of the text of the landscape he decided to reproduce for his readers.

Within contextual Scriptural Geographies we almost have a return to the quotidian understanding of colonial domination, and yet George Adam Smith's project was different yet again. Smith had the arsenal of modern Western scientific methodology, and modern Western theology, at his disposal. He could encapsulate the Orient not only in the descriptive terms of prose, poetry and picture, he could also use the newly-available archaeological, geographical and textual data to support his opinions that a change in understanding of the biblical text was often necessary, in methodological and theological contrast to his predecessors.

Spaces of Writing and Living

The spatial biographies of writers tend to affect the character of their output. An understanding of the micro-geographical spaces that a writer moves in is a crucial factor in understanding and analyzing their works. We have noted that Michael Russell's Holy Land was an entirely textual construct. Having never visited the land that he wrote about, Russell was dependent upon other texts, and our analysis has indicated a particular moral topography in the texts which Russell chose to use. Russell's own writings are texts which do not benefit from any propinquity to the Holy Land. Their sense of distance from the sites which they describe is a significant factor in their constitution. Livingstone argues that 'Attending to the spaces of writing opens up new dimensions to the historical geography of science',[16] and Russell's spatial separation from the Holy Land is important as we consider the nature of geographical writing. Russell lacked the sensibility of a writer who is on the spot and he could not therefore claim for himself any epistemological privilege based on an existential experience of the holy landscape; however, for the didactic

Scriptural Geography project such a trait is unnecessary. Within Russell's intellectual milieu his entire hermeneutic textual engagement with the Holy Land could be conducted in the space of his study in Scotland: rather than casting his view across the hilly vistas of Palestine, Russell ran his eye along the bookshelves of his study, and through the envelopes of his mail, and there found the materials for his writing. It was in this vital micro-geographical space that Russell's Holy Land was constructed, that his research was conducted and his writing crafted. This particular mode of intellectual inquiry created for Russell a particular geographical imaginary of the Holy Land, and one that served his purposes entirely adequately. Said would doubtless identify Russell as an agent in the self-referential archive of Orientalist knowledge, and position Russell towards the metropolitan end of the Orientalist machine, noting his particular citationary architecture.[17]

We have considered Smith's time in Germany as well as his Holy Land trips, but the micro-geography of the quayside at Port Said was important too. George Adam Smith's chance meeting with William Robertson Smith in Port Said was an event whose significance we have not overlooked. The two Smiths had much in common, and said much to each other. Smith's letter home from Cairo noted how '[William Robertson Smith] spoke freely of his case, but I had better not repeat all that he said...' Smith went on to note how William Robertson Smith had said that for anyone of his theological position to 'leave the church if he is deposed' would be a 'great mistake'.[18] This comment from one whom we have noted that George Adam Smith admired so much, coming as it did, at the beginning of Smith's first Holy Land tour, was perhaps a decisive factor in determining how Smith would integrate his German theological knowledge with the actual geography of the Holy Land that he was about to experience.

In the same biographical space where we read of Porter's appreciation of Oriental architecture we discovered how the micro-geography of the interior of the new Chapel at the Presbyterian College in Belfast was a significant site for Porter. It was in this space that his ideas about Oriental architecture clashed with the conservatism of Irish Presbyterianism in the nineteenth century. Porter's conception of the Holy Land geography to which he had been exposed was evidently that it was not an embedded phenomenon, and that Oriental architectural ideas could be transported back to Ireland without causing problems. He learned of the naivety of this idea when organizing the designs of the Presbyterian College Chapel windows.

Science and Theology

We have remarked upon the changing role of the knowledge generated by modern western science in understanding the geography of the Holy Land through the didactic, polemical and contextual phases of the Scriptural Geography enterprise. It is not unimportant to note also that, to some extent, each Scriptural Geography author's relationship with the Holy Land, involving whatever conception of science, is at least in part the result of their intellectual and spatial biography. Russell's treatment of scientific knowledge was of a straightforward, unproblematic nature. In his oeuvre science was an ally of Christian theology, and served to illustrate the scriptural record, bringing into focus many of the obscure and puzzling references of the Bible. Russell was engaging with a science that was, at that time, largely unthreatening to religious belief. Moreover, Russell's conception of Scripture did not require it to be literally true, and he was not troubled by the issues raised by new interpretations of biblical texts. His international scholarly outlook, demonstrated by his footnotes and his citizenship of the Republic of Letters,[19] meant that he was open to new ideas on biblical texts. While higher criticism was in its infancy in the 1830s, Russell had no problems, as we have seen, taking a spacious view of the interpretation of Scripture.

In contrast, for Porter, the advent of higher criticism and the apparent consequential loss in scriptural authority were dire circumstances, and the role of his Scriptural Geography was to counteract these, just as much as it was to undermine speculative scientific ideas, and validate the moral basis of a society founded on biblical ideals. In the conservative foundationalist views of J.L. Porter, the geography of the Holy Land fed into a 'self-authenticating positivism of revelation',[20] which unproblematically, for Porter, allowed him to induce knowledge of a variety apparently superior to that provided by scientific speculation, when considering the weighty matters of human origins and the teleology of the Universe. Porter's relationship with science was cautious, yet seemed to vary according to where he was located. We have noted Porter's carefully timed journeys and notes taken on the spot, his classifications of landscape features and wild-life in the Holy Land, and yet we have seen how he decried the ideas of scientists who worked in the West.

In Smith's textual landscape things were different from that of Russell or Porter, Smith's project was a broader and a more complex one, for Smith the Holy Land existed in an altogether dissimilar way to what it did for them. Smith's Holy Land writing is based on his imagined geography of the land, his understanding of the biblical text and his existential experiences in the land, however, unlike Russell and Porter, Smith's understanding of the biblical text was complicated by his time in Germany. His reading of the Bible was one that would have seemed innovative to Russell, and threatening to Porter. While Porter's writing was designed, in part, to disprove the results of higher criticism, Smith's travel narratives were where these results were employed, tested, and allowed to challenge prevailing ideas. Smith, like Porter and unlike Russell, wrote his works mainly on the spot, but for Smith the spot was one which had a different meaning, because of the spatial biography that Smith had lived out. Smith's works employed new theological ideas and practices, including higher criticism, to the utmost, and proudly noted that this was the case. He was able to use his own field data in association with the insights of higher criticism to inform his readers' understanding of the biblical text. George Adam Smith's employment of science was full and unabashed: he had no difficulty in accepting the merits of a science, dramatically changed since the days of Russell, enjoying a different status than in the days of Porter, and allowing its evidence to modify his religious belief.

The History of Geographical Knowledge

The import of our studies for the more general history of geographical knowledge must not be forgotten. The material which has been analyzed and the data revealed have touched upon several key concerns of current scholarship.

It has been in attempting to problematize the monolithic construction of Holy Land geographers that we encounter a multiplicity of geographies of the Holy Land, and a multiplicity of methodologies that were pursued in writing them. Further, we have observed how each text is situated in a messy set of circumstances, and is a distillation of the influences of its context, but is at the same time more than a series of epiphonema of social prejudices.

It has been in attempting to probe the strange silence of Edward Said with regard to the Scriptural Geography enterprise that we have noted how Said did not deal with Scriptural Geography as a genre at all. His only engagement with this part of the Orientalist canon was to deal with a few Scriptural Geography texts in their role as pilgrim accounts, and to argue that these were texts aimed at 'redeeming' the Holy Land from its present condition:

> Chateaubriand puts the whole idea in the Romantic redemptive terms of a Christian mission to revive a dead world, to quicken in it a sense of its own potential, one which only a European can discern underneath a lifeless and degenerate surface. For the traveller this means that he must use the Old Testament and the Gospels as his guide in Palestine, only in this way can the apparent degeneration of the modern Orient be gotten beyond.[21]

We must broaden our understanding of Orientalism therefore, to include Scriptural Geographies as particular constellations of Oriental knowledge in their own right, and to note how the geographical data contained in them are much more than straightforward colonialist appropriations of a landscape to which some right was claimed. A more nuanced reading of them is needed: fully contextualized studies of Scriptural Geographies are required to entirely comprehend the authors' intentions.

It has been in attempting to problematize the role of geographical, scientific, intellectual, philosophical, and social contexts of Scriptural Geography that we have noted how the site of knowledge creation, the motivation for the creation of that knowledge and the uses to which that knowledge is eventually put, are key formative ingredients in determining the content of the geographies in which those pieces of knowledge are employed. Our investigations have shown just how powerful location is as an influence on the processes of research and writing.

These studies have helped us to approach the understanding of the story of Scriptural Geography and having gestured at what I believe are the important aspects of the story of the idea of the Holy Land, I have come to believe that the changing role of science in the culture of the intellectual economy of the Western world is the medium through which the history of Scriptural Geography must be told. With an eye to the spatial we have noted the consonant and dissonant features of various Scriptural Geographies, and our study has displayed that there have been different motivations for writing Scriptural Geography, different methods of doing so and a selection of different intellectual perspectives brought to bear, or avoided, in each of the three orders of Scriptural Geography. We have traced this genre's genealogy, with a closer focus on the nineteenth century than other eras, and have noted the shifting intellectual currents at the broadest level, the more localized concerns of the biographies of authors' lives and the micro-geographies of various events in their experience, all of which have affected their engagements with the textual surfaces of the Bible, contemporary geographies and the text of the holy landscape.

This story has been a powerful colophonic exemplification of how the threads of scientific knowledge, theological belief, geographical context and hermeneutic engagements run through the history of society and culture. Our investigations have shown the importance of setting about understanding the changing constitution of society's, and individuals', ideas about what are appropriate intellectual strategies for engaging with the world. The story works in the opposite sense also, as recent commentators on studies in the geography of religion have noted the importance of religious practice in shaping a society and managing its alteration: 'in order to understand the construction and meaning of society and space, it is vital to acknowledge that religious practices, in terms of both institutional organization and personal experience, are central not only to the spiritual life of society, but also to the constitution and reconstruction of that society'.[22]

The story of Scriptural Geography can be set into the broader concerns of a triumvirate of space, knowledge, and science in a geographical context, and so aid us in our understanding of just how geographers understand the world.

EPILOGUE

I asked if it was possible to climb [Mount Ararat].
'It is forbidden', he said. 'Since 1991 no one has been to the top'.
'Is there anything to see?'
'If you believe something, you can see. If you don't believe, you cannot see'.[23]

The Scriptural Geography project continues today, for a surprising number of people. A recent resurgence of interest in the Middle East and the Holy Land, following the events of contemporary world history, has seen the publication of a wealth of scholarly, fictional and political works. Holy Land titles are still a feature of many publishers' catalogues, and their numbers seem to be increasing.

Recently, Edward Fox has told the story of the American archaeologist Albert Glock, whose work was finding the remains of what some have considered to be the erased history of Palestinian peoples in what is now Eretz-Israel.[24] Fox tells of the events leading up to the assassination of Glock in the West Bank in 1992, and delves into the sticky quagmire of contemporary Holy Land archaeology, attempting to grasp just what it is about the discipline that can lead its practitioners to be killed. Whatever interpretation we put on stories like that of Glock, they remind us that for many the study of the Holy Land remains an emotive and inflammatory business, not at all an irrelevance, or a thing of the past.

The Palestine Exploration Fund continues its work. *Palestine Exploration Quarterly* continues to be published, albeit triannually, and lecture series are still organized by the Fund.

The ongoing debacle over the teaching of human origins in the United States education system has reminded us that the concepts that polemical Scriptural Geographers were trying to defend are still important tenets of the faith of many, and, as we saw above the apologetic project with reference to the sacred landscape carries on, in a variety of publications and via the Internet.

More broadly, the consumption of sacred geography is an incessant affair, and as recently as 2005 expeditions have been launched to find Noah's Ark, while in January 2006 an international conference was organized on the theme of finding Noah's Ark.[25] There seems to be little abatement of the public's appetite for the discovery of physical artefacts of the Bible which reach down to our time.

As J.L. Porter noted many years ago, 'Nazareth is still a sacred spot to the Christian',[26] and Holy Land tourism continues to thrive, despite the new threats of global terror. Millions each year still want to see the sites/sights of the land where their faith was born. And it is not only for the conservative evangelical branches of Christianity that pilgrimage and a spatial sense of religious hope remains a strong tradition: even the sophisticated, apparently placeless, ethereal notions of postmodern ethical thought seem to require a place in which to belong, with theorists like David Harvey couching their arguments in terms indicating that the answer to the world's moral problems is geographical – in a spatially constructed utopia.[27]

It seems that the lure of a sacred and holy land and the quest for its (imagined) geography will continue to occupy the spaces of the human mind for a while yet.

Notes

CHAPTER 1

1   van Dyke, Henry., *Out-of-doors in the Holy Land: Impressions of Travel in Body and Spirit* (New York, 1908), pp. 3, 4
2   Butlin, Robin A., 'Ideological Contexts and the Reconstruction of Biblical Landscapes in the Seventeenth and Early Eighteenth Centuries: Dr Edward Wells and the Historical Geography of the Holy Land', in Baker, Alan H.R. and Biger, G. (eds.) *Ideology and Landscape in Historical Perspective: Essays on the Meanings of Some Places in the Past* (Cambridge, 1992), 31–62
3   Butlin: 'Ideological Contexts', p. 45
4   Butlin, Robin A., *Historical Geography: Through the Gates of Space and Time* (London, 1993), p. 2
5   Shepherd, Naomi, *The Zealous Intruders: the Western Rediscovery of Palestine* (San Francisco, 1987), p. 45
6   Butlin: *Historical Geography*, p. 4
7   Butlin: 'Ideological Contexts', pp. 45, 46
8   Butlin: 'Ideological Contexts', p. 46
9   Shepherd: *Zealous Intruders*, p. 43
10 Shepherd: *Zealous Intruders*, p. 43
11 Shepherd: *Zealous Intruders*, p. 73
12 Shepherd: *Zealous Intruders*, p. 77; Repcheck, Jack, *The Man who Found Time: James Hutton and the Discovery of the Earth's Antiquity* (London, 2003), demonstrates the difficulty with which Hutton's theory of an earth millions of years old was received by his contemporary geologists.
13 A host of polemical websites, including <http://www.bibleandscience.com/>, <http://www.christiananswers.net/> and <http://www.gnmagazine.org/archaeology.htm> perpetuate the project. Sites accessed on 7 September 2005
14 Lock, C., 'Bowing Down to Wood and Stone: One Way to be a Pilgrim', *Journeys,* 3/1 (2002), pp. 110–132, p. 113
15 Butlin: *Historical Geography*, p. 7
16 Butlin: *Historical Geography*, p. 4
17 Lozovsky, Natalia, *'The Earth is Our Book': Geographical Knowledge in the Latin West ca. 400–1000* (Ann Arbor MI, 2000), p. 14
18 Lozovsky: *Geographical Knowledge*, p. 34
19 Friedman, John Block, *The Monstrous Races in Medieval Art and Thought* (Cambridge, MA, 1981), p. 76

20 Campbell, Mary B., *The Witness and the Other World: Exotic European Travel Writing, 400–1600* (Ithaca, 1988), p. 19
21 Taylor, Joan, in Eusebius of Caesarea (ed. Joan E. Taylor; tr. G.S.P. Freeman-Grenville), *The Onomasticon by Eusebius of Caesarea with Jerome's Latin translation and Expansion in Parallel From the Edition of E. Klostermann*, (Jerusalem, 2003)
22 Taylor: *Onomasticon*, p. 2
23 Eusebius of Caesarea: *Onomasticon*, 8
24 Eusebius of Caesarea: *Onomasticon*, 160
25 Taylor: *Onomasticon*, p. 1
26 Wilkinson, John, *Egeria's Travels: Newly Translated with Supporting Documents and Notes* (London, 1971)
27 Wilkinson: Pilgrim of Bordeaux, 585.7, in *Egeria's travels*, p. 153
28 Wilkinson: Pilgrim of Bordeaux, 596, in *Egeria's travels*, p. 160
29 Hunt, E.D., 'The Itinerary of Egeria: Reliving the Bible in Fourth-century Palestine', in. Swanson, R.N (ed.) *The Holy Land, Holy Lands and Christian history* (Woodbridge, 2000), pp. 34–54, pp. 39, 40
30 Wilkinson: *Egeria's travels*, 3.3
31 Wilkinson: *Egeria's travels*, 10.7
32 Wilkinson: *Egeria's travels*, 4.8
33 Wilkinson: Peter the Deacon, P2, in *Egeria's travels*, p. 191
34 Meserve, Margaret, 'Introduction', in John Mandeville, *The travels of Sir John Mandeville* (Mineloa NY, 2006), pp. v–xiv, p. v
35 Mandeville: *Travels*, p. 3
36 Mandeville: *Travels*, p. 49
37 Ellis, Henry, (ed.) *The Pylgrymage of Sir Richard Guylforde to the Holy Land, A.D. 1506. From a Copy Believed to be Unique, From the Press of Richard Pyson*. (London, 1851), fol. x
38 Ellis: *Pylgrymage*, fol. xi
39 Staphorst, Nicholas (ed.), *A Collection of Curious Travels and Voyages. In Two Parts. The first Containing Dr Leonhart Rauwolff's Itinerary into the Eastern Countries; as Syria, Palestine, or the Holy Land, Armenia, Mesopotamia, Assyria, Chaldea & c. Translated from the High Dutch by Nicholas Staphorst*. (London, 1705), unpaged
40 Rauwolff: *Curious Travels*, p. 220
41 Staphorst: *Curious Travels*, unpaged
42 Staphorst: *Curious Travels*, unpaged
43 Sandys, George, *Sandys Travels, Containing a History of the Original and Present State of the Turkish Empire ... A Description of the Holy Land; of the Jews, and Several Sects of Christians Living There; of Jerusalem, Sepulchre of Christ, Temple of Solomon; and what else Either of Antiquity or Worth Observation* (London, 1673), p. 110
44 Sandys: *Sandys Travels*, p. 111, capitalization and italicization original.
45 Sandys: *Sandys Travels*, p. 135
46 R.B. in Bünting, Heinrich, *Itinerarium Totius Sacrae Scripturae, or, The Travels of the Holy Patriarchs, Prophets, Judges, Kings, our Saviour Christ and his Apostles, as they are Related in the Old and New Testaments with a Description of the Towns and Places to which they Travelled* (London, 1682), unpaged
47 Bünting: *Itinerarium*, unpaged
48 Bünting: *Itinerarium*, unpaged
49 Hasselquist, Frederick, *Voyages and Travels in the Levant; in the Years 1749, 50, 51, 52, Containing Observations in Natural History, Physick, Agriculture, and*

Commerce: Particularly on the Holy Land, and the Natural History of the Scriptures (London, 1766)
50 Hasselquist: *Voyages and Travels*, p. 118
51 Hasselquist: *Voyages and Travels*, p. 126
52 Hasselquist: *Voyages and Travels*, p. 123
53 Hasselquist: *Voyages and Travels*, p. 126

CHAPTER 2

1   Larsen, T., 'Thomas Cook, Holy Land pilgrims, and the Dawn of the Modern Tourist Industry', in R.N. Swanson (ed.) *The Holy Land, Holy Lands, and Christian History* (Woodbridge, 2000), p. 336
2   Silberman, Neil A., *Digging for God and Country: Exploration, Archaeology, and the Secret Struggle for the Holy Land 1799–1917* (New York, 1982), pp. 5, 6
3   Bannister, J.T., A *Survey of the Holy Land; its Geography, History and Destiny. Designed to Elucidate the Imagery of Scripture and Demonstrate the Fulfilment of Prophecy* (Bath, 1844), p. iii
4   Butlin, Robin A., 'Ideological Contexts and the Reconstruction of Biblical Landscapes in the Seventeenth and Early Eighteenth Centuries: Dr Edward Wells and the Historical Geography of the Holy Land', in A.H.R. Baker and G. Biger (eds), *Ideology and Landscape in Historical Perspective: Essays on the Meanings of Some Places in the Past* (Cambridge, 1992), p. 45
5   Brooke, John H., *Science and Religion: some Historical Perspectives* (Cambridge, 1991)
6   Glacken, Clarence, *Traces on the Rhodian Shore: Nature and Culture in Western Thought from Ancient Times to the End of the Eighteenth century* (Berkeley, 1967), p. 203
7   Bannister: *Survey*, pp. iv, v
8   Bannister: *Survey*, p. v
9   Bannister: *Survey*, pp. vii, viii
10 Forster, Charles, 1984. *The Historical Geography of Arabia*. 2 vols. (London, 1984)
11 Forster: *Historical Geography*, i, p. vi
12 Forster: *Historical Geography*, i, p. vii
13 Forster: *Historical Geography*, i, pp vii, viii
14 Wylie, James A., *The Modern Judea, Compared with Ancient Prophecy. Some Scenes Illustrative of Biblical Subjects* (Glasgow, 1841)
15 Wylie: *Modern Judea*, p. 6
16 Wylie: *Modern Judea*, p. 16
17 Anon. *Scripture Sites and Scenes, from Actual Survey, in Egypt, Arabia, and Palestine. Chiefly for the use of Sunday Schools* (London, c. 1849), p. 2, emphasis original.
18 Anon.: *Scripture Sites*, p. 10
19 Bowes, J., *A Text-book of the Geography of Palestine, Phoenecia, Philistia, the Seven Churches of Asia, and the Travels of S. Paul. Illustrated by a Map of Palestine. Compiled for use in Day and Sunday schools. To which are Appended Useful Notes and Memory Tablets. The whole Arranged on a Plan Specially Adapted to the Purposes of Tuition* (Manchester, 1867)
20 Bowes: *Geography of Palestine*, p. iii
21 Kitto, J., *The History of Palestine from the Patriarchal Age to the Present Time with Introductory Chapters on the Geography and Natural History of the Country, and on the Customs and Institutions of the Hebrews* (Edinburgh, 1851).

22 Kitto: *History of Palestine*, p. v
23 It is interesting to note that a subsequent edition of Kitto's work was edited and enlarged by J.L. Porter, whose influence turned it into a polemical Scriptural Geography.
24 Burckhardt, J.L., Leake, W.M. (ed.) *Travels in Syria and the Holy Land; by the late John Lewis Burckhardt. Published by the Association for Promoting the Discovery of the Interior Parts of Africa* (London, 1822).
25 Leake himself was a Holy Land traveller, making journeys to Egypt, Syria and Palestine, among many other places. Wagstaff, J.M., 'Leake, William Martin (1777–1860)', *The Oxford Dictionary of National Biography*. <http://www.oxforddnb.com/view/article/16242>. Accessed 10 September 2005
26 Leake, W., 'Preface' in Leake, W. (ed.) *Travels in Syria and the Holy Land; by the late John Lewis Burckhardt. Published by the Association for Promoting the Discovery of the Interior Parts of Africa* (London, 1822), i–xxiii, pp. iv, v
27 Burckhardt: *Travels*, p. 318
28 Burckhardt: *Travels*, p. 336
29 Burckhardt: *Travels*, p. 406
30 Thomson, W.M., *The Land and the Book*; however, quotations in this work are taken from the much expanded *Popular edition*, in 3 volumes (New York, 1880)
31 Thomson: *Land and the Book*, i, p. iv
32 Thomson: *Land and the Book*, ii, p. 200
33 Thomson: *Land and the Book*, ii, p. 223
34 Dixon, W.H., 1867. *The Holy Land*. 3 edn. (London, 1867), p. vii
35 Dixon: *Holy Land*, p. vii
36 Dixon: *Holy Land*, p. vii
37 Dixon: *Holy Land*, p. 99, capitalization original.
38 Palmer, R., *The Bible Atlas, or Sacred Geography Delineated, in a Complete Series of Scriptural Maps, Drawn from the Best Authorities, Ancient and Modern* (London, 1831), p. v, capitalization original.
39 Palmer: *Bible Atlas*, pp. vi, vii
40 Goodrich-Freer, A., *In a Syrian Saddle* (London, 1905)
41 McEwan, Cheryl, 'Paradise or pandemonium: West African landscapes in the travel accounts of Victorian women' *Journal of Historical Geography* 22/1 (1996), pp. 68–83
42 Goodrich-Freer: *Syrian saddle*, p. 1
43 S.C.M. 'Three months in the Holy Land', *The Journal of Sacred Literature and Biblical Record* 6/12, (1858), 273–294, p. 294, capitalization original.
44 Livingstone, David N. *Darwin's Forgotten Defenders: the Encounter Between Evangelical Theology and Evolutionary Thought* (Edinburgh, 1987), p. 51
45 Livingstone: *Forgotten Defenders*, p. 51
46 Bowler, Peter J. *Charles Darwin: the Man and his Influence* (Oxford, 1990), p. 2
47 Greene, J.C. *Debating Darwin: Adventures of a Scholar* (Claremont, 1999), p. 51, emphasis original.
48 Greene: *Debating Darwin*, p. 51
49 Romans, i.18 ff.
50 Livingstone: *Forgotten Defenders*
51 Livingstone: *Forgotten Defenders*
52 Brooke: *Science and Religion*, p. 197
53 Livingstone: *Forgotten Defenders*
54 Brooke: *Science and Religion*

55 Darwin, Charles R., *On the Origin of Species by Means of Natural Selection* (London, 1859)
56 Livingstone: *Forgotten Defenders*
57 Bowler: *Darwin*, p. 8
58 Desmond, Adrian and Moore, Jim, *Darwin* (London, 1991), p. 191
59 Desmond and Moore: *Darwin* p. 221
60 Greene: *Debating Darwin* p. 48
61 Brooke: *Science and Religion*, p. 276
62 Bowler, Peter J., *Reconciling Science and Religion: the Debate in Early-Twentieth-century Britain* (Chicago, 2001)
63 Livingstone: *Forgotten Defenders*
64 Livingstone: *Forgotten Defenders*, p. 35
65 Rogerson, James W., *Old Testament Criticism in the Nineteenth Century: England and Germany* (Minneapolis, 1985)
66 Shepherd, Naomi, *The Zealous Intruders: the Western Rediscovery of Palestine* (San Francisco, 1987) p. 45
67 Comaroff, Jean and John L., *Of Revelation and Revolution: Christianity, Colonialism, and Consciousness in South Africa* (Chicago, 1991)
68 Fulleylove, John and Kelman, John, *The Holy Land: Painted by John Fulleylove R.I.: Described by John Kelman D.D.* 2nd edn. (London, 1923), p. 1
69 Stanley, A.P., *Sinai and Palestine in Connection with their History* (London, 1873
70 Stanley: *Sinai and Palestine*, p. xiii
71 Stanley: *Sinai and Palestine*, p. xviii
72 Stanley: *Sinai and Palestine*, p. xix
73 Stanley: *Sinai and Palestine*, p. xix
74 Stanley: *Sinai and Palestine*, p. xx
75 Stanley: *Sinai and Palestine*, p. xxi
76 Stanley: *Sinai and Palestine*, pp. 190, 191, 194
77 Tristram, Henry Baker, *Bible Places; or, the Topography of the Holy Land: a Succinct Account of all the Places, Rivers, and Mountains of the Land of Israel, Mentioned in the Bible, so far as They have been Identified: Together with their Modern Names and Historical References.* (London, 1871), p. vi
78 Tristram: *Bible Places*, p. 45, italicization original.
79 Kinns, Samuel. *Graven in the Rock; or, the Historical Accuracy of the Bible Confirmed, by Reference to the Assyrian and Egyptian Monuments in the British Museum and Elsewhere* (London, 1891)
80 Kinns: *Graven in the Rock*, p. 1
81 Kinns: *Graven in the Rock*, p. xv
82 Kinns: *Graven in the Rock*, p. xvi
83 Kinns: *Graven in the Rock*, p. 47
84 Kinns: *Graven in the Rock*, pp. 195–197, italicization original.
85 Hackett, H.B. *Illustrations of Scripture: Suggested by a Tour Through the Holy Land* (London, 1857)
86 Hackett: *Illustrations*, p. iii
87 Hackett: *Illustrations*, p. 113
88 Hackett: *Illustrations*, pp. 113, 114
89 Hackett: *Illustrations*, p. 114
90 Hackett: *Illustrations*, pp. 124, 125
91 Hackett: *Illustrations*, pp. 117, 118
92 Conder, C.R., *Tent Work in Palestine: a Record of Discovery and Adventure* 2 vols. (London, 1878), i, p. xxi
93 Conder: *Tent Work*, i, p. xxv
94 Conder: *Tent Work*, i, p. 86

95 Conder: *Tent Work*, i, p. 82
96 Anon., Book Review: 'An account of Palmyra and Zenobia', *Journal of the Anthropological Institute of Great Britain and Ireland* 25 (1896), p. 284, p. 284
97 Wright, W., *Palmyra and Zenobia: with Travels and Adventures in Bashan and the Desert* (London, 1895), pp. 78, 80
98 Wright, William 1892. 'The Hittites' in Anon. (ed.) *The City and the Land: a Course of Seven Lectures on the Work of the Society: Delivered in Hanover Square in May and June, 1892.* (London, 1892), 138–183.
99 Wright: *Palmyra and Zenobia*, p. 130
100 Wright: *Palmyra and Zenobia*, p. xix
101 Wright: *Palmyra and Zenobia*, p. 373
102 Wright: *Palmyra and Zenobia*, p. 1
103 Wright: *Palmyra and Zenobia*, p. 385
104 Wright: *Palmyra and Zenobia*, p. 385
105 Wright: *Palmyra and Zenobia*, p. 386
106 Wright's 1884 work, *The Empire of the Hittites*. (London), was much less subtle in the polemical line. In this book he listed his discoveries proving the existence of the Hittites, a group often mentioned in the Old Testament, but whose existence modern scholarship had questioned, as no physical evidence of their existence had been found prior to Wright's discoveries.
107 Goodspeed, Frank L., *Palestine: 'A Fifth Gospel': Four Lectures on the Christian Evidence Borne by the Holy Land as it is Today.* (Springfield MA, 1901)
108 Goodspeed: *Palestine*, p. 7
109 Goodspeed: *Palestine*, pp. 27, 28
110 Goodspeed: *Palestine*, p. 28
111 Goodspeed: *Palestine*, p. 137
112 Miller, M.S., *Footprints in Palestine: Where the East begins.* (New York, 1936), p. 10
113 Miller: *Footprints*, p. 44
114 Davis, G.T.B., *Seeing Prophecy Fulfilled in Palestine.* (London, n.d.)
115 Davis: *Prophecy Fulfilled*, p. 126.
116 Merrill, Selah, 'Modern researches in Palestine', *Journal of the American Geographical Society of New York* 9 (1877), 109–125, p. 109
117 Merrill: 'Modern researches', p. 110
118 Merrill: 'Modern researches', p. 110
119 Merrill: 'Modern researches', p. 110
120 Merrill: 'Modern researches', p. 118
121 *East of the Jordan: a Record of Travel and Observation in the Countries of Moab, Gilead, and Bashan.* (London, 1881)
122 Merrill: *East of the Jordan*, p. 218
123 Merrill: *East of the Jordan*, p. 133
124 Merrill: *East of the Jordan*, p. 217
125 Merrill: *East of the Jordan*, pp. 232, 233
126 Merrill: *East of the Jordan*, p. 327. 'J.L.P.' is J.L. Porter, the noted polemical Scriptural Geographer.
127 Merrill: *East of the Jordan*, p. 288
128 Merrill: *East of the Jordan*, p. 387
129 Gunn, B. (rev. Gurney, O.R.), 'Sayce, Archibald Henry (1845–1933)'. *The Oxford Dictionary of National Biography*, 2004. <http://www.oxforddnb.com/view/article/35965>. Accessed 11 September 2005
130 Sayce, A.H., *The 'Higher Criticism' and the Verdict of the Monuments.* 4 edn. (London, 1894), pp. ix–xi
131 Sayce: *Higher Criticism*, p. v

132 Sayce: *Higher Criticism*, p. 3
133 Sayce: *Higher Criticism*, pp. 5, 6
134 Sayce: *Higher Criticism*, p. 6
135 Sayce: *Higher Criticism*, pp. 24, 25
136 Sayce: *Higher Criticism*, p. 174
137 Geikie, Cunningham, *The Holy Land and the Bible: a book of Scripture Illustrations Gathered in Palestine*. (London, 1891), p. v
138 Geikie: *The Holy Land*, p. 818
139 Driver, S.R., 'Hebrew Authority' in D.G. Hogarth (ed.) *Authority and Archaeology: Sacred and Profane*. (London, 1899), 3–153, p. 8
140 Driver: 'Hebrew Authority', p. 9
141 Driver: 'Hebrew Authority', p. 34
142 Driver: 'Hebrew Authority', p. 145
143 Cooke, A.W., *Palestine in Geography and in History*. 2 vols. (London, 1901), i, p. v
144 Cooke: *Palestine*, i, p. vi
145 Cooke: *Palestine*, i, p. vi
146 Kelman and Fulleylove: *The Holy Land*, p. 3. It is notable that John Kelman was assistant minister to the famous contextual Scriptural Geographer, George Adam Smith, during Smith's time as minister of Queen's Cross Church in Glasgow.
147 Blunt, A.W.F., 'Introduction', in Caiger, S.L. 1935. *Bible and Spade: an Introduction to Biblical Archaeology* (Oxford, 1935), xi–xii, p. xi
148 Wright, G. Ernest, *An Introduction to Biblical Archaeology*. (London, 1960), p. ix.
149 Wright: *Biblical Archaeology*, pp. ix, x
150 Wright: *Biblical Archaeology*, p. x
151 de Boer, P.A.H. 'Preface', in Franken, H.J. and Franken-Battershill, C.A. *A Primer of Old Testament Archaeology*. (Leiden, 1963), xiii–xiv, p. xiv
152 Franken and Franken-Battershill: *Old Testament Archaeology*, p. 5
153 Livingstone, David N., *The Geographical Tradition: Episodes in the History of a Contested Enterprise*. (Oxford, 1992), p. 28

CHAPTER 3

1 Russell, Michael, *Palestine, or the Holy Land; from the Earliest Period to the Present Time. With nine Engravings*. 4 edn. (Edinburgh, 1837), p. 8
2 Russell, Michael, *View of Ancient and Modern Egypt; with an Outline of its Natural History. With a Map and ten Engravings by Branston*. (Edinburgh, 1831)
3 Russell, Michael, *Nubia and Abyssinia: Comprehending the Civil History, Antiquities, Arts, Religion, Literature, and Natural History. Illustrated by a Map, and twelve Engravings, chiefly by Jackson*. (Edinburgh, 1833)
4 Walker, W., *Three Churchmen: Sketches and Teminiscences of the Right Rev Michael Russell LLD, DCL, Bishop of Glasgow: the Right Rev Charles Hughes Terrot, DD, Bishop of Edinburgh: and George Grubb, LLD, Professor of Law in the University of Aberdeen*. (Edinburgh, 1893)
5 Henderson, T.F. (rev. Strong, R.) 'Michael Russell.' *The Oxford Dictionary of National Biography*, 2004 <http://www.oxforddnb.com/view/article/24331>. Accessed 29 April 2005
6 Nothing else is known of Russell's early life.
7 Russell apparently omitted the academic session 1804-5; Walker: *Three Churchmen*

8   Walker: *Three Churchmen*
9   Walker: *Three Churchmen*
10 Walker: *Three Churchmen*
11 Walker: *Three Churchmen*
12 Walker: *Three Churchmen*
13 Walker: *Three Churchmen*, p. 14
14 Walker: *Three Churchmen*, p. 14
15 Walker: *Three Churchmen*. At that stage all the bishops in the Scottish Episcopal Church continued in normal parish incumbency as well as conducting their episcopalian duties.
16 Walker: *Three Churchmen*, p. 17
17 Walker: *Three Churchmen*, p. 43
18 Walker: *Three Churchmen*, p. 43
19 Walker: *Three Churchmen*, p. 44
20 (London, 1834)
21 *The History and Present Condition of the Barbary States: Comprehending a View of their Civil Institutions, Antiquities, Arts, Religion, Literature, Commerce, Agriculture, and Natural Productions. With a Map, and eleven Engravings by Jackson.* (Edinburgh, 1835)
22 *A Connection of Sacred and Profane History, From the Death of Joshua to the Decline of the Kingdoms of Israel and Judah, Intended to Complete the Works of Shuckford and Prideaux.* 2 vols. (London, 1827/37)
23 Russell: *Connection*, i, pp. viii, ix
24 (Edinburgh, 1829)
25 Russell: *Oliver Cromwell*, i, p. 9
26 Russell: *Oliver Cromwell*, i, pp. 9, 10
27 Livingstone, David N., *The Geographical Tradition: Episodes in the History of a Contested Enterprise* (Oxford, 1992), p. 5
28 Russell: *Oliver Cromwell*, i, p. 10
29 Russell: *Oliver Cromwell*, i, p. 17
30 *Discourses on the Millennium, the Doctrine of Election, Justification by Faith: and on the Historical Evidence for the Apostolical Institution of Episcopacy, together with Preliminary Remarks on the Principles of Scriptural Interpretation* (Edinburgh, 1830)
31 Walker: *Three Churchmen*, pp. 56, 57
32 Mayhew, Robert, 'Mapping Science's Imagined Community: Geography as a Republic of Letters, 1600–1800', *British Journal for the History of Science* 38/1 (2005), pp. 73–92
33 Mayhew: 'Imagined Community', p. 73
34 Mayhew: 'Imagined Community', p. 74
35 Mayhew: 'Imagined Community', p. 74
36 Mayhew: 'Imagined Community', p. 74
37 Mayhew: 'Imagined Community', p. 76
38 Mayhew: 'Imagined Community', p. 77
39 Russell, *Egypt*, pp. 5, 6. Planat's work, referred to by Russell, was published in Paris in 1830, otherwise Planat's life remains obscure to history. 'Mr Salt' is undoubtedly Henry Salt (1780–1827) who was an early Egyptologist and collector of antiquities, many of which ended up in the British Museum and the Louvre. He was British Consul General in Egypt from 1816 until his death. He published numerous Egyptology works on antiquities, Hieroglyphs and cultural matters as well as drawing many Egyptian scenes. The present author's personal communication from Deborah Manley (24 July 2005) suggests that it is likely that he entered a correspondence with Russell, al-

though no letters have been found. Russell's mention of 'successive communications' does not refer to any known published volume. Manley, Deborah and Rée, Peta, *Henry Salt: Artist, Traveller, Diplomat, Egyptologist* (Oxford, 2001)

40 Said, Edward W., *Orientalism: Western Conceptions of the Orient* (Harmondsworth, 1978)
41 Gregory, Derek, 'Scripting Egypt: Orientalism and the Cultures of Travel', In Duncan, James and Gregory, Derek (eds), *Writes of Passage: Reading Travel Writing.* (London, 1999), 114–150
42 Gregory, Derek, *The Colonial Present* (Malden MA, 2004)
43 Russell: *Egypt*, p. 26
44 Russell: *Egypt*, p. 32
45 Russell: *Egypt*, p. 33
46 Russell: *Egypt*, p. 34
47 Russell: *Egypt*, p. 34
48 Russell: *Egypt*, p. 35. Presumably George W. Browne (1768–1813) author of numerous works of Eastern travel and scholarship, most notably *Travels in Africa, Egypt and Syria*, published in London in 1799, which is most probably the volume that Russell was using. Browne travelled in Egypt between 1792 and 1798. He sympathized with the French Revolutionaries, and so his works were poorly received in Britain, yet they are used by Russell. R. Garnett. (rev. Baigent, E.). 'William George Browne.' *The Oxford Dictionary of National Biography*, 2004. <http://www.oxforddnb.com/view/article/3710>. Accessed 2 August 2005
49 Russell: *Egypt*, p. 39. Undoubtedly this refers to Claude Étienne Savary, author in 1787 of *Letters on Egypt*. (London : G.G.J. & J. Robinson), and the 1788 work *Lettres sur la Grece, Faisant Suite de Celles sur l'Égypte*. (Paris: Chez Onfroi)
50 Russell: *Egypt*, p. 39. Shaw was Secretary of the Royal Geographical Society from its inception in 1830 and a well known traveller of the nineteenth century.
51 Russell: *Egypt*, p. 39. Constantin François de Volney, Count, had his *Travels Through Syria and Egypt*, published in an English translation in 1787.
52 Russell: *Egypt*, p. 50. Giovanni Battista Belzoni's *Narrative of the Operations and Recent Discoveries Within the Pyramids, Temples, Tombs, and Excavations in Egypt and Nubia* was first published in London by John Murray in 1820.
53 Russell: *Egypt*, p. 56; Antes, John, Observations on the Manners and Customs of the Egyptians (London, 1800)
54 Russell: *Egypt*, p. 61. Dominique Vivant Denon. [tr. F. Blagdon], *Travels in Upper and Lower Egypt During the Campaigns of General Bonaparte* (London, 1802)
55 Mengin, F., *Histoire de l'Égypte sur le Gouvernement de Mohammed-Aly*. 2 vols. (Paris, 1823)
56 This name belongs to a dynasty of French geographers in the nineteenth century, famed for atlases and general, global geographies.
57 Russell: *Egypt*, pp. 66, 67. When commenting on Manetho's Tract, Russell says 'the accuracy of which cannot be called into question', p. 69. Diodorus is also referred to as 'a writer of the highest credit', p. 198
58 Russell: Egypt, p. 357. Lushington, Mrs Charles, *Narrative of a Journey From Calcutta to Europe, by way of Egypt* (London, 1829)
59 Russell: *Egypt*, pp. 5, 6
60 Russell: *Egypt*, p. 64

61 This is the uniform size of The Edinburgh Cabinet Library. A foolscap sheet folded octavo gives a page of 6¼ by 4¼ inches when trimmed.
62 Gregory:'Scripting Egypt'
63 Russell: *Egypt*, p. 31
64 Russell: *Egypt*, p. 32
65 Russell: *Egypt*, p. 76
66 Russell: *Egypt*, p. 6
67 Egypt is described as 'the cradle of science' *Egypt*, p. 18
68 Russell: *Egypt*, p. 453
69 Russell: *Egypt*, p. 453
70 Russell: *Egypt*, p. 432
71 Said: *Orientalism*
72 Russell: *Egypt*, p. 18
73 Russell: *Egypt*, p. 174
74 Russell: *Egypt*, p. 353
75 It has suggested that he derived this opinion largely from Henry Salt, who greatly admired Mohammed Ali. Author's personal correspondence with Deborah Manley, Oxford (24 July 2005).
76 Russell: *Egypt*, p. 361
77 Russell: *Egypt*, p. 442. Maillet is most probably Bénôit de Maillet, whose memoirs were collated and published as *Description de l'Égypte, Composé sur les Mémoires de M. de Maillet* in Paris in 1735.
78 Russell: *Egypt*, p. 436
79 Russell: *Egypt*, p. 444
80 Russell: *Egypt*, p. 440. To prove his point Russell went on to do just that.
81 Gregory, Derek, 'Between the Book and the Lamp: Imaginative Geographies of Egypt, 1849–50', *Transactions of the Institute of British Geographers*, NS 20/1 (1995), pp. 29–57, p. 29
82 Russell: *Egypt*, p. 3
83 (Edinburgh, 1831). Throughout this book however quotations are from the fourth edition of 1837, which differs little, the main change having been an updated section on the present state of Palestine.
84 Russell: *Palestine*, p. 5
85 Russell: *Palestine*, p. 5
86 This is most probably either Fuller, Thomas, *A Historie of the Holy Warre*. (Cambridge, 1647) or Fuller, Thomas, *A Pisgah-sight of Palestine and the Confines Thereof* (London, 1650)
87 Wilken is a figure lost to history, whose writings may not have been published.
88 Presumably Michaud, Jean-François, *History of the Crusades*. 3 vols. (Paris, 1812–1817)
89 This may be either Mills, Thomas, *The History of the Holy War began in 1095 Against the Turks for the Recovery of the Holy Land*. 2 vols. (London, 1685); or Mills, Charles, *The History of the Crusades: for the Recovery and Possession of the Holy Land*. 2 vols. (London, 1820–1828). Russell would plausibly have used either work, and possibly both.
90 Russell: *Palestine*, p. 7
91 Jean Doubdan was a celebrated seventeenth century French cartographer who produced various maps of the Holy Land.
92 Maundrell refers to Henry Maundrell's account of *A journey from Aleppo to Jerusalem at Easter, AD 1697* (Oxford, 1703).
93 Pococke, Richard, *A Description of the East and Some Other countries*. 2 vols. (London, 1743). Pococke was Bishop of Ossory and subsequently of Meath.

94 Probably a reference to Sandys, George, *A Relation of a Journey Begun An. Dom. 1610. Foure Books. Containing a Description of the Turkish Empire, of Ægypt, of the Holy Land, of the Remote Parts of Italy, and Ilands Adjoining* (London, 1615)
95 de Thévenot, Jean, The Travels of Monsieur de Thévenot into the Levant. (London, 1687)
96 Lucas, Paul, *Voyage Fait en 1714 dans la Turquie, l'Asie, Sourie, Palestine, Haute et Basse Égypte.* 3 vols. (Rouen, 1719)
97 Giovanni Francesco Gemelli-Careri's *Voyage Round the World* was first published in English in 1732 and may be the source to which Russell refers.
98 François René de Chateaubriand's famous *Itinérarie de Paris à Jerusalem et de Jerusalem à Paris, en Allant par le Grèce, et Revenant par l'Égypte, la Barbarie, et l'Espagne* was first published in an English translation in London by Henry Colburn in 1811.
99 Robert Richardson's 1822 book *Travels Along the Mediterranean and Parts Adjacent* was published by T. Cadell in London. Dr Richardson was the Earl of Belmore's physician on his journeys to the East.
100 Russell: *Palestine*, pp. 7, 8
101 Russell: *Palestine*, p. 6
102 Russell: *Palestine*, p. 8
103 Russell: *Palestine*, p. 7
104 Elsner, Jas and Rubiés, Jean-Pau, 'Introduction', in Elsner, Jas and Rubiés, Jean-Pau (eds) *Voyages and Visions: Towards a Cultural History of Travel* (London, 1999), 1–56
105 Russell: *Palestine*, pp. 138, 139
106 Russell: *Palestine*, pp. 146, 147
107 Foucault, Michel [Tr. Sheridan Smith, A.M.], *The Archaeology of Knowledge* (London, 1972), p. 183
108 Russell: *Palestine*, p. 138
109 Melman, Billie, 'The Middle East / Arabia: 'The Cradle of Islam'.' In Hulme, P. and Young, T. (eds) *The Cambridge Companion to Travel Writing* (Cambridge, 2002), 105–121, p. 107
110 Russell: *Palestine*, p. 6
111 Russell: *Palestine*, p. 28
112 Russell: *Palestine*, p. 33
113 Russell: *Palestine*, p. 34
114 Russell: *Palestine*, p. 222
115 Goren, Haim, 'Sacred but not Surveyed: Nineteenth Century Surveys of Palestine', *Imago Mundi*, 54 (2002), pp. 87–110, p. 88
116 Russell: *Palestine*, pp. 36, 37
117 Russell: *Palestine*, p. 369
118 Russell: *Palestine*, p. 362
119 Russell: *Palestine*, p. 8
120 Russell: *Palestine*, pp. 29, 30
121 Russell: *Palestine*, p. 274
122 Ben-Arieh, Yehoshua, *The Rediscovery of the Holy Land in the Nineteenth Century* (Jerusalem, 1979), p. 12
123 Russell: *Palestine*, p. 372
124 Russell: *Palestine*, pp. 6, 7
125 Russell: *Palestine*, p. 120
126 Russell: *Palestine*, p. 35
127 Russell: *Palestine*, p. 222
128 Russell: *Palestine*, p. 225
129 Russell: *Palestine*, p. 22

130 Graber, Linda H., *Wilderness as Sacred Space*. (Washington DC, 1976), p. 3
131 Russell: *Palestine*, p. 132, 133
132 Russell: *Palestine*, p. 26
133 Tuan, Yi-Fu, 'Geopiety: a Theme in Man's Attachment to Nature and to Place.' in Lowenthal, D. and Bowden, M. (eds) *Geographies of the Mind: Essays in Historical Geosophy* (New York, 1976), pp. 11–39
134 Tuan: 'Geopiety', p. 12
135 Russell: *Palestine*, p. 26
136 Russell: *Palestine*, p. 276
137 Russell: *Palestine*, p. 273
138 Russell: *Palestine*, p. 174
139 Russell: *Palestine*, p. 27
140 Russell: *Palestine*, p. 173
141 Russell: *Palestine*, p. 160
142 Lock, C., 'Bowing Down to Wood and Stone: One Way to be a Pilgrim', *Journeys* 3/1 (2002), pp. 110–132, p. 124
143 Russell: *Palestine*, p. 175
144 Walker: *Three Churchmen*, p. 69
145 Cited in Walker: *Three Churchmen*, p. 69
146 Henderson: 'Michael Russell'
147 Walker: *Three Churchmen*, p. 20
148 Combe published works including *Lectures on Popular Education, Delivered to the Edinburgh Philosophical Association for Procuring Instruction in Useful and Entertaining Science, in April and November, 1833.* (Edinburgh, 1833) Presumably these were similar to the lectures that Russell attended.
149 Edinburgh, National Library of Scotland, MS 7385, fo. 239. Letter from Mr George Combe to Rev Michael Russell, 6 March 1832
150 Edinburgh, National Library of Scotland, MS 7229, fo. 71. Letter from Rev Michael Russell to Mr George Combe, 7 March 1832
151 Edinburgh, National Library of Scotland, MS 7229, fo. 69. Letter from Rev Michael Russell to Mr George Combe, 24 March 1832
152 Edinburgh, National Library of Scotland, MS 7385, fo. 462. Letter from Mr George Combe to Rev Michael Russell, 11 February 1833
153 Walker: *Three Churchmen*, p. 19
154 Russell, Michael, *The Agency of Human Means in the Propagation of the Gospel: a Sermon Preached in St John's Episcopal Chapel, Edinburgh, on Thursday, March 13, 1828; in the Presence of the District Committee of the Society for Promoting Christian Knowledge.* (Edinburgh, 1828), p. 25
155 Russell: *Human Means*, p. 27
156 Russell: *Human Means*, p. 27
157 Russell, Michael, Various entries in Smedley, E., Rose, H.J. and Rose, H.J. (eds) *Encyclopaedia Metropolitana: or, Universal Dictionary of Knowledge, on an Original Plan: Comprising the Twofold Advantage of a Philosophical and an Alphabetical Arrangement, with Appropriate Engravings.* 29 vols. (London, 1833)
158 Russell, Michael, 'Egypt' in Smedley, Rose and Rose, *Encyclopaedia Metropolitana*, x, 337–353
159 Russell: 'Egypt' p. 337
160 Russell: 'Egypt' p. 341
161 Walker: *Three Churchmen*, cited on p. 54
162 Walker: *Three Churchmen*, p. 54
163 *Observations on the Advantages of Classical Learning.* (Edinburgh, 1836)
164 Russell: *Classical Learning*, p. 17

165 Walker: *Three Churchmen*, p. 35. The quotation is from a letter of Russell's from Leith, to Primus Skinner on 23 October 1841
166 Walker: *Three Churchmen*, p. 42.
167 *Polynesia: or, an Historical Account of the Principal Islands of the South Sea, including New Zealand; the Introduction of Christianity; and the Actual Condition of the Inhabitants in Regard to Civilisation, Commerce, and the Arts of Social Life. With a Map and Vignette.* (Edinburgh, 1842)
168 Russell: *Polynesia*, p. 9
169 Barnes, Trevor J., 'Geography and Science (including Science Studies)' in Johnston, R.J., Gregory, D., Pratt, G. and Watts, M. (eds), *The Dictionary of Human Geography.* 4th edn. (Oxford, 2000), pp. 727–729, p. 728.
170 Said: *Orientalism*, p. 44
171 Mitchell, T., *Colonising Egypt* (Cambridge, 1988), p. 22
172 Strong, Rowan, '"A Church for the Poor": High Church Slum Ministry in Anderston, Glasgow, 1845–1851', *Journal of Ecclesiastical History* 50/2 (1999), pp. 279–302
173 Walker: *Three Churchmen*, p. 19
174 Walker: *Three Churchmen*, p. 13

CHAPTER 4

1   Porter, Josias Leslie, 'Report', *The Missionary Herald of the Presbyterian Church in Ireland.* 84/November (1850) pp. 864–867, p. 864.
2   Porter, Josias Leslie, *Five Years in Damascus: Including an Account of the History, Topography, and Antiquities of that City; with Travels and Researches in Palmyra, Lebanon and the Hauran.* 2 vols. (London, 1855), i, pp. 202–204
3   Materials found in the unsorted archive of the Overseas Board of the Presbyterian Church in Ireland, Belfast, The Gamble Library, have contributed to this story of Porter's life and work.
4   Anon. [Porter, Josias Leslie], *A Handbook for Travellers in Syria and Palestine; Including an Account of the Geography, History, Antiquities, and Inhabitants of These Countries, the Peninsula of Sinai, Edom, and the Syrian Desert; with Detailed Descriptions of Jerusalem, Petra, Damascus, and Palmyra. Maps and plans.* 2 parts. (London, 1858). Porter was author of the first two editions. Later editions were edited and reworked by others. This series of travel guidebooks and maps flourished in the nineteenth century, with 63 volumes covering Britain, the Continent and Asia. The bulk of the series ran from the mid-nineteenth century and some volumes were still being published in the 1970s.
5   Murray, Virginia, John Murray Publishers Ltd., London. Personal correspondence with author, (15 May 2001).
6   Porter, Josias Leslie, *Science and Revelation: their Distinctive Provinces: with a Review of the Theories of Tyndall, Huxley, Darwin & Herbert Spencer* (Belfast, 1874); Porter, Josias Leslie 1863. *Bishop Colenso on the Pentateuch Reviewed* (Belfast, 1863)
7   For example: Porter, Josias Leslie, 'Geography', in W.L. Alexander (ed.) *A Cyclopaedia of Biblical Literature* (Edinburgh, 1864), 106–109. Several other articles in this volume, and some geographical entries in the *Encyclopaedia Britannica*.
8   Porter, Josias Leslie, *The Life and Times of Henry Cooke D.D., LL.D.* (Belfast, 1871)

9   Barkley, J.M., *Fasti of the General Assembly of the Presbyterian Church in Ireland 1840–1870* (Belfast, 1986). Craig was later the first PCI Missionary to the Jews, in Hamburg.

10   Hamilton, T., 'Josias Leslie Porter', in Lee, S. (ed.) *The Dictionary of National Biography*, 26 vols. (London, 1909), xvi, pp. 187–188

11   Hutchinson, Samuel, 'The Salvation of Israel: the Story of the Jewish Mission', in Thompson, Jack (ed.), *Into all the World: a History of 150 Years of the Overseas Work of the Presbyterian Church in Ireland* (Belfast, 1990), pp. 125–143, p. 125

12   Anon., News item in *The Missionary Herald of the Presbyterian Church in Ireland*, 83/November (1849) p. 731

13   Anon., Eighth Annual Report of the Assembly's Jewish Mission: presented to the General Assembly [of the Presbyterian Church in Ireland] at its Meeting in Belfast, July 1850. (Belfast, 1850)

14   Porter: *Five years,* ii, p. 3

15   Porter: *Five years*, ii, p. 2

16   It is interesting to note the considerable sales of this work, with an initial print run of 1,250 in December 1855 and a further run of 1,500 in March 1870. The plates were finally melted in 1907. Author's personal correspondence with Virginia Murray, John Murray Publishers Ltd., London (15 May 2001).

17   Porter: *Five Years*, i, p. 190, n. 6

18   Porter: *Five Years*, i, pp. 199, 200, n. 2

19   Anon.: *Handbook*, p. xi

20   Anon.: *Handbook*, p. 9

21   Anon.: *Handbook*, p. xvii, capitalization original.

22   Porter: 'Geography', pp. 106, 107, italicization original.

23   Porter: 'Geography' p. 108

24   *The Giant Cities of Bashan and Syria's Holy Places.* (London, 1865); Porter, Josias Leslie, *The Giant Cities of Bashan and the Northern Border Land.* (Philadelphia, n.d. [c. 1865])

25   Porter: *Giant Cities*, p. ii

26   Porter: *Giant Cities*, p. iii

27   Porter: *Giant Cities*, pp. iii, iv

28   Porter: *Giant Cities*, p. iv, capitalization original. This passage stands in resplendent contrast to the preface of *Five Years in Damascus*, which reads: 'My sextant and compass were my constant companions on every excursion', i, p. vi

29   Porter: *Giant Cities and the Northern Border Land*, p. 18, capitalization original.

30   Porter: *Giant Cities and the Northern Border Land*, pp. 75, 76

31   Porter: *Giant Cities and the Northern Border Land*, p. 76

32   Porter: *Giant Cities and the Northern Border Land*, p. 86

33   Porter, Josias Leslie, *The Life and Times of Henry Cooke D.D. LL.D. People's Edition.* (Belfast, 1875), p. vi. Porter retained his interest in his father-in-law's life and work, and Porter was a member of a delegation which attended a meeting of Belfast Town Council on 1 April 1876 to hand over a newly-completed statue of Dr Cooke to the Council's care. Belfast, Public Record Office of Northern Ireland. LA/7/2EA/12, Minute Book of the Belfast Corporation, p. 203

34   Porter: *Science and Revelation*

35   Porter: *Science and Revelation*, p. 35

36   Porter, Josias Leslie, *Illustrations of Bible Prophecy and History from Personal Travels in Palestine* (Belfast, 1883), p. 46

37   Porter, Josias Leslie, *Egypt: Physical and Historical* (London, 1885), p. 3
38   Porter: *Egypt*, p. 2
39   Porter, Josias Leslie, *Jerusalem, Bethany and Bethlehem* (London, 1887); *"Through Samaria" to Galilee and the Jordan: scenes in the early life and labours of our Lord* (London, 1889)
40   Porter: *Jerusalem, Bethany and Bethlehem*, p. 127
41   Porter: *Through Samaria*, unpaginated
42   Porter: *Five years*, i, p. 37, italicization mine.
43   Porter: *Giant Cities and the Northern Border Land*, p. 5
44   Porter: *Giant Cities and the Northern Border Land*, p. 16
45   Gregory, Derek, *The Colonial Present*. (Malden, MA, 2004)
46   Anon.: *Handbook*, p. xi
47   Porter: *Egypt*, p. 19
48   Makdisi, U., 'Mapping the Orient: Non-Western Modernization, Imperialism, and the End of Romanticization', in Michie, H. and Thomas, R.R. (eds) *Nineteenth Century Geographies: the Transformation of Space from the Victorian Age to the American Century* (London, 2002), pp. 40–54, p. 40
49   Porter: *Five Years*, i, p. 141
50   Urry, John, *The Tourist Gaze: Leisure and Travel in Contemporary Societies* (London, 1990), p. 45
51   Porter: *Five Years*, i, p. 148
52   Anon.: *Handbook*, p. xvii
53   Porter: *Five Years*, i, p. 32
54   Porter: *Five Years*, i, p. 30
55   Porter: *Five Years*, i, pp. 32, 33
56   Purity of Worship Defence Association, in connection with the Irish Presbyterian Church, *Address to the Ministers, Elders, and Members of the Church* (Belfast, 1875), p. 2.
57   Allen, R.A., *The Presbyterian College Belfast: 1853–1953* (Belfast, 1954)
58   These were particularly prominent in the issues for late 1878.
59   Allen: *Presbyterian College*, p. 131
60   Allen: *Presbyterian College*
61   This later proved to be a member of the Dublin Presbyterian merchant family, the Findlaters, whose family crest appears in one pair of the chapel windows. Findlater, A. *Findlaters – the story of a Dublin merchant family 1774–2001*. (Dublin, 2001).
62   Anon., News item in *The Witness*, 18 October 1878, p. 5
63   Anon.: News item, p. 5.
64   Purity of Worship Defence Association: *Address*, p. 8
65   Crinson, M., *Empire Building: Orientalism and Victorian Architecture*. (London, 1996), p. 9
66   This opinion is expressed by Allen: *Presbyterian College*, p. 134
67   The following story is also dealt with by Allen: *Presbyterian College*, pp. 130–133
68   Rodgers, J.M., Letter to *The Witness*, 21 October 1878, p. 8. Some of the quotations of Porter's speech made by Maxwell were not actually included in Porter's original words.
69   A 'visitation' of a Presbyterian congregation is a ten-yearly inspection of that congregation's activities by a representation of the Presbytery to which that congregation belongs.
70   Belfast, Board of Finance and Administration, Presbyterian Church in Ireland, Church House: MS Minutes of the Presbytery of Belfast, 5 November 1878. Unpaginated.

71 Porter, Josias Leslie, Letter to *The Witness*, 8 November 1878, p. 5
72 Belfast, Board of Finance and Administration, Presbyterian Church in Ireland, Church House: MS Minutes of the Presbytery of Belfast, 5 November 1878. Unpaginated.
73 Porter: Letter, p. 5
74 Porter: *Giant Cities and the Northern Border Land*, p. 221
75 Porter: *Giant Cities*, p. 3
76 Porter, Josias Leslie, 'The Old City of Adraha (Dera) and the Roman Road from Gerasa to Bostra', *Palestine Exploration Quarterly* 12 (1881), pp. 77–79, p. 77
77 Porter: *Five Years*, i, p. 255
78 Driver, Felix, *Geography Militant: Cultures of Exploration and Empire*. (Oxford, 2001), pp. 12, 13
79 Among them: Barnes, B., *Scientific Knowledge and Sociological Theory* (London, 1974); Beaver, B.de B., 'Possible Relationships Between the History and Sociology of Science' in Gaston, J (ed.), *Sociology of Science* (San Francisco, 1978), pp. 140–161; Latour, B., *Pandora's Hope: Essays in the Reality of Science Studies* (Cambridge MA, 1999)
80 Porter: *Five Years*, i, p. 219
81 Porter, Josias Leslie, 'The Hittites', *Palestine Exploration Quarterly* 12 (1881) pp. 218–220, pp. 218, 219
82 Porter: *Five Years*, ii, p. 7
83 Said, Edward W., *Orientalism: Western Conceptions of the Orient* (Harmondsworth, 1978), p. 1
84 Porter: *Five Years*, ii, pp. 281, 219
85 Makdisi: 'Mapping the Orient', p. 43
86 Porter: *Five Years*, ii, p. 304
87 Livingstone, David N., *Darwin's Forgotten Defenders: the Encounter Between Evangelical Theology and Evolutionary Thought* (Edinburgh, 1987)
88 Porter: *Five Years*, i, p. vi ; a section of the map was also published in the *Journal of the Royal Geographical Society* 26 (1856) pp. 43–55, on a larger scale, with an extensive and fairly typical memoir.
89 Edney, Matthew H., *Mapping an empire: the geographical construction of British India, 1765–1843*. (Chicago, 1997), p. 39
90 Keay, John, *The Great Arc: the Dramatic Tale of how India was Mapped and Everest was Named*. (London, 2000), pp. 83, 84
91 Porter's blunt statement that 'I have already found it to be rather an expensive amusement to conduct scientific investigations in a country like Syria, when one is dependent wholly on his own resources' may well have been a plea for funding for more ambitious scientific projects. Porter, Josias Leslie 'Memoir on the Map of Damascus, Hauran and the Lebanon Mountains', *Journal of the Royal Geographical Society* 26 (1856) pp. 43–55, p. 55
92 Porter: *Giant Cities*, pp. 210, 211
93 Said: *Orientalism*, p. 20
94 Porter: *Five Years*, i, pp. 1, 2
95 Porter: *Five Years*, i, p. 2
96 Sack, Robert David, *Homo Geographicus: a Framework for Action, Awareness, and Moral Concern*. (Baltimore MD, 1997), pp. 127, 128
97 Sack: *Homo Geographicus*, p. 66
98 Porter: *Giant Cities*, pp. 2, 3
99 Porter: *Five Years*, i, p.142.
100 Porter: *Five Years*, ii, p. 93

101 In the terms of Comaroff, John L. and Comaroff, Jean, *Of Revelation and Revolution: Christianity, Colonialism and Consciousness in South Africa.* (Chicago, 1991). A 'power encounter' is an intellectual circumstance where missionaries use superior knowledge to manipulate their target groups into a religious commitment.
102 Comaroff and Comaroff: *Revelation and Revolution*
103 Porter: *Five Years*, i, p. 145
104 Porter: *Five Years*, i, p. 145
105 Porter: *Five Years*, i, p. 186, italicization original.
106 Warfield, Benjamin Breckinridge, cited in Livingstone, David N. and Wells, Ronald A., *Ulster-American Religion: Episodes in the History of a Cultural Connection* (Notre Dame IN, 1999), p. 15
107 Livingstone and Wells: *Ulster-American Religion*
108 Marsden, G., 'The Collapse of American Evangelical Academia', in Plantinga, Alvin and Wolterstorff, N. (eds) *Faith and Rationality: Reason and Belief in God* (Notre Dame IN, 1983), pp. 219–264, p. 225
109 Marsden: 'Collapse'
110 Noll, Mark A., *The Scandal of the Evangelical Mind.* (Grand Rapids MI, 1994), p. 85
111 This characterization is used by Noll, Mark A. 'Common Sense traditions in American evangelical thought', *American Quarterly* 37 (1985), pp. 216–238
112 Noll: 'Common sense', p. 221
113 Hoeveler, J.D., Jr., *James McCosh and the Scottish Intellectual Tradition: from Glasgow to Princeton* (Princeton, 1981), p. 117
114 Livingstone and Wells: *Ulster-American religion*, p. 16
115 McBride, Ian, 'The school of virtue: Francis Hutcheson, Irish Presbyterians and the Scottish Enlightenment', in Boyce, D.G., Eccleshall, Robert and Geoghan, Vincent (eds.) *Political Thought in Ireland Since the Seventeenth Century*. (London, 1993), pp. 73–99, p. 79
116 Hoeveler, *James McCosh*, p. 116
117 McCosh, cited in Livingstone and Wells, *Ulster-American Religion*, p. 15
118 Hoeveler: *James McCosh*, p. 116
119 Hoeveler: *James McCosh*, p. 116
120 Hoeveler: *James McCosh*, p. 121
121 Noll: 'Common sense', p. 229
122 Noll: 'Common sense', p. 224
123 Noll: 'Common sense', p. 226
124 Hoeveler: *James McCosh*, p. 114
125 Hoeveler: *James McCosh*, p. 116
126 Hoeveler: *James McCosh*
127 Hoeveler: *James McCosh*, p. 113
128 McBride: 'School of Virtue', p. 74
129 Sloane, W.M. (ed.), *The life of James M'Cosh: a Record Chiefly Autobiographical. With Portraits.* (Edinburgh, 1896), pp. 172, 173
130 Hoeveler: *James McCosh*
131 Allen: *Presbyterian College*, p. 162
132 Livingstone and Wells: *Ulster-American religion*
133 Porter: *Five Years*, i, pp. v, vi
134 Porter: *Five Years*, ii, p. 7
135 Porter: *Five Years*, i, p. 9
136 Porter's *Through Samaria* contains a significant amount of natural history material.
137 Porter: *Science and Revelation*, p. 4

138 Porter: *Science and Revelation*, p. 5
139 Porter: *Science and Revelation*, p. 3
140 A mode of understanding detailed by Glacken, Clarence, *Traces on the Rhodian Shore: Nature and Culture in Western Thought from Ancient Times to the end of the Eighteenth Century* (Berkeley CA, 1967)
141 Porter: *Science and Revelation*, p. 6
142 Porter: *Science and Revelation*, p. 35
143 Macloskie, George, 'Concessions to Science', *Presbyterian Review* 10 (1889), pp. 220–228, p. 224
144 Macloskie: 'Concessions', pp. 225, 226
145 Porter: *Colenso Reviewed*, p. 12, emphasis original.
146 Porter: *Colenso Reviewed*, p. 12
147 Porter: *Travels in Palestine*, pp. 5, 6
148 Porter: *Travels in Palestine*, p. 6
149 Porter: *Giant Cities and the Northern Border Land*, p. 108, capitalization original.
150 Porter: *Giant Cities and the Northern Border Land*, p. 106
151 Tuan, Yi-Fu, 'Geopiety: a Theme in Man's Attachment to Nature and to Place', in Lowenthal, David and Bowden, M. (eds), *Geographies of the Mind: Essays in Historical Geosophy* (New York, 1976), pp. 11–39; Wright, J.K. '*Terrae Incognitae*: the Place of the Imagination in Geography', *Annals of the Association of American Geographers* 37/1 (1947), pp. 1–15
152 Knorr-Cetina, K.D., *The Manufacture of Knowledge: an Essay on the Constructivist and Contextual Nature of Science* (Oxford, 1981)
153 Porter: *Giant Cities and the Northern Border Land*, p. 125
154 Porter: *Giant Cities and the Northern Border Land*, p. 122
155 Porter: *Travels in Palestine*, p. 47
156 Porter: *Travels in Palestine*, p. 10
157 Porter: *Giant Cities*, p. 198
158 Porter: *Five Years*, i, p. 234
159 Porter: *Five Years*, i, p. v
160 Porter: *Travels in Palestine*, pp. 46, 47
161 Porter: *Jerusalem, Bethany and Bethlehem*, p. 78, italicization original.
162 Porter: *Jerusalem, Bethany and Bethlehem*, p. 99
163 Porter: *Jerusalem, Bethany and Bethlehem*, p. 127
164 Gregory, Derek, 'Scripting Egypt: Orientalism and the Cultures of Travel', in Duncan, James and Gregory, Derek (eds), *Writes of Passage: Reading Travel Writing*. (London, 1999), pp. 114–50
165 Porter: *Through Samaria*, p. 29
166 Porter: *Five Years*, i, p. 305
167 Porter: *Through Samaria*, pp. 24, 25, capitalization original.
168 Gregory, Derek, *Geographical Imaginations* (Oxford, 1994)
169 Porter: *Through Samaria*, p. 13
170 Gregory: 'Scripting Egypt'
171 Porter: *Five Years*, ii, pp. 2, 3
172 Gregory, Derek, *The Colonial Present* (Malden MA, 2004)
173 Porter: *Five Years*, i, p. 213
174 Porter: *Science and Revelation*, p. 6
175 Porter: *Five Years*, i, p. 233, italicization original.
176 Porter: *Five Years*, i. p. 297.
177 Belfast. The Archive of The Queen's University of Belfast: Damp press copy out letter book of Rev Josias Leslie Porter, President of Queen's College, Belfast and his successor, Rev Thomas Hamilton, 1882–1889, pp. 74–77. Letter

of President Porter to L. L'Hévétier regarding Natural Philosophy and Experimental Physics in the matriculation curriculum of the Queen's College, dated 5 January 1884, p. 75, emphasis original.
178 Greene, J.C., *Debating Darwin: Adventures of a Scholar.* (Claremont CA, 1999), p. 51, emphasis original.
179 Livingstone, David N., *Putting Science in its Place: Geographies of Scientific Knowledge* (Chicago, 2003), p. 47
180 Livingstone, *Science in its Place*, p. 20

CHAPTER 5

1 Smith, Lilian Adam, *George Adam Smith: a Personal Memoir and Family Chronicle.* (London, 1943), p. 49
2 The story is recounted in Smith: *George Adam Smith*, p. 1
3 In acknowledgement of his lofty academic status he was awarded honorary degrees by Aberdeen, Cambridge, Dublin, Durham, Edinburgh, Glasgow, Oxford, St Andrews, Sheffield, Western Reserve and Yale Universities.
4 Cook, S.A. 'George Adam Smith: 1856–1942', *Proceedings of the British Academy*, 28 (1942) pp. 325–346, p. 325
5 Smith, George Adam, *Our Common Conscience: Addresses Delivered in America During the Great War.* (London, N.D. [c. 1918])
6 Smith, George Adam, *The Early Poetry of Israel in its Physical and Social Origins. The Schweich Lectures, 1910* (Oxford, 1912).
7 *The Geography of British India: Political and Physical.* (London, 1882).
8 Smith: *George Adam Smith*, p. 13
9 Smith: *George Adam Smith*
10 Smith, George Adam, *Jerusalem: the Topography, Economics and History from the Earliest Times to AD 70.* 2 vols. (London, 1907).
11 For these dates I rely on Campbell, Iain D. *Fixing the Indemnity: the Life and Work of Sir George Adam Smith* (1856–1942) (Carlisle, 2004), p. 30
12 Edinburgh, National Library of Scotland, Acc 9446/13. Sketch Map of Leipzig, attached to letter of 24 April [1878] to George Adam Smith's sister, Isabel.
13 Riesen, Richard A., *Criticism and Faith in Late Victorian Scotland.* (Lanham MD, 1985), p. 45
14 Simpson, P.C.,*The life of Principal Rainy.* 2 vols. (London, 1909), i, p. 272
15 His teacher at New College, A.B. Davidson, was in favour of higher criticism, and may well have sent Smith to Germany to experience it more directly.
16 Edinburgh, National Library of Scotland, Acc 9446/13. Summary of George Adam Smith's Personal Expenses in Tübingen, April – June 1876.
17 Edinburgh, National Library of Scotland, Acc 9446/13. Letter from George Adam Smith to his father, Summer 1876.
18 Fell, Winandus, *Canones Apostolorum Æthiopice* (Lipsiae, 1871).
19 Smith: *George Adam Smith*
20 Edinburgh, National Library of Scotland, Acc 9446/13. Letter of 26 May 1876, from George Adam Smith to Janet Smith. Smith records his experience of hearing Diestel's history of the place of the Old Testament at first hand.
21 Smith: George Adam Smith
22 Rogerson, J.W. goes so far as to call Delitzsch 'an original and adventurous thinker' but opines that 'he stayed much closer to orthodoxy' than many of his contemporaries. *Old Testament Criticism in the Nineteenth Century: England and Germany* (Minneapolis, 1985), p. 104
23 Rogerson: *Old Testament criticism*, p. 114

24 Riesen: *Criticism and Faith*, p. xx
25 Riesen: *Criticism and Faith*, p. xx
26 Howard, T.A., *Religion and the Rise of Historicism: W.M.L. de Wette, Jacob Burck-hardt, and the theological origins of nineteenth-century historical consciousness.* (Cambridge, 2000), p. 2
27 Howard: *Rise of Historicism*, p. 3
28 Howard: *Rise of Historicism*, p. 8
29 Howard: *Rise of Historicism*, p. 8
30 Anon., 'Memorial to the College Committee of the United Free Church of Scotland', Appendix I to the Special report by the College Committee to the General Assembly of 1902, Report XI-A, Reports to the General Assembly of the United Free Church of Scotland, 1902. (Edinburgh, 1902). One page only.
31 Smith: *George Adam Smith*, p. 18
32 Smith: *George Adam Smith*, p. 18
33 Duncan, James and Gregory, Derek, 'Introduction', in Duncan, James and Gregory, Derek (eds), *Writes of Passage: Reading Travel Writing.* (London, 1999), 1–13
34 Smith: *George Adam Smith*, p. 18
35 Smith: *George Adam Smith*, p. 18
36 Smith: *George Adam Smith*, p. 18
37 Edinburgh, New College Library Special Collections: 'Sir George Adam Smith': MSS SMI 1.1.4.1. Letter of 11 April 1880 from George Adam Smith to his brother.
38 Edinburgh, New College Library Special Collections: 'Sir George Adam Smith': MSS SMI 1.1.4.1. Letter of 19 April 1880 from George Adam Smith to his mother.
39 Edinburgh, New College Library, Special Collections: 'Sir George Adam Smith': MSS SMI 1.1.4.1. Letter of 27 April 1880 from George Adam Smith to his mother.
40 Edinburgh, New College Library, Special Collections: 'Sir George Adam Smith': MSS SMI 1.1.4.1. Letter of 15 April 1880 from George Adam Smith to his father. Punctuation in the manuscript letters of George Adam Smith is often necessarily silently reconstructed, or silently inserted by the present author, to aid the reader's understanding.
41 Edinburgh, New College Library, Special Collections: 'Sir George Adam Smith': MSS SMI 1.1.4.1. Letter of 15 April 1880 from George Adam Smith to his father.
42 Smith, George Adam, *The Historical Geography of the Holy Land: Especially in Relation to the History of Israel and the Early Church.* (London, 1894), p. xiii
43 A vertical (|) is used to indicate a new paragraph in the manuscript.
44 Edinburgh, New College Library, Special Collections: 'Sir George Adam Smith': MSS SMI 1.1.4.1. Letter of 15 April 1880 from George Adam Smith to his father.
45 Edinburgh, New College Library, Special Collections: 'Sir George Adam Smith': MSS SMI 1.1.4.1. Letter of 15 April 1880 from George Adam Smith to his father.
46 Lock, C., Bowing down to Wood and Stone: One Way to be a Pilgrim. *Journeys* 3/1 (2002), pp. 110–132
47 Edinburgh, New College Library, Special Collections: 'Sir George Adam Smith': MSS SMI 1.1.4.1. Letter of 15 April 1880 from George Adam Smith to his father.

48 Edinburgh, New College Library, Special Collections: 'Sir George Adam Smith': MSS SMI 1.1.4.1. Letter of 19 April 1880 from George Adam Smith to his mother.
49 Edinburgh, New College Library, Special Collections: 'Sir George Adam Smith': MSS SMI 1.1.4.1. Letter of 19 April 1880 from George Adam Smith to his mother.
50 Edinburgh, New College Library, Special Collections: 'Sir George Adam Smith': MSS SMI 1.1.4.1. Letter of 15 April 1880 from George Adam Smith to his father.
51 Edinburgh, New College Library, Special Collections: 'Sir George Adam Smith': MSS SMI 1.1.4.1. Letter of 19 April 1880 from George Adam Smith to his mother.
52 Edinburgh, New College Library, Special Collections: 'Sir George Adam Smith': MSS SMI 1.1.4.1. Letter of 19 April 1880 from George Adam Smith to his mother.
53 Edinburgh, New College Library, Special Collections: 'Sir George Adam Smith': MSS SMI 1.1.4.1. Letter of 19 April 1880 from George Adam Smith to his mother.
54 Lock: 'Bowing Down'
55 Edinburgh, New College Library, Special Collections: 'Sir George Adam Smith': MSS SMI 1.1.4.1. Letter of 19 April 1880 from George Adam Smith to his mother.
56 This indicates a word which is indecipherable in the original manuscript.
57 Edinburgh, New College Library, Special Collections: 'Sir George Adam Smith': MSS SMI 1.1.4.1. Letter of 19 April 1880 from George Adam Smith to his mother.
58 Lock: 'Bowing Down', p. 123
59 Edinburgh, New College Library, Special Collections: 'Sir George Adam Smith': MSS SMI 1.1.4.1. Letter of 19 April 1880 from George Adam Smith to his mother.
60 Gregory, Derek, *The Colonial Present* (Malden MA, 2004)
61 Smith, William Robertson, 'Bible' in Baynes, T.S. (ed.), *The Encyclopaedia Britannica: a Dictionary of Arts, Sciences and General Literature*. 9th edn. 25 vols. (Edinburgh, 1875), iii, pp. 634–638
62 Burleigh, J.H.S. *A Church History of Scotland* (London, 1960), p. 359
63 Smith, George Adam, *The life of Henry Drummond*. 9th edn. (London, 1907), p. 129
64 Livingstone, David N. 'Oriental travel, Arabian Kinship and Ritual Sacrifice: William Robertson Smith and the Fundamental Institutions', *Environment and Planning D: Society and Space*, 22 (2004), pp. 639–657, p. 652
65 Riesen: *Criticism and Faith*, p. xv
66 Riesen: *Criticism and Faith*, p. xiv
67 Riesen: *Criticism and Faith*, p. xiv
68 Riesen: *Criticism and Faith*, p. xv
69 Hunter, A.G., 'The Indemnity: William Robertson Smith and George Adam Smith', in Clines, D.J.A. and Davies, P.R. (eds) *William Robertson Smith: essays in reassessment* (Sheffield, 1995) pp. 60–66.
70 Campbell: *Fixing the Indemnity*, p. 35
71 George Adam Smith notes that he had 'a chat' with William Robertson Smith at this chance meeting. Edinburgh, National Library of Scotland, Acc 9446/16. Letter of 21 December 1879 from George Adam Smith in Cairo, to his mother.
72 Smith: *George Adam Smith*, p. 19

73 Campbell: *Fixing the indemnity*, p. 37
74 Smith: *George Adam Smith*, p. 23
75 Smith: *George Adam Smith*
76 Smith, George Adam, *The Forgiveness of Sins and other Sermons* (London, 1904)
77 For example: Smith, George Adam 'The Twenty-Third Psalm', *The Expositor* 1 (1900) pp. 33–44
78 Smith: *George Adam Smith*
79 His father had been one of the founders of the Society in 1884, and served on its council. Baigent, Elizabeth, 'George Adam Smith (1856–1942)' *Oxford Dictionary of National Biography*. Oxford University Press. <http://www.oxforddnb.com/view/article/36139>. Accessed 1 June 2005
80 Campbell, Iain D., 'In search of the physical: George Adam Smith's journeys to Palestine and their importance', *History and anthropology* 13/4 (2002), pp. 291–299, letter from James Black to Lillian Smith, 5 March 1942, cited on pp. 291, 292
81 Smith: *George Adam Smith*
82 Smith: *George Adam Smith*
83 Riesen: *Criticism and Faith*, p. 10
84 Smith, George Adam, *The Book of Isaiah: in Two Volumes*. (London, [1888] 1900), i, p. xiii
85 Edinburgh, New College Library Special Collections: 'Sir George Adam Smith': MSS SMI 1.7.2
86 Smith, George Adam 'The New Edition of Baedeker's "Palestine"', *The Expositor*, 4th series, 4 (1891) pp. 467–468, p. 467.
87 Smith: Baedeker's "Palestine", p. 467
88 Smith: *George Adam Smith*
89 Smith, George Adam, 'Duhm's Isaiah and the New Commentary to the Old Testament', *The Expositor*, 4th series, 6 (1892) pp. 312–318, p. 312
90 Smith, George Adam, *The Preaching of the Old Testament to the Age*. (London, 1893), p. 7
91 Smith: *Preaching of the Old Testament*, p. 32
92 Smith: *Preaching of the Old Testament*, p. 35
93 Smith: *Historical Geography*
94 Schürer, book review of Smith, *Historical Geography*, in Theologische Literatur-Zeitung, cited in publisher's back matter of Smith, *Modern Criticism and the Preaching of the Old Testament*.
95 Anon. in the *Speaker*, book review, of Smith, *Historical Geography*, cited in publisher's back matter of Smith, *Modern Criticism and the Preaching of the Old Testament*.
96 Butlin, Robin A., 'George Adam Smith and the Historical Geography of the Holy Land: Contents, Contexts and Connections', *Journal of Historical Geography*, 14/4 (1988), pp. 381–404, p. 387
97 Robertson, C.J., 'Scottish geographers: the first hundred years', *Scottish Geographical Magazine*, 89 (1973), pp. 5–18, p. 7
98 While I have been unable to obtain sight of a Hebrew copy myself, I thank Prof Haim Goren for this information.
99 Edinburgh, New College Library, Special Collections: MSS SMI 1.4.2.
100 Edinburgh, New College Library, Special Collections: MSS SMI 1.4.2, Letter from Edw. C. Goldberg, Tunbridge, Kent, 13 October 1895, to George Adam Smith.
101 Schürer: Book Review
102 Lock: 'Bowing Down', p. 123
103 Smith: *George Adam Smith*

104 Gregory, Derek, 'Between the Book and the Lamp: Imaginative Geographies of Egypt, 1849–1850', *Transactions of the Institute of British Geographers*, NS 20 (1995), pp. 29–57, p. 50

105 Among these, Smith made frequent use of Charles Doughty's work, *Travels in Arabia Deserta*. 2 vols. (Cambridge, 1888); C. Conder's. *Tent work in Palestine*. 2 vols. (London, 1878); A. Henderson's *The historical geography of Palestine* (Handbooks for Bible classes and private students; M. Dods (the Younger) and A. Whyte, 1884); along with selection of German sources and many of the materials produced by the Palestine Exploration Fund.

106 Smith: *Historical Geography*, pp. 93, 94. The italicized words are original and, in the pattern of the book, are a biblical quotation, from Isaiah, xxxv.2, though the reference is not given in Smith's text.

107 Smith: *Historical Geography*, p. 119

108 Smith: *Historical Geography*, pp. 644, 645

109 Smith: *Historical Geography*, p. 645

110 Smith: *Historical Geography*, p. 646

111 Smith: *Historical Geography*, p. 504

112 Smith: *Historical Geography*, p. 67

113 Smith: *Historical Geography*, p. 523

114 Smith: *Historical Geography*, pp. 6, 7

115 Smith: *Historical Geography*, p. 209

116 Smith: *Historical Geography*, p. 65. The italicized text is original, and is a quotation from 2 Samuel, xxiii.20

117 Smith: *Historical Geography*, p. 141

118 Duncan and Gregory: 'Introduction'; Gregory, Derek, 'Geography and Travel Writing', in Johnston, R.J., Gregory, D., Pratt, G. and Watts, M. (eds), *The Dictionary of Human Geography*. 4th edn. (Oxford, 2000) pp. 857–859

119 Smith: *Historical Geography*, p. 99

120 Rajchman, J. 'Foucault's art of seeing', in *Philosophical Events: Essays of the 80s*. (New York, 1991), pp. 68–102, p. 81

121 Gregory, Derek, 'Scripting Egypt: Orientalism and the Cultures of Travel', in Duncan, James and Gregory, Derek (eds), *Writes of Passage: Reading Travel Writing*. (London, 1999), pp. 114–150

122 Smith: *Historical Geography*, p. 40

123 Smith: *Historical Geography*, pp. 99, 100

124 Mitchell, Timothy, *Colonising Egypt* (Cambridge, 1988)

125 Lock: 'Bowing down', p. 121

126 Smith: *Historical Geography*, p. 123

127 Smith: *Historical Geography*, p. 59

128 Smith: *Historical Geography*, pp. 74, 75

129 Smith: *Historical Geography*, p. 31

130 Smith: *Historical Geography*, p. 421

131 Said, Edward W., *Orientalism: Western Conceptions of the Orient* (Harmondsworth, 1978).

132 Smith: *Historical Geography*, p. 422

133 Smith: *Historical Geography*, p. 113

134 Smith: *Historical Geography*, pp. 431, 432

135 Smith: *Historical Geography*, p. 29

136 Mitchell, Timothy, 'Orientalism and the Exhibitionary Other' in Dirks, N. (ed), *Colonialism and Culture*. (Ann Arbor MI, 1992), pp. 289–318

137 Smith: *Historical Geography*, p. x

138 Smith: *Historical Geography*, p. xiv

139 Smith, George Adam and Bartholomew, John G. (eds), *Atlas of the Historical Geography of the Holy Land.* (London, 1915). This work was dedicated to A.B. Davidson and William Robertson Smith, amongst others, p. v
140 Smith: *George Adam Smith*
141 'Recent German Literature on the Old Testament', *The Expositor*, 4th series, 10 (1894) pp. 150–160, p. 150. Budde was a lifelong friend of Smith.
142 *The Book of the Twelve Prophets: Commonly Called Minor.* 2 vols. (London, 1896/1898)
143 Smith: *Twelve Prophets*, i, p. xi
144 Smith: *Twelve Prophets*, ii, p. 177
145 Smith: *Twelve Prophets*, i, pp. 72, 73
146 Smith: *Twelve Prophets*, i, p. 73
147 Smith: *Twelve Prophets*, i, pp. 73, 74
148 Smith: *Twelve Prophets*, i, p. 74
149 *The Life of Henry Drummond.* (London, 1899). Quotations in this book are however from the 9th edition of 1907.
150 Smith: *Life of Henry Drummond*, p. 130
151 Smith: *Life of Henry Drummond,* p. 131
152 Smith: *Life of Henry Drummond,* p. 136
153 Smith, George Adam, *Modern Criticism and the Preaching of the Old Testament: Eight Lectures on the Lyman Beecher Foundation, Yale University, U.S.A.* (London, 1901), p. 68
154 Smith: *Modern Criticism*, p. 40
155 Smith: *Modern Criticism*, p. 70
156 Smith: *Modern Criticism*, p. 2
157 Smith: *Modern Criticism*, p. 72
158 Campbell, Iain D., The Church in Scotland 1840–1940: an overview. *Quodlibet*, 1/8, unpaginated. <http://www.quodlibet.net/>. Accessed 29 February 2004.
159 Anon., 'Memorial to the College Committee of the United Free Church of Scotland', Appendix I to Special Report by the College Committee to the General Assembly of 1902, Report XI-A, in Anon. Reports to the General Assembly of the United Free Church of Scotland, 1902. (Edinburgh, 1902). Unpaginated.
160 Anon.: 'Memorial'
161 Smith, George Adam, 'Statement to the Sub-Committee of the College Committee of the United Free Church of Scotland, anent a Memorial against the volume Modern Criticism and the Preaching of the Old Testament', Appendix II to the Special Report by the College Committee to the General Assembly of 1902. Report XI-A in Anon. Reports to the General Assembly of the United Free Church of Scotland, 1902. (Edinburgh, 1902), p. 9
162 Smith: 'Statement', p. 9
163 Anon., 'UFCS Assembly in St Andrew's Halls, Glasgow', *The Union Magazine* May 1902, p. 193
164 Teka, 'Assembly Side-Lights', *The Union Magazine* July 1902, pp. 305–309, p. 307
165 Teka: 'Assembly Side-Lights', p. 307
166 Simpson: *Life of Principal Rainy*, i, p. 272
167 Anon., Special Report by the College Committee to the General Assembly of 1902. Report XI-A, Reports to the General Assembly of the United Free Church of Scotland, 1902 (Edinburgh, 1902), p. 3
168 Anon.: *Special Report*, p. 6
169 Anon., 'The Assembly and the Bible', *The Union Magazine*, July 1902, p. 290

170 *A Layman's Reply to Prof George Adam Smith's "Modern Criticism and the Preaching of the Old Testament"* (Glasgow, 1902)
171 Smith: *George Adam Smith*
172 Lines from 'Attock-on-the-Indus: a rhyming geography' cited in D. Middleton, D. 'George Adam Smith: 1856–1942', *Geographers: Biobibliographical Studies*, 1 (1977), pp. 105–106, p. 105
173 Smith: *Forgiveness of Sins*, p. 34
174 Smith: *Forgiveness of Sins*, p. 35
175 Smith: *Forgiveness of Sins*, p. 35
176 Press cutting preserved in Edinburgh, National Library of Scotland, Acc 9446/142
177 Press cutting preserved in Edinburgh, National Library of Scotland, Acc 9446/142
178 Smith: *Jerusalem*, i, p. 4
179 Smith: *Jerusalem*, i, p. 25
180 Smith: *Jerusalem*, i, p. 20
181 Smith: *Jerusalem*, i, p. 50
182 Smith: *Jerusalem*, i, p. x
183 Smith: *Jerusalem*, i, p. 4
184 Smith: *George Adam Smith*
185 Smith: *Schweich Lectures*, p. x
186 Smith: *Our Common Conscience*, p. 151
187 Smith, George Adam, *Syria and the Holy Land*. (London, 1918), p. 37
188 Smith, George Adam, *Jeremiah: being the Baird Lecture for 1922*. (London, 1923), p. 68
189 Smith: *Jeremiah*, p. 68
190 Smith, George Adam, 'Science and Faith: a Sermon Preached Before the Members of the British Association in Aberdeen, and Broadcast, on September 9', *The Listener*, 26 September 1934 pp. 529–530, p. 529
191 Smith: 'Science and faith', p. 530
192 Riesen: *Criticism and Faith*, p. 21
193 Riesen: *Criticism and Faith*, p. 22
194 Riesen: *Criticism and Faith*, p. 42
195 Smith: *George Adam Smith*, p. 20
196 Riesen: *Criticism and Faith* ; Hunter: 'The indemnity'
197 Smith: *Modern Criticism*, pp. 11, 12
198 Cook: 'George Adam Smith', p. 341
199 Smith: *Modern Criticism*, p. 16
200 Smith: *Life of Henry Drummond*, p. 129
201 Riesen: *Criticism and Faith*, p. xix
202 Campbell points out that 'Part of the significance of Smith's life is that he ministered in three denominations: the Free Church of Scotland (from 1882–1900), the United Free Church of Scotland (1900–1929) and the Church of Scotland (1929–1935).' Church in Scotland, unpaginated.
203 Smith: *George Adam Smith*
204 Gregory, Derek, *Geographical Imaginations* (Cambridge MA, 1994)
205 Livingstone, David N., *Putting Science in its Place* (Chicago, 2003) p. xi
206 Gregory: 'Book and the lamp'
207 Smith: *Historical Geography*, p. 114
208 Smith: *Modern Criticism*, p. 57
209 Smith: *Modern Criticism*, p. 68
210 Smith: *Modern Criticism*, p. 76
211 Rajchman: 'Foucault's art', pp. 71, 72

212 Campbell states that many of Smith's conclusions 'are still being widely debated and discussed among scholars, both liberal and evangelical', *Fixing the Indemnity*, p. 9
213 For example: Miller, J.M,. 'The Ancient Near East and Archaeology', in Mays, J.L., Petersen, D.L. and Richards, K.H. (eds), *Old Testament Interpretation: Past, Present and Future: Essays in Honour of Gene M. Tucker*. (Edinburgh, 1995), 245–260, who refers to Smith, pp. 250f

CHAPTER 6

1   Twain, Mark, *The Innocents Abroad: or, the New Pilgrim's Progress* (Hartford, 1869), p. 319
2   Livingstone, David N., *Nathaniel Southgate Shaler and the Culture of American Science*. (Tuscaloosa, 1987), cited on p. 3
3   Livingstone, David N., *The Geographical Tradition: Episodes in the History of a Contested Enterprise*. (Oxford, 1992), p. 5
4   Gange, David, 'Religion and Science in Late Nineteenth-Century Egyptology', *The Historical Journal*, 49/4 (2006), pp. 1083–1103
5   Walker, P.W.L., *Holy city, Holy places? Christian Attitudes to Jerusalem and the Holy Land in the Fourth Century* (Oxford, 1990), p. vii
6   Long, Burke O., *Imagining the Holy Land: Maps, Models and Fantasy Travels*. (Bloomington IN, 2003), p. 208
7   Whiting, C., 'Geographical imaginations of the 'Holy Land': Biblical Topography and Archaeological Practice', *Nineteenth-Century Contexts*, 29/2–3, pp. 237–250, p. 237
8   Theorists such as Homi Bhabha, Gayatri Spivak, and Robert Young have made such arguments in many places.
9   Livingstone: *Geographical Tradition*, p. 27
10 Livingstone, David N., 'Text, Talk and Testimony: Geographical Reflections on Scientific Habits. An Afterword', *British Journal for the History of Science* 38/1 (2005), pp. 93–100
11 King, R., *Orientalism and Religion: Post-colonial Theory, India and the Mystic East*. (London, 1999), p. 62
12 Livingstone, David N., *Science, Space and Hermeneutics: Hettner-Lecture 2001*. (Heidelberg, 2002), pp. 34, 35
13 Ball, C.J., *Light from the East: or the Witness of the Monuments. An Introduction to the Study of Biblical Archaeology*. (London, 1899), p. vii
14 Ball: *Witness of the Monuments*, pp. vii, viii
15 Marten, Michael, *Attempting to Bring the Gospel Home: Scottish Missions to Palestine, 1839–1917*. (London, 2006), p. 142
16 Livingstone: 'Afterword', p. 95
17 Said, Edward W., *Orientalism: Western Conceptions of the Orient* (Harmondsworth, 1978)
18 Edinburgh, National Library of Scotland, Acc 9446/16. Letter of George Adam Smith, 21 December 1879, to his mother.
19 Mayhew, Robert, 'Mapping Science's Imagined Community: Geography as a Republic of Letters, 1600–1800', *British Journal for the History of Science*, 38/1 (2005), pp. 73–92
20 A term from van Huyssteen, W., 'Theology and Science: the Quest for a New Apologetics', in *Essays in Postfoundationalist Theology*. (Grand Rapids, 1997), pp. 215–237, p. 226
21 Said: *Orientalism*, p. 172

22   Brace, C., Bailey, A.R. and Harvey, D.C., 'Religion, Place and Space: a Framework for Investigating Historical Geographies of Religious Identities and Communities', *Progress in Human Geography* 30/1 (2006), pp. 28–43, p. 29
23   Feiler, Bruce, *Walking the Bible: a Journey by Land Through the Five Books of Moses.* (New York, 2001), p. 6
24   Fox, Edward, *Palestine Twilight: the murder of Dr Albert Glock and the Archaeology of the Holy Land* (London, 2001); Fox, Edward, *Sacred Geography: a Tale of Murder and Archeology in the Holy Land.* (New York, 2001)
25   Anon. <http://www.noahsarksearch.com/>. Accessed 31 March 2006
26   Porter, Josias Leslie, Report. *Missionary Herald*, November 1850 pp. 864–867, p. 865
27   Harvey, David, *Spaces of Hope* (Edinburgh, 2000)

Bibliography

ARCHIVAL SOURCES

Edinburgh, The National Library of Scotland: Acc. 9446: 'George Adam Smith'
Edinburgh, The National Library of Scotland: MSs 7229, 7385
Edinburgh, New College Library, Special Collections: MSS SMI: 'Sir George Adam Smith Archive'
Belfast, Board of Finance and Administration, The Presbyterian Church in Ireland, Church House: Minute Book of the Presbytery of Belfast
Belfast, The Gamble Library: Archive of the Overseas Board of the Presbyterian Church in Ireland
Belfast, The Archive of The Queen's University of Belfast: Damp press copy out letter book of Rev Josias Leslie Porter, President of Queen's College, Belfast and his successor, Rev Thomas Hamilton, 1882–1889: QUB/B/2/1/15
Belfast, The Public Record Office of Northern Ireland: LA/7/2EA, Minute Book of the Belfast Corporation

UNPUBLISHED SOURCES

Author's personal correspondence with Deborah Manley, Oxford, 2005
Author's personal correspondence with Virginia Murray, John Murray Publishers Ltd., London, 2001

PRIMARY PUBLISHED TEXTS

Anon. *Scripture Sites and Scenes, from Actual Survey, in Egypt, Arabia, and Palestine. Chiefly for the use of Sunday Schools.* (London, 1849)
——, News item in *The Missionary Herald of the Presbyterian Church in Ireland*, 83 (November 1849), p. 731

——, *Eighth Annual Report of the Assembly's Jewish Mission: presented to the General Assembly* [of the Presbyterian Church in Ireland] *at its Meeting in Belfast, July 1850*

——, [Porter, J.L.], *A Handbook for Travellers in Syria and Palestine; Including an Account of the Geography, History, Antiquities and Inhabitants of these Countries, the Peninsula of Sinai, Edom, and the Syrian Desert; with Detailed Descriptions of Jerusalem, Petra, Damascus, and Palmyra. Maps and Plans.* 2 parts. (London, 1858)

——, News items and opinion pieces in *The Witness*. 18, 21 October and 8 November 1878

——, Review: *An Account of Palmyra and Zenobia. Journal of the Anthropological Institute of Great Britain and Ireland*. 25 (1896), p. 284

——, 'Memorial to the College Committee of the United Free Church of Scotland,' Appendix I to *Special report by the College Committee to the General Assembly of 1902*, Report XI-A, in Anon. (ed.), *Reports to the General Assembly of the United Free Church of Scotland, 1902* (Edinburgh, 1902)

——, *Special Report by the College Committee to the General Assembly of 1902.* Report XI-A, *Reports to the General Assembly of the United Free Church of Scotland, 1902* (Edinburgh, 1902)

——, 'UFCS Assembly in St Andrew's Halls, Glasgow', *The Union Magazine*, May 1902, p.193

——, 'The Assembly and the Bible,' *The Union Magazine*, July 1902, p. 290

——, <http://www.bibleandscience.com>. Accessed 7 September 2005

——, <http://www.christiananswers.net>. Accessed 7 September 2005

——, <http://www.gnmagazine.org/archaeology>. Accessed 7 September 2005

——, <http://www.noahsarksearch.com/>. Accessed 31 March 2006

Antes, John, *Observations on the Manners and Customs of the Egyptians* (London, 1800)

Ball, C.J., *Light from the East: or the Witness of the Monuments. An Introduction to the Study of Biblical Archaeology* (London, 1899)

Bannister, J.T., *A Survey of the Holy Land; its Geography, History and Destiny. Designed to Elucidate the Imagery of Scripture, and Demonstrate the Fulfilment of Prophecy* (Bath, 1844)

Belzoni, G.B., *Narrative of the Operations and Recent Discoveries Within the Pyramids, Temples, Tombs, and Excavations in Egypt and Nubia* (London, 1820)

Blunt, A.W.F., 'Introduction', in Caiger, S.L. *Bible and Spade: an Introduction to Biblical Archaeology* (Oxford, 1935), xi–xii

de Boer, P.A.H., Preface to Franken, H.J. and Franken-Battershill, C.A. *A Primer of Old Testament Archaeology* (Leiden, 1963), xiii–xiv

Bowes, John, *A Text-book of the Geography of Palestine, Phoenecia, Philistia, the Seven Churches of Asia, and the Travels of S. Paul. Illustrated by a Map of Palestine. Compiled for use in Day and Sunday schools. To which are Appended Useful Notes and Memory Tablets. The Whole Arranged on a Plan Specially Adapted to the Purposes of Tuition* (Manchester, 1867)

Browne, George William, *Travels in Africa, Egypt and Syria* (London, 1799)

de Chateaubriand, F.R., *Itinérarie de Paris à Jerusalem et de Jerusalem à Paris, en Allant par le Grèce, et Revenant par l'Égypte, la Barbarie, et l'Espagne* (London, 1811)

Combe, George, *Lectures on Popular Education, Delivered to the Edinburgh Philosophical Association for Procuring Instruction in Useful and Entertaining Science, in April and November, 1833* (Edinburgh, 1833)

Conder, Claude R., *Tent work in Palestine: a Record of Discovery and Adventure. With Illustrations by J.W. Whymper.* 2 vols. (London, 1878)

Cooke, A.W., *Palestine in Geography and in History.* 2 vols. (London, 1901)

Darwin, Charles R., 1859. *On the Origin of Species by Means of Natural Selection* (London, 1859)

Davis, G.T.B., *Seeing Prophecy Fulfilled in Palestine* (London, n.d.)

Denon, D.V., [tr. F. Blagdon] 1802. *Travels in Upper and Lower Egypt During the Campaigns of General Bonaparte* (London, 1802)

Dixon, W.H., *The Holy Land.* 3 edn. (London, 1867)

Doughty, Charles M., *Travels in Arabia Deserta* (Cambridge, 1888)

Driver, S.R., 'Hebrew Authority', in Hogarth, D.G. (ed.), *Authority and Archaeology: Sacred and Profane* (London, 1899), 3–153

van Dyke, H., *Out-of-doors in the Holy Land: Impressions of Travel in Body and Spirit* (New York, 1908)

Ellis, Henry (ed.), *The Pylgrymage of Sir Richard Guylforde to the Holy Land, AD 1506. From a Copy Believed to be Unique, from the Press of Richard Pyson.* (London, 1851)

Eusebius of Caesarea, *The Onomasticon with Jerome's Latin Translation and Expansion in Parallel from the edition of E. Klostermann* (Jerusalem, 2003)

Feiler, Bruce, *Walking the Bible: a Journey by Land Through the Five Books of Moses* (New York, 2001)

Fell, Winandus, *Canones Apostolorum Æthiopice* (Lipsiae, 1871)

Forster, Charles, *The Historical Geography of Arabia; or, the Patriarchal Evidences of Revealed Religion: a Memoir, with Illustrative Maps; and an Appendix Containing Translations, with an Alphabet and Glossary, of the Hamyaritic Inscriptions Recently Discovered at Hadramaut.* 2 vols. (London, 1984)

Franken, H.J. and Franken-Battershill, C.A., *A Primer of Old Testament Archaeology* (Leiden, 1963)

Fulleylove, J. and Kelman, J., *The Holy Land: Painted by John Fulleylove, R.I. and Described by John Kelman, D.D.* 2 edn. (London, 1923)

Fuller, T., *A Historie of the Holy Warre* (Cambridge, 1647)

——, *A Pisgah-sight of Palestine and the Confines Thereof* (London, 1650)

Geikie, Cunningham, *The Holy Land and the Bible: a Book of Scripture Illustrations Gathered in Palestine* (London, 1891)

Gemelli-Careri, G.F., *Voyage Round the World* (London, 1732)

Goodrich-Freer, A., *In a Syrian Saddle* (London, 1905)

Goodspeed, Frank L., *Palestine: 'A Fifth Gospel': Four Lectures on the Christian Evidence Borne by the Holy Land as it is Today* (Springfield, MA, 1901)

Hackett, Horatio B., *Illustrations of Scripture: Suggested by a Tour Through the Holy Land* (London, 1857)

Hasselquist, Frederick, *Voyages and Travels in the Levant; in the Years 1749, 50, 51, 52. Containing Observations in Natural History, Physick, Agriculture, and Commerce: Particularly on the Holy Land, and the Natural History of the Scriptures* (London, 1766)

Henderson, A., *The Historical Geography of Palestine* (Edinburgh, 1884)

Kinns, Samuel, *Graven in the Rock; or, the Historical Accuracy of the Bible Confirmed, by Reference to the Assyrian and Egyptian Monuments in the British Museum and Elsewhere* (London, 1891)

Kitto, John, *The History of Palestine from the Patriarchal Age to the Present Time with Introductory Chapters on the Geography and Natural History of the Country, and on the Customs and Institutions of the Hebrews* (Edinburgh, 1851)

Leake, W.M. (ed.), *Travels in Syria and the Holy Land; by the late John Lewis Burckhardt. Published by the Association for Promoting the Discovery of the Interior Parts of Africa* (London, 1822)

Logie, William, *A Layman's Reply to Prof George Adam Smith's 'Modern Criticism and the Preaching of the Old Testament'* (Glasgow, 1902)

Lucas, P., *Voyage Fait en 1714 dans la Turquie, l'Asie, Sourie, Palestine, Haute et Basse Égypte.* 3 vols. (Rouen, 1719)

Lushington, C. (Mrs), *Narrative of a Journey from Calcutta to Europe, by way of Egypt* (London, 1829)

de Maillet, B., *Description de l'Égypte, Composé sur les Mémoires de M de Maillet* (Paris, 1735)

Maundrell, H., *A Journey from Aleppo to Jerusalem* (London, 1703)

Mengin, F., *Histoire de l'Égypte sur le Gouvernement de Mohammed-Aly.* 2 vols. (Paris, 1823)

Merrill, Selah, 'Modern researches in Palestine', *Journal of the American Geographical Society of New York*, 9 (1877), pp. 109–125

——, *East of the Jordan: a Record of Travel and Observation in the Countries of Moab, Gilead and Bashan* (London, 1986)

Michaud, J.-F., *History of the Crusades.* 3 vols. (Paris, 1812–17)

Miller, M.S., *Footprints in Palestine: Where the East Begins* (New York, 1936)

Mills, C., *The History of the Crusades: for the Recovery and Possession of the Holy Land.* 2 vols. (London, 1820–28)

Mills, T., *The History of the Holy War began in 1095 Against the Turks for the Recovery of the Holy Land.* 2 vols. (London, 1685)

Palmer, R., *The Bible Atlas, or Sacred Geography Delineated, in a Complete Series of Scriptural Maps, Drawn From the Best Authorities, Ancient and Modern* (London, 1831)

Planat, Jules, *Histoire de la Régénération de l'Égypte* (Paris, 1830)

Pococke, R., *A Description of the East and Some Other Countries.* 2 vols. (London, 1743)

Porter, Josias Leslie, 'Report', *The Missionary Herald of the Presbyterian Church in Ireland*, November 1850, pp. 864–867

——, *Five Years in Damascus: Including an Account of the History, Topography, and Antiquities of that City, with Researches in Palmyra, Lebanon and the Hauran.* 2 vols. (London, 1855)

——, 'Memoir on the Map of Damascus, Hauran and the Lebanon Mountains', *Journal of the Royal Geographical Society* 26 (1856), pp. 43–55

——, *Bishop Colenso on the Pentateuch Reviewed* (Belfast, 1863)

——, 'Geography' in Alexander, W.L. (ed.), *A Cyclopedia of Biblical Literature. 3 edn.* (Edinburgh, 1864), pp. 106–109

——, *The Giant Cities of Bashan and Syria's Holy Places* (London, 1865)

——, *The Giant Cities of Bashan, and the Northern Border Land* (Philadelphia, n.d. [c. 1865])

——, *The Life and Times of Henry Cooke, DD LlD* (Belfast, 1871)

——, *Science and Revelation: their Distinctive Provinces: with a Review of the Theories of Tyndall, Huxley, Darwin & Herbert Spencer* (Belfast, 1874)

——, *The Life and Times of Henry Cooke, DD LlD People's Edition* (Belfast, 1875)

——, Letter to *The Witness*, 18 October 1878, p. 5

——, 'The Old City of Adraha (Dera) and the Roman Road from Gerasa to Bostra', *Palestine Exploration Quarterly* 12 (1881), pp. 77–79

——, 'The Hittites', *Palestine Exploration Quarterly*, 12 (1881), pp. 218–220

——, *Illustrations of Bible Prophecy and History from Personal Travels in Palestine* (Belfast, 1883)

——, *Egypt: Physical and Historical* (London, 1885)

——, *Jerusalem, Bethany and Bethlehem* (London, 1887)

——, *Through Samaria to Galilee and the Jordan: Scenes in the Early Life and Labours of our Lord* (London, 1889)

Purity of Worship Defence Association (In Connection with the Irish Presbyterian Church), *Address to the Ministers, Elders, and Members of the Church* (Belfast, 1875)

R.B. in Bünting, Heinrich, *Itinerarium Totius Sacrae Scripturae, or, The Travels of the Holy Patriarchs, Prophets, Judges, Kings, our Saviour Christ and his Apostles, as they are Related in the Old and New Testaments with a Description of the Towns and Places to which they Travelled* (London, 1682)

Richardson, R., *Travels along the Mediterranean and Parts Adjacent* (London, 1822)

Rodgers, J.M., Letter to *The Witness*, 21 October 1878, p. 8

Russell, Michael, *A Connection of Sacred and Profane History, from the Death of Joshua to the Decline of the Kingdoms of Israel and Judah, Intended to Complete the Works of Shuckford and Prideaux.* 2 vols. (London, 1827–37)

——, *The Agency of Human Means in the Propagation of the Gospel: a Sermon Preached in St John's Episcopal Chapel, Edinburgh, on Thursday, March 13, 1828; in the Presence of the District Committee of the Society for Promoting Christian Knowledge* (Edinburgh, 1828)

——, *Life of Oliver Cromwell.* 2 vols. (Edinburgh, 1829)

——, *Discourses on the Millennium, the Doctrine of Election, Justification by Faith: and on the Historical Evidence for the Apostolical Institution of Episcopacy, together with Preliminary Remarks on the Principles of Scriptural Interpretation.* (Edinburgh, 1830)

——, *View of Ancient and Modern Egypt; with an Outline of its Natural History. With a Map and Ten Engravings by Branston* (Edinburgh, 1831)

——, *Palestine, or the Holy Land; from the Earliest Period to the Present Time. With Nine Engravings* (Edinburgh, 1831)

——, 'Egypt', in Smedley, E., Rose, H.J. and Rose, H.J. (eds.), *Encyclopaedia Metropolitana: or, Universal Dictionary of Knowledge, on an Original Plan: Comprising the Twofold Advantage of a Philosophical and an Alphabetical Arrangement, with Appropriate Engravings*. 29 vols. (London, 1833), x, pp. 337–353

——, *Nubia and Abyssinia: Comprehending the Civil History, Antiquities, Arts, Religion, Literature, and Natural History. Illustrated by a Map, and Twelve Engravings, chiefly by Jackson* (Edinburgh, 1833)

——, *History of the Church in Scotland* (London, 1834)

——, *The History and Present Condition of the Barbary States: Comprehending a View of their Civil Institutions, Antiquities, Arts, Religion, Literature, Commerce, Agriculture, and Natural Productions. With a Map, and Eleven Engravings by Jackson* (Edinburgh, 1835)

——, *Observations on the Advantages of Classical Learning* (Edinburgh, 1836)

——, *Polynesia: or, an Historical Account of the Principal Islands of the South Sea, including New Zealand; the Introduction of Christianity; and the Actual Condition of the Inhabitants in Regard to Civilisation, Commerce, and the Arts of Social Life. With a Map and Vignette* (Edinburgh, 1842)

Sandys, George, *A Relation of a Journey Begun An. Dom. 1610. Foure Books. Containing a Description of the Turkish Empire, of Ægypt, of the Holy Land, of the Remote Parts of Italy, and Ilands adjoining* (London, 1615)

Sandys, George, *Sandys Travels, Containing a History of the Original and Present State of the Turkish Empire ... A Description of the Holy Land; of the Jews, and Several Sects of Christians Living There; of Jerusalem, Sepulchre of Christ, Temple of Solomon; and What Else either of Antiquity or Worth Observation* (London, 1673)

Savary, C.É., *Letters on Egypt* (London, 1787)

——, *Lettres sur la Grece, Faisant Suite de Celles sur l'Égypte* (Paris, 1788)

Sayce, A.H., *The 'Higher Criticism' and the Verdict of the Monuments. 4 edn.* (London, 1894)

——, *Patriarchal Palestine* (London, 1895)

S.C.M. 'Three Months in the Holy Land', *The Journal of Sacred Literature and Biblical Record* 6/12 (1858), pp. 273–294

Smith, George Adam and Bartholomew, J.G. (eds.), *Atlas of the Historical Geography of the Holy Land* (London, 1915)

Smith, George Adam, 'The New Edition of Baedeker's "*Palestine*"', *The Expositor*, 4th series 4 (1891), pp. 467–468

——, 'Duhm's *Isaiah* and the *New Commentary to the Old Testament*', *The Expositor*, 4th series 6 (1892), pp. 312–318

——, *The Preaching of the Old Testament to the Age* (London, 1893)

——, *The Historical Geography of the Holy Land: Especially in Relation to the History of Israel and of the early Church. With Four Maps* (London, 1894)

——, 'Recent German Literature on the Old Testament', *The Expositor*, 4th series 10 (1894), pp. 150–160

——, *The Book of the Twelve Prophets: Commonly Called Minor*. 2 vols. (London, 1896–98)

——, 'The Twenty-third Psalm', *The Expositor*, 1 (1900), pp. 33–44

——, *The Book of Isaiah: in Two Volumes* (London, 1900)

——, *Modern Criticism and the Preaching of the Old Testament: Eight Lectures on the Layman Beecher Foundation, Yale University, U.S.A.* 2 edn. (London, 1901)

——, 'Statement to the Sub-Committee of the College Committee of the United Free Church of Scotland, anent a Memorial against the Volume *Modern Criticism and the Preaching of the Old Testament*.' Appendix II to *Special Report by the College Committee to the General Assembly of 1902.* Report XI-A, in Anon. (ed.), *Reports to the General Assembly of the United Free Church of Scotland, 1902* (Edinburgh, 1902)

——, *The Forgiveness of Sins and Other Sermons* (London, 1904)

——, *The Book of the Twelve Prophets: Commonly Called Minor. In Two Volumes.* 9 edn. (London, 1906)

——, *Jerusalem: the Topography, Economics and History from the Earliest Times to AD 70.* 2 vols. (London, 1907)

——, *The Life of Henry Drummond.* 9 edn. (London, 1907)

——, *The Early Poetry of Israel in its Physical and Social Origins. The Schweich Lectures, 1910* (Oxford, 1912)

——, *Our Common Conscience: Addresses Delivered in America During the Great War* (London, n.d. [c. 1918])

——, *Syria and the Holy Land* (London, 1918)

——, *Jeremiah: Being the Baird Lecture for 1922* (London, 1923)

——, 'Science and Faith: a Sermon Preached Before the Members of the British Association in Aberdeen, and Broadcast, on September 9', *The Listener*, 26 September 1934, pp. 529–530

Smith, George, *The Geography of British India: Political and Physical* (London, 1882)

Smith, William Robertson, 'Bible', in Baynes, T.S. (ed.), *The Encyclopaedia Britannica: a Dictionary of Arts, Sciences and General Literature.* 9 edn. 25 vols. (Edinburgh, 1875), iii, pp. 634–638

Stanley, Arthur Penrhyn, *Sinai and Palestine in Connection with their history* (London, 1873)

Staphorst, Nicholas (ed.), *A Collection of Curious Travels and Voyages. In Two Parts. The First Containing Dr Leonhart Rauwolff's Itinerary into the Eastern Countries; as Syria, Palestine, or the Holy Land, Armenia, Mesopotamia, Assyria, Chaldea & c. Translated from the High Dutch by Nicholas Staphorst* (London, 1705)

Teka, 'Assembly Side-lights', *The Union Magazine*, July 1902, pp. 305–309

de Thévenot, J., *The Travels of Monsieur de Thévenot into the Levant* (London, 1687)

Thomson, William M., *The Land and the Book; or, Biblical Illustrations Drawn from the Manners and Customs, the Scenes and Scenery of the Holy Land* (London, 1876)

——, *The Land and the Book; or, Biblical Illustrations Drawn From the Manners and Customs, the Scenes and Scenery of the Holy Land. Popular Edition.* 3 vols. (New York, 1880)

Tristram, Henry Baker, *Bible Places; or, the Topography of the Holy Land: a Succinct Account of all the Places, Rivers, and Mountains of the Land of Israel,*

Mentioned in the Bible, so far as they have been Identified: Together with their Modern Names and Historical References (London, 1871)

Twain, Mark, *The Innocents Abroad: or, the New Pilgrim's Progress* (Hartford, 1869)

de Volney, C.F., *Travels through Syria and Egypt* (London, 1787)

Wilkinson, John, *Egeria's Travels: Newly Translated with Supporting Documents and Notes* (London, 1971)

Wright, G.E., *An Introduction to Biblical Archaeology* (London, 1960)

Wright, William, *The Empire of the Hittites* (London, 1884)

——, 'The Hittites' in Anon (ed.), *The City and the Land: a Course of Seven Lectures on the Work of the Society: Delivered in Hanover Square in May and June, 1892* (London, 1892), pp. 138–183

——, *Palmyra and Zenobia: with Travels and Adventures in Bashan and the Desert* (London, 1987)

Wylie, James Aitken, *The Modern Judea, Compared with Ancient Prophecy. Some Scenes Illustrative of Biblical Subjects* (Glasgow, 1841)

SECONDARY PUBLISHED TEXTS

Allen, R.A., *The Presbyterian College Belfast: 1853–1953* (Belfast, 1954)

Anon. Book review: *The Historical Geography of the Holy Land,* in *The Speaker.* Cited in publisher's back matter of Smith, *Modern Criticism.*

Baigent, E., 'George Adam Smith (1856–1942)' *The Oxford Dictionary of National Biography.* Oxford University Press.<http://www.oxforddnb.com/view/article/36139>. Accessed 1 June 2005

Barkley, J.M., *Fasti of the General Assembly of the Presbyterian Church in Ireland 1840–1870.* (Belfast, 1986)

Barnes, B., *Scientific Knowledge and Sociological Theory* (London, 1974)

Barnes, Trevor J. 'Geography and Science (including science studies)', in Johnston, ,R.J., Gregory, D. Pratt, G. and Watts, M. (eds.), *The Dictionary of Human Geography 4 edn* (Oxford, 2000), pp. 727–729

Beaver, B.de B., 'Possible Relationships Between the History and Sociology of Science', in Gaston, J. (ed.), *Sociology of Science* (San Francisco, 1978), pp. 140–161

Ben-Arieh, Y., *The Rediscovery of the Holy Land in the Nineteenth Century* (Jerusalem, 1979)

Bowler, Peter J., *Darwin: the Man and his Influence* (Oxford, 1990)

——, *Reconciling Science and Religion: the Debate in the Early Twentieth Century* (Chicago, 2001)

Brace, C., Bailey, A.R. and Harvey, D.C., 'Religion, Place and Space: a Framework for Investigating Historical Geographies of Religious Identities and Communities', *Progress in Human Geography* 30/1 (2006), pp. 28–43

Brooke, John H., *Science and Religion: Some Historical Perspectives* (Cambridge, 1991)

Burleigh, J.H.S., *A Church History of Scotland* (London, 1960)

Butlin, Robin A., 'George Adam Smith and the Historical Geography of the Holy Land: Contents, Contexts and Connections', *Journal of Historical Geography*, 14/4 (1988), pp. 381–404

——, 'Ideological Contexts and the Reconstruction of Biblical Landscapes in the Seventeenth and Early Eighteenth Centuries: Dr Edward Wells and the Historical Geography of the Holy Land', in Baker, A.H.R. and Biger, G. (eds.), *Ideology and Landscape in Historical Perspective: Essays on the Meanings of Some Places in the Past* (Cambridge, 1992) pp. 31–62

——, *Historical Geography: Through the Gates of Space and Time* (London, 1993)

Campbell, I.D., 'The Church in Scotland 1840–1940: an Overview', *Quodlibet*, 1/8 (1999), <http://www.quodlibet.net/>. Accessed 29 February 2004

——, 'In Search of the Physical: George Adam Smith's Journeys to Palestine and their Importance', *History and Anthropology* 13/4 (2002), pp. 291–299

——, *Fixing the Indemnity: the Life and Work of Sir George Adam Smith (1856–1942)* (Carlisle, 2004)

Campbell, Mary B., *The Witness and the Other World: Exotic European Travel Writing, 400–1600* (Ithaca, 1988)

Cook, S.A., 'George Adam Smith: 1856–1942', *Proceedings of the British Academy*, 28 (1942), pp. 325–346

Comaroff, J.L. and Comaroff, J., *Of Revelation and Revolution: Christianity, Colonialism and Consciousness in South Africa* (Chicago, 1991)

Crinson, M., *Empire Building: Orientalism and Victorian Architecture* (London, 1996)

Desmond, A. and Moore, J., *Darwin* (London, 1991)

Driver, Felix, *Geography Militant: Cultures of Exploration and Empire* (Oxford, 2001)

Duncan, J. and Gregory, D., 'Introduction' in Duncan, J. and Gregory, D. (eds.), *Writes of Passage: Reading Travel Writing* (London, 1999), pp. 1–13

Edney, M. H., *Mapping an Empire: the Geographical Construction of British India, 1765–1843* (Chicago, 1997)

Elsner, J. and Rubiés, J.-P., 1999. 'Introduction', in Elsner, J. and Rubiés, J.-P. (eds.), *Voyages and Visions: Towards a Cultural History of Travel* (London, 1999), pp. 1–56

Findlater, A., *Findlaters – the Story of a Dublin Merchant Family 1774–2001* (Dublin, 2001)

Foucault, M. [Tr. Sheridan Smith, A.M.], *The Archaeology of Knowledge* (London, 1972)

Fox, E., *Palestine Twilight: the Murder of Dr Albert Glock and the Archaeology of the Holy Land* (London, 2001)

——, *Sacred Geography: a Tale of Murder and Archeology in the Holy Land* (New York, 2001)

Friedman, John Block, *The Monstrous Races in Medieval Art and Thought* (Cambridge, MA, 1981)

Gange, David, 'Religion and Science in Late Nineteenth-century Egyptology', *The Historical Journal*, 49/4 (2006), pp. 1083–1103

Garnett, R. (rev. Baigent, E.), 'William George Browne.' *The Oxford Dictionary of National Biography.* <http://www.oxforddnb.com/view/article/ 3710>. Accessed 2 August 2005

Glacken, C., *Traces on the Rhodian shore: Nature and Culture in Western Thought from Ancient Times to the End of the Eighteenth Century* (Berkeley, 1967)

Goren, Haim, 'Sacred but Not Surveyed: Nineteenth Century Surveys of Palestine', *Imago Mundi*, 54 (2002), pp. 87–110

Graber, L.H., *Wilderness as Sacred Space* (Washington, 1976)

Greene, J.C., *Debating Darwin: Adventures of a Scholar* (Claremont, 1999)

Gregory, Derek, *Geographical Imaginations* (Cambridge, MA, 1994)

——, 'Between the Book and the Lamp: Imaginative Geographies of Egypt, 1849–1850', *Transactions of the Institute of British Geographers,* NS 20/1 (1995), pp. 29–57

——, 'Scripting Egypt: Orientalism and the Cultures of Travel', in Duncan, J. and Gregory, D. (eds.), *Writes of Passage: Reading Travel Writing* (London, 1999), pp. 114–150

——, 'Geography and Travel Writing', in Johnston, R.J., Gregory, D., Pratt, G. and Watts, M. (eds.), *The Dictionary of Human Geography. 4 edn.* (Oxford, 2000), pp. 857–859

——, *The Colonial Present* (Malden, MA, 2004)

Gunn, B. (rev. Gurney, O.R.), 'Sayce, Archibald Henry (1845–1933)', *The Oxford Dictionary of National Biography*, 2004, <http://www.oxforddnb. com/view/article/35965>. Accessed 11 September 2005

Hamilton, T., 'Josias Leslie Porter', in Lee, S. (ed.), *The Dictionary of National Biography*, 26 vols. (London, 1909), xvi, pp. 187–188

Harvey, David, *Spaces of Hope* (Edinburgh, 2000)

Henderson, T.F. (rev. Strong, R.), 'Michael Russell', *The Oxford Dictionary of National Biography*, 2004, <http://www.oxforddnb.com/view/article/ 24331>. Accessed 29 April 2005

Hoeveler, J.D., *James McCosh and the Scottish Intellectual Tradition: From Glasgow to Princeton* (Princeton, 1981)

Howard, T.A., *Religion and the Rise of Historicism: W.M.L. de Wette, Jacob Burckhardt, and the Theological Origins of Nineteenth-century Historical Consciousness* (Cambridge, 2000)

Hunt, E.D., 'The Itinerary of Egeria: Reliving the Bible in Fourth-century Palestine', in Swanson, R.N. (ed.), *The Holy Land, Holy Lands and Christian History* (Woodbridge, 2000), pp 34–54

Hunter, A.G., 'The Indemnity: William Robertson Smith and George Adam Smith', in Clines, D.J.A. and Davies, P.R. (eds.), *William Robertson Smith: Essays in Reassessment* (Sheffield, 1995), pp. 60–66

Hutchinson, Samuel. 'The Salvation of Israel: the Story of the Jewish Mission', in Thompson, J. (ed.), *Into All the World: a History of 150 Years of the Overseas Work of the Presbyterian Church in Ireland* (Belfast, 1990), pp. 125–143

van Huyssteen, W., 'Theology and Science: the Quest for a New Apologetics', in *Essays in Postfoundationalist Theology* (Grand Rapids, 1997), pp. 215–237

Keay, J., *The Great Arc: the Dramatic Tale of how India was Mapped and Everest was Named* (London, 2000)

King, R., *Orientalism and Religion: Post-colonial Theory, India and the Mystic East* (London, 1999)

Knorr-Cetina, K.D., *The Manufacture of Knowledge: an Essay on the Constructivist and Contextual Nature of Science* (Oxford, 1981)

Larsen, T., 'Thomas Cook, Holy Land Pilgrims, and the Dawn of the Modern Tourist Industry', in Swanson, R.N. (ed.), *The Holy Land, Holy Lands and Christian History*. (Woodbridge, 2000), pp. 329–342

Latour, Bruno, *Pandora's Hope: Essays in the Reality of Science Studies* (Cambridge, MA, 1999)

Livingstone, D.N. and Wells, R.A., *Ulster-American Religion: Episodes in the History of a Cultural Connection* (Notre Dame, 1999)

Livingstone, D.N., *Nathaniel Southgate Shaler and the Culture of American Science* (Tuscaloosa, 1987)

——, *Darwin's Forgotten Defenders: the Encounter Between Evangelical Theology and Evolutionary Thought* (Grand Rapids, 1987)

——, *The Geographical Tradition: Episodes in the History of a Contested Enterprise* (Oxford, 1992)

——, *Science, Space and Hermeneutics: Hettner-Lecture 2001* (Heidelberg, 2002)

——, *Putting Science in its Place: Geographies of Scientific Knowledge* (Chicago, 2003)

——, 'Oriental Travel, Arabian Kinship and Ritual Sacrifice: William Robertson Smith and the Fundamental Institutions', *Environment and Planning D: Society and Space* 22 (2004), pp. 639–657

——, 'Text, Talk and Testimony: Geographical Reflections on Scientific Habits. An afterword', *British Journal for the History of Science*, 38/1 (2005) pp. 93–100

Lock, C., 'Bowing Down to Wood and Stone: One Way to be a Pilgrim', *Journeys* 3/1 (2002), pp. 110–132

Long, Burke O., *Imagining the Holy Land: Maps, Models and Fantasy Travels* (Bloomington, IN, 2003)

Lozovsky, Natalia, *'The Earth is our Book': Geographical Knowledge in the Latin West ca. 400–1000* (Ann Arbor, MI, 2000)

McBride, I., 'The School of Virtue: Francis Hutcheson, Irish Presbyterians and the Scottish Enlightenment', in Boyce, D.G., Eccleshall, R. and Geoghan, V. (eds.), *Political Thought in Ireland Since the Seventeenth Century* (London, 1993), pp. 73–99

McEwan, Cheryl, 'Paradise or Pandemonium: West African Landscapes in the Travel Accounts of Victorian Women', *Journal of Historical Geography*, 22/1 (1996), pp. 68–83

Macloskie, G., 'Concessions to Science', *Presbyterian Review*, 10 (1889), pp. 220–228

Makdisi, U., 'Mapping the Orient: Non-western Modernization, Imperialism, and the End of Romanticization', in Michie, H. and Thomas, R.R. (eds.), *Nineteenth Century Geographies: the Transformation of Space from the Victorian Age to the American Century* (London, 2002), pp. 40–54

Manley, D. and Rée, P., *Henry Salt: Artist, Traveller, Diplomat, Egyptologist* (Oxford, 2001)

Marsden, G., 'The Collapse of American Evangelical Academia', in Plantinga, A. and Wolterstorff, N. (eds.), *Faith and Rationality: Reason and Belief in God* (Notre Dame, IN, 1983), pp. 219–264

Marten, Michael, *Attempting to Bring the Gospel Home: Scottish Missions to Palestine, 1839–1917* (London, 2006)

Mayhew, Robert, 'Mapping Science's Imagined Community: Geography as a Republic of Letters, 1600–1800', *British Journal for the History of Science*, 38/1 (2005), pp. 73–92

Melman, B., 'The Middle East / Arabia: 'the Cradle of Islam'', in Hulme, P. and Young, T. (eds.), *The Cambridge Companion to Travel Writing* (Cambridge, 2002), pp. 105–121

Meserve, Margaret, 'Introduction', in Mandeville, John *The Travels of Sir John Mandeville* (Mineloa, NY, 2006), pp. v–xiv

Middleton, D., 'George Adam Smith: 1856–1942', *Geographers: Biobibliographical Studies*, 1 (1977), pp. 105–106

Miller, J.M., 'The Ancient Near East and Archaeology', in Mays, J.L., Petersen, D.L. and Richards, K.H. (eds.), *Old Testament Interpretation: Past, Present and Future: Essays in honour of Gene M. Tucker* (Edinburgh, 1995), pp. 245–260

Mitchell, T., *Colonising Egypt* (Cambridge, 1988)

——, 1992. 'Orientalism and the Exhibitionary Other', in Dirks, N. (ed.), *Colonialism and Culture* (Ann Arbor, 1992), pp. 289–318

Noll, M.A., 'Common Sense Traditions and American Evangelical Thought', *American Quarterly*, 37 (1985), pp. 216–238

——, *The Scandal of the Evangelical Mind* (Grand Rapids, 1994)

Rajchman, J., 'Foucault's Art of Seeing', in *Philosophical Events: Essays of The 80s* (New York, 1991), pp. 69–102

Repcheck, J., *The Man Who Found Time: James Hutton and the Discovery of the Earth's Antiquity* (London, 2003)

Riesen, R.A., *Criticism and Faith in Late Victorian Scotland* (Lanham, 1985)

Robertson, C.J., 'Scottish geographers: the first hundred years', *Scottish Geographical Magazine*, 89 (1973), pp. 5–18

Rogerson, J.W., *Old Testament Criticism in the Nineteenth Century: England and Germany* (Minneapolis, 1985)

Sack, R.D., *Homo Geographicus: a Framework for Action, Awareness, and Moral Concern* (Baltimore, 1997)

Said, Edward W., *Orientalism: Western Conceptions of the Orient* (Harmondsworth, 1978)

Schürer. Book review *The Historical Geography of the Holy Land*, in *Theolgische Literatur-Zeitung*. Cited in publisher's back matter of Smith, *Modern Criticism*.

Shepherd, Naomi, *The Zealous Intruders: the Western Rediscovery of Palestine* (San Francisco, 1987)

Silberman, Neil Asher, *Digging for God and Country: Exploration, Archeology, and the Secret Struggle for the Holy Land 1799–1917* (New York, 1982)

Simpson, P.C., *The Life of Principal Rainy*. 2 vols. (London, 1909)

Sloane, W.M. (ed.), *The Life of James M'Cosh: a Record Chiefly Autobiographical. With Portraits* (Edinburgh, 1896)

Smith, Lilian Adam, *George Adam Smith: a Personal Memoir and Family Chronicle* (London, 1943)

Strong, Rowan, '"A Church for the Poor": High Church Slum Ministry in Anderston, Glasgow, 1845–1851', *Journal of Ecclesiastical History*, 50/2 (1999), pp. 279–302

Taylor, Joan E., in Eusebius of Caesarea, Taylor, J.E. (ed.), *The Onomasticon by Eusebius of Caesarea with Jerome's Latin Translation and Expansion in Parallel From the Edition of E. Klostermann*, (Jerusalem, 2003)

Tuan, Y.-F., 'Geopiety: a Theme in Man's Attachment to Nature and to Place', in Lowenthal, D. and Bowden, M. (eds.), *Geographies of the Mind: Essays in Historical Geosophy* (New York, 1976), pp. 11–39

Urry, J., *The Tourist Gaze: Leisure and Travel in Contemporary Societies* (London, 1990)

Wagstaff, J.M., 'Leake, William Martin (1777–1860).' *The Oxford Dictionary of National Biography*, 2004, <http://www.oxforddnb.com/view/article/16242>. Accessed 10 September 2005

Walker, P.W.L., *Holy City, Holy Places? Christian Attitudes to Jerusalem and the Holy Land in the Fourth Century* (Oxford, 1990)

Walker, W., *Three Churchmen: Sketches and Reminiscences of the Right Rev Michael Russell LLD, DCL, Bishop of Glasgow: the Right Rev Charles Hughes Terrot, DD, Bishop of Edinburgh: and George Grubb, LLD, Professor of Law in the University of Aberdeen* (Edinburgh, 1893)

Whiting, C., 'Geographical Imaginations of the 'Holy Land': Biblical Topography and Archaeological Practice', *Nineteenth-century Contexts*, 29/2–3, pp. 237–250

Wright, John K., '*Terrae Incognitae*: the Place of the Imagination in Geography', *Annals of the Association of American Geographers*, 37/1 (1947), pp. 1–15

Index

Diodorus 71
Dixon, W.H. 25, 26
Dods, Marcus 169
Doubdan, Jean 72
Driver, S.R. 49, 50
Drummond, Henry 166, 167, 178

Edinburgh Cabinet Library 60, 63, 67, 72, 73, 85, 86
Edinburgh University 93, 120, 135
Egeria 7, 8
Egyptology 49, 98
environmental determinism *see* determinism
Episcopalianism 58–60, 82
Eratosthenes 65
Eusebius of Caesarea 3, 6, 38, 65
Euthemenes 65

Fell, Winand 137
Forster, Charles 22
Foucault, Michel 74, 184
foundationalism 117, 118, 193
Franken, H.J. 52
Franken-Battershill, C.A.A. 52
Free Church College Glasgow 152, 167
Fuller, Thomas 72

Geikie, Cunningham 47, 48
Gemelli-Careri, G.F. 73
geographical knowledge, authority of 17, 33, 108, 163, 163, 168
geographical knowledge, popularization of 2, 68, 93, 98, 187
geographical knowledge, religion and 5
geographies, imagined 43, 65, 67, 71, 74, 79, 80, 99, 100 108, 114, 115, 127, 144, 160, 161, 166, 175, 187, 188, 190, 192, 194
geology 4, 17, 43, 49, 52, 67, 68, 76, 77, 117, 129, 174, 175
Glasgow University 57, 60, 91, 93, 120
Goodrich-Freer, A. 27
Goodspeed, Frank 40, 41
Graf, K.H. 168
Gregory, Derek 71, 99, 127, 128, 139, 160, 182
Guylforde, Sir Richard 10, 11

Hackett, Horatio B. 35, 36, 37
Hasselquist, Frederick 15, 16
Helena, The Empress 18, 26

Herodotus 65, 71
Holzinger, H. 168
Howard, Thomas 138
Hupfeld, H. 168
Hutcheson, Francis 117

imagined geographies *see* geographies, imagined
India 134
inspiration, biblical 28, 63, 123, 126, 146, 169, 182
intellectual crisis, Victorian 27, 28, 109, 138

Jaffa *see* Joppa
Jaffe *see* Joppa
Jericho 7, 9, 10, 17, 76
Jerom *see* Jerome
Jerome 15, 38
Jerusalem 5, 7, 10, 14, 15, 17, 74, 126, 141, 143–145, 172, 174, 175
Johnston, William 106
Joppa 10, 159
Jordan, River 9, 10, 79, 94, 144, 159
Josephus 14, 26, 65, 73, 128, 135, 141

Kautzsch, E.F. 168
Keil, Karl 45, 137
Kelman, John 51
Kinns, Samuel 34, 35
Kitto, John 24
Kuenen, A.K. 164

Leake, William Martin 24
Leipzig 135–137, 141
Leith 59, 88
literalism, biblical 4, 27, 45, 49, 96, 126, 146, 193
Livie 15
Livingstone, David N. 28, 29, 118, 130, 131, 182, 188, 191
Logie, William 172
Lucan 65
Lucas, Paul 73
Lucretius 65
Lyell, Charles 121

Macnaughtan, John 106
Mandeville, Sir John 10, 11
Manetho 65
Maundrell, Henry 72
McCosh, James 118, 120, 121
Mengin, Felix 65